24147851

8/00

The Last CONQUISTADOR

Mansio Serra de Leguizamón
and the conquest of the incas

STUART STIRLING

SUTTON PUBLISHING

First published in 1999 by
Sutton Publishing Limited · Phoenix Mill
Thrupp · Stroud · Gloucestershire · GL5 2BU

British Library Cataloguing in Publication Data
A catalogue record for this book is available from the British Library

ISBN 0 7509 2246 X

™ ALAN SUTTON™ and SUTTON™ are the
trade marks of Sutton Publishing Limited

Typeset in 10/14.5 pt Photina.
Typesetting and origination by
Sutton Publishing Limited.
Printed in Great Britain by
Butler & Tanner, Frome, Somerset.

To the memory of
María Díez de Medina de Peláez,
my grandmother,
and Ofelia Díez de Medina,
descendants of the conquistador

At the time the Spaniards first entered the city of Cuzco the gold image of the sun from its temple was taken in booty by a nobleman and conquistador by the name of Mansio Serra de Leguizamón, who I knew and who was still alive when I came to Spain, which he lost in a night of gambling, and where, according to the Father Acosta, was born the refrain: He gambled the sun before the dawn.

Garcilaso de la Vega,
Comentarios Reales de los Incas

CONTENTS

PROLOGUE

On 1 August 1619, a small caravan of horses and mules, accompanying several wagons and escorted by outriders, could be seen making its way across the mountains to the city of Arequipa, its white-washed buildings, monasteries and churches lying at the foot of the snow-capped volcano of the Misti. On that morning, His Grace the Friar Bishop Don Pedro de Perea y Díez de Medina finally entered his see and formally took possession of the newest of all the bishoprics of the Indies of Peru.[1] Aged sixty-three and worn down by the years of political intrigue that had robbed him of any one of the great episcopates of Spain, a scholarly and austere figure, his only known work was a treatise supporting the contention of the Immaculate Conception he dedicated to the theologian Agustín Antolínez, Archbishop of Santiago de Compostela. His talents, so greatly admired in his youth, at Rome and at the university of Pavia, appeared almost meaningless among the faces that greeted him in the city's council chamber: whose distrust and condemnation he would within the years earn by his high handed and authoritarian manner in a dispute with regard to the building of his cathedral church, in which even the King would be forced to intervene.

Among the presbyters who had supported the Friar Bishop was an Andalusian, Miguel Pérez Romero, whom he appointed to administer his diocese when he was later forced to travel to the viceregal capital at Lima to face the censure of both the Viceroy and the colony's Archbishop. The relationship had further been strengthened by the subsequent marriage of the presbyter Romero's daughter to the Bishop's nephew Don Pablo Díez de Medina, a hidalgo and lawyer from his native township of Briones, in La Rioja. On 28 May 1630, the Friar Bishop died at Lima. His will shows him

Arms of the Friar Bishop Pedro de Perea y Díez de Medina, Capilla del Sagrario, sculptured by Domingo de Arregui, Briones. (Author)

Sculpture of the Friar Bishop by Juan Bazcardo, Capilla del Sagrario, Briones. (Author)

to have left much of his considerable fortune to the Augustinian convent at Burgos and to the church at Briones for the founding of a chapel, and where his sculptured features can still be seen under a grill awning of his coat of arms, bearing the ten Moors heads and title name of his family, awarded his ancestor for killing single handed ten Moors in the medina, citadel, of the castle of Tíscar, in the reconquest of Andalusia.[2]

Shortly before the Friar Bishop's death a manuscript had come into his possession, which, because of its antiquity and historical interest, he had entrusted to the care of his fellow Augustinian Antonio de la Calancha y Benavides. A creole from Sucre, Calancha had for several years been researching Inca history and traditions, together with his Order's missionary role in Peru. The manuscript, written a year after the defeat of the Spanish Armada, was addressed to King Philip II, and was the last will and testament of the Conquistador Mansio Serra de Leguizamón, the grandfather of the presbyter Romero's wife.* The preamble of the will Calancha included in his history *Corónica Moralizada del Orden de San Agustín en el Perú*, published in Barcelona in 1639.[3]

Among the other papers in the possession of Romero's wife was a copy of her grandfather's *Probanza de Méritos*,† his testimonial of his past service to the Crown, also addressed to King Philip II. The 154 folio pages record the testimony of twenty witnesses, six of whom had been present with him at the killing of the Inca Atahualpa at Cajamarca, and several of whom had been pardoned for their part in the rebellions against the Crown which had lasted intermittently for seventeen years. The text, published for the first time, forms the basis of a portrait of an almost unknown soldier, who had been the last conquistador to die in Peru, and, as his will demonstrates, one of the very few of Pizarro's veterans to have expressed his remorse for his role in the conquest of the Incas.

---

* See Appendix 1.
† See Appendix 2.

ACKNOWLEDGEMENTS

Principally I acknowledge my mother, without whose encouragement this book would never have been written. I would also like to thank Luis Roldán Jordán and Josefa García Tovar, of the Seminario de Historia Local de Pinto, Madrid. I am grateful to my brother Alexander Stirling and Nicholas du Chastel for taking photographs for me in La Paz, Potosí and Cuzco. I am also grateful to Dr Barry Taylor, of the British Library, for his advice and the staffs of the Archivo General de Indias, Escuela de Estudios Hispano-Americanos, Seville, the Archivo Nacional de la Nación, Lima, Canning House, the British Library and the Institute of Historical Research, London.

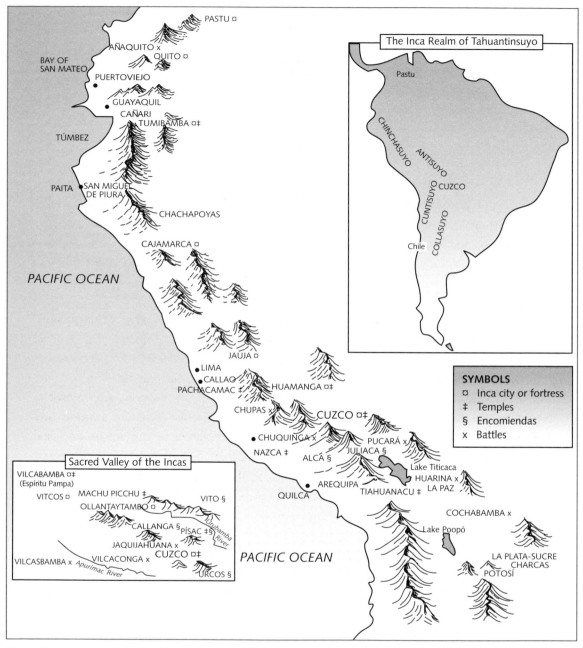

Map of Peru.

1

HEIRS OF THE CID

When in ancient or modern times has so great an enterprise been undertaken by so few against so many odds, and to so varied a climate and seas, and at such great distances, to conquer the unknown?

Francisco López de Jerez
Verdadera Relación de la Conquista del Perú

The history of Spain's conquest of the Inca empire of Tahuantinsuyo is as much a history of the destruction of a civilization as it is of its protagonists and victims: conquistador and Indian alike, some of whose names are recorded by history, and others forgotten in the faded parchments of some distant archive. As with much of colonial history, it was a history of a conquered people written by its conquerors, and revised in part by the chronicles of later missionaries and Crown officials. Almost nothing in any great biographical detail is recorded of their lives. As illiterate as the people they had conquered, their silence was to prove their greatest defence of the wealth they accumulated, and of the inhumanity with which they had established their empire: a social and economic infrastructure which would still be evident in Andean America until the agrarian reforms of the present century.

That each of the conquistadors of the New World was tainted with the blood and brutality of their conquest is without dispute. Neither was their role any different from that of their forefathers who had fought in the *reconquista* of Muslim Spain and shared in the booty of its destruction, nor can their undoubted courage be denied them. Their story is not of a great religious crusade but of explorers and would-be mercenaries, whose treatment of the natives they subjugated was possibly no more bloody than the crusading armies which had ransacked their fellow Christians at Constantinople on the way to the Holy Land three hundred years previously, or in any of the later religious wars of Europe. With scant knowledge of handling the arms they purchased or borrowed, and united solely by their poverty and the dream of riches that had brought each of them to the Indies, they were to conquer one of the greatest empires of the Americas. Nor as colonists did they differ in their sense of racial superiority to any other latter day European colonist; nor was the plight of the people they conquered any less humane than that of an African, North American Indian or Aborigine. Neither was their racism dissimilar to that of any other European, nor even of the humanist Erasmus who chided the Spaniards for having too many Jews in their country.[1]

The legacy of their cruelty would transcend the centuries, inspired in part by the writings of the Dominican Bartolomé de las Casas, whose condemnation of the treatment of the natives of the New World would later be revived by Protestant pamphleteers in elaborating the *leyenda negra*, black legend, of Spain's conquest. 'There are many who were never witnesses to our deeds, who are now our chroniclers,' the Conquistador Mansio Serra de Leguizamón complained in his old age, 'each one recording his impressions, often in prejudice of the actions of those who had taken part in the Conquest . . . and when they are read by those of us who were the discoverers and conquistadors of these realms, of whom they write, it is at times impossible to believe that they are the same accounts and of the same personages they portend to portray.'[2]

The homelands and social hierarchies the conquistadors left behind in their poverty stricken villages of Castile, Estremadura and Andalusia had evolved in the feudalism of the Middle Ages: an era that had transformed Spain from an amalgamation of semi-autonomous Visigoth and Arab kingdoms into a nation of imperial power. It had also been an age that had seen the throne of Spain inherited by the Flemish-born grandson of Queen Isabella of Castile and her consort King Ferdinand of Aragón, who as Charles V would be elected Holy Roman Emperor and succeed to the great Burgundian inheritance of the Low Countries and to the kingdom of Naples: a legacy which would divide the political and religious map of Europe, and in time witness Spain's hegemony of the New World.

The realm the young Austrian Prince Charles of Habsburg inherited from his Spanish mother and grandparents was a land steeped in the exorcism of its past Arab and Judaic civilization, the last symbolic vestige of which had been the surrender of the kingdom of Granada in 1492. This was the same year his grandmother's Genoese Admiral Columbus had first set foot on the Caribbean island of Guanahaní he had believed to be the gateway to India, and for which reason the Americans would be known as Indians. In the eighth century possibly 1 million Arabs and North African Berbers had crossed the Strait of Gibraltar and had settled in the Iberian Peninsula, three-quarters of which by the eleventh century had been under Muslim rule,[3] populated not only by Christians but by a large urban Jewish community. It was a land separated as much by its geographical contrasts as by its racial division.

Only in the mid-thirteenth century had Spain's Christian armies re-established its former Visigoth capital, at Toledo. The reconquered territories were placed under the protection of encomiendas, lands entrusted by the Crown to families of old Christian lineage, *Cristianos viejos*, and held in lieu of feudal service. Evangelical as well as territorial in its purpose, it was a system that would dominate the social structure of a vanquished people, destroying both their identity and traditions. With similar effect it would be introduced by the conquistadors to the colonies of the New World, and which in all but name would become a licence for slavery. The fate of the country's Jews had followed a similar course of persecution. The tax returns of Castile in the year 1492, whose kingdom comprised three-quarters of the Peninsula's populace of an estimated 7 million people, record some 70,000 Jews, almost half of whom would refuse to accept conversion and face exile in Portugal[4] or North Africa.[5] Those who remained, known as conversos, as in previous centuries, would be assimilated into a society governed by the tenets of a religious Inquisition, in which they would face the stigma of their race in the proofs of *limpieza de sangre*, racial purity – an anachronism that would perpetuate unabated well into the nineteenth century.[6] Even St Teresa of Avila, venerated by king and courtier alike, would never disclose the ignominy shown her grandfather, a converso, who had been publicly flogged in Toledo at an *auto-da-fé* for his apostasy.[7]

It was an image of a people in every level of their existence: of a predominant and mainly destitute peasant society governed by its Church and feudal nobility, which owned 95 per cent of the land;[8] and of a small urban middle class, of tradesmen, artisans and clerks, many of them incorporated in the Hermandades, guilds, dependent on the Crown for their privileges. The hidalgo – *hijo de algo*, son of a man of rank – represented an untitled nobility which for generations had served the Crown as soldiers, or as warrior monks in the Military Orders modelled on the crusading Orders of the Holy Land. Bound by their distinct codes of chivalry, they had traditionally derived their livelihood from the booty of war and from the rents of their small country estates, regarding trade and any form of commerce as below their dignity; a stance that brought many of them to penury, and which Cervantes satirized in the characterization of the hidalgo Don Quijote de la Mancha. Some were landless and lived in townships or in the garrison castles of the Orders: Calatrava, founded in 1158 for the defence of Toledo by Ramón Sierra, Benedictine abbot of the Navarre monastery of Santa María de Fitero; Alcántara, founded in about 1170 for the defence of Estremadura; and Montesa, founded in 1317 by King James II of Aragón as the result of the disbandment of the Templar Order, whose lands he acquired.

The Order of Santiago, founded in about 1160, was however the most prominent of all the Orders, owning some quarter of a million acres of land. It was established by knights of León for the protection of pilgrims to the shrine of St James the Apostle, at Compostela in Galicia, where, according to tradition, his body was buried. Proclaimed patron of Spain and its armies because of his legendary apparition at the Battle of Clavijo in the ninth century, his image as *Santiago mata moros*, slayer of Moors, mounted on a white horse in full armour would emblazon its banners during its wars in Europe and in the conquest of both Mexico and Peru. St James' emblem of the cockleshell owes its origin to the legend that at Clavijo a Christian knight discovered his chain mail studded with cockleshells after making his escape across the River Ebro: a symbol

Mansio's signature. (Patronato 126, AGI, Seville)

synonymous with pilgrimage to his shrine at Compostela. With the demise of Muslim Spain the Orders would witness the end of their crusading role, their lands and wealth prey to the political and financial demands of the Crown.[9] It would also symbolize the end of the hidalgo as a crusader knight, relegating him to the romances of a bygone age, and his title to a mere appendage of nobility.

The conquistador Mansio Serra de Leguizamón was one of the few hidalgos to have taken part in the discovery and conquest of Peru,[10] most of whose 330 known volunteers were from the humblest backgrounds, the sons of yeomen and tradesmen. He was born in the year 1512, three years before the birth of St Teresa of Avila, in the township of Pinto in the realm of Toledo, in an age that could still recall the reconquest of Granada and had witnessed the discovery of the New World. He was the son of Juan Serra de Leguizamón, a Vizcayan,[11] and of María Jiménez, whose Castilian family had lived in the township for generations.[12]

Mansio's father, who probably typified the plight of the impoverished hidalgo at the turn of the century, was descended from the families of Serra, of Ceánuri and of Leguizamón, of Echévarri near Bilbao, the arms of which the Conquistador bore, and whose faded carving can still be seen on the portico of his mansion in Cuzco. From time immemorial Iberia's northern province on the shores of the Bay of Biscay, bordering the Basque lands and Pyrennean kingdom of Navarre, had possessed its own language and *fueros*, privileges, as subjects of its feudal lordship, which only in the fourteenth century had been assimilated into the Crown of Castile. The Victorian writer Richard Ford, who travelled widely across its mountainous land, referring to the language of its people, quotes a common saying that the Devil had studied

Seigneurial families of the Vizcaya at Guernica, El Besamanos, Francisco de Mendieta, 1609. (Diputación Foral de Vizcaia)

Vizcayan for seven years and had accomplished only three words. 'A people,' he wrote, obsessed by their independence and lineage, '. . . whose armorial shields, as large as the pride of their owners, are sculptured over the portals of their houses, and contain more quarterings than there are chairs in the drawing rooms or eatables in the larder . . . and well did Don Quijote know how to annoy a Viscayan by telling him he was no gentleman'.[13] According to the fifteenth-century Vizcayan chronicler and genealogist Lope García de Salazar,[14] the Leguizamón were descended from Alvar Fáñez de Minaya, a cousin of Rodrigo Díaz de Vivar, known to history and legend by his Moorish title of el Cid, the Lord: both of whose names would embellish the ballads of the Middle Ages and inspire the epic poem of that name.

> Of the lineage of Alvar Fáñez de Minaya, cousin of the Cid of Vivar, succeeded a knight who came to settle the lands known as Leguizamón, and there founded the House of Leguizamón the old many years before Bilbao was populated, and from father to son was succeeded by Diego Pérez de Leguizamón, a fine knight and held as the noblest of his name, who bore for arms horizontal bars as borne by the said Alvar Fáñez de Minaya in his sepulchre at San Pedro de Gumiel de Hizán where he is buried, and which this lineage bears, and who in turn was succeeded by Sancho Díaz de Leguizamón who was killed in the vega of Granada . . .[15]

Arms of Leguizamón: Azure, three bars Or,
Palacio de Leguizamón, Echévarri, Bilbao.
(Author)

What history records of Rodrigo Díaz de Vivar is that he was born in the mid-eleventh century and that for several years he had served King Sancho of Castile as his constable until his murder at Zamora in 1072.[16] Exiled from Castile by Sancho's heir and brother Alfonso VI, for eighteen years he commanded the armies of the Emir al-Mu'tamin of Saragosa and his own Castilian and Moorish mercenaries, eventually capturing the Muslim city and kingdom of Valencia, where he died in 1099. His exploits and life were recorded in the twelfth-century poem chronicle *Carmen Campi Doctoris*, Song of the Campeador, and then later by a prose chronicle *Historia Roderici*, and in the epic medieval poem *Mio Cid*.[17] Though Alvar Fáñez de Minaya is depicted in *Mio Cid* as his trusted commander, there is no evidence that he ever accompanied him in his exile as the poem purports. In the *Poema de Almería*, written in about 1152, Minaya is described as the most renowned of the Christian warrior knights, second only to the Cid: *Mio Cidi primus fuit, Alvarus atque secundus*.[18] In 1091 he is recorded as commanding one of the armies of Alfonso VI against the Berber Almoravides which was defeated at Almodóvar del Rio. Six years later, Alfonso appointed him governor of the fortress of Zorita and then of Toledo, which he defended against the Berber siege. In 1114, while in the service of Alfonso's sister, the Infanta Doña Urraca, he was killed in the defence of the castle city of Segovia.

The pride of the Leguizamón in their descent from Minaya was personified by the boastfulness of their motto: 'Let none doubt my lineage nor dispute me in combat, for my arms recall my descent from the Cid.' As one of the seigneural families of Vizcaya, *parientes mayores*, the Leguizamón for several centuries had governed the *fueros* of Vizcaya and of the Basque provinces, which the kings of Castile and León traditionally swore to uphold at Guernica, a city which was raised to the ground during the Spanish Civil War, and whose destruction is depicted in Picasso's painting of that name. García de Salazar records the family's recurring involvement in Vizcaya's turbulent civil wars, in which one of the Conquistador's forbears met his death.

In this year [1443] Tristán de Leguizamón, the younger, and Martín de Zaballa, entering the township of Bermeo at dead of night and armed with their swords,

Boda en Begoña, Francisco de Mendieta, *c.* 1600. (Museo de Bellas Artes, Bilbao)

killed in the street of the fishermen Ochoa López de Arcayche and Pedro de Arna, who were partisans of the Zurbarán . . . in the year of Our Lord, 1446, the Leguizamón and Zurbarán fought in the square of Bilbao, and Tristán de Leguizamón, the younger, who had been asleep in his house, and armed with only a shield entered the square and was struck by an arrow in the chest, dying shortly after he was taken to his house . . .[19]

Since 1382 the family had also held the patronage and lordship of Vizcaya's shrine of the Virgin of Begoña, awarded by the illegitimate son and heir of the last feudal lord of Vizcaya to his uncle, as recorded in his deed of gift:

Be it known that We, Don Pedro Nuñez de Lara y Leguizamón, Conde de Mayorga and Lord of Castroverde, donate to thee Martín Sánchez de Leguizamón, my uncle, in

Nuestra Señora de Begoña. (Museo de Bellas Artes, Bilbao)

recompense of your loyalty and the many services you have rendered me, and continue to render me each day, in free gift and in perpetuity to you, your wife, children and heirs, the monastery and sanctuary of Santa María de Begoña and its lordship, and all its goods, lands, fruit trees, waters and mountains and fields . . .[20]

Established as a centre of pilgrimage in about 1300 in the mountain above Bilbao, the shrine and its adjacent tower and later palace dominated the approach to the city. It remained in the family's patronage for several generations until its partial destruction by Napoleon's troops, who stabled their horses in its monastery church and desecrated the Leguizamón tombs – a pillage the shrine and palace would again suffer in the Carlist wars of the nineteenth century.

No record survives as to the year the Conquistador's father left Vizcaya and settled in the Castilian township of Pinto, lying a few miles south of Madrid, and which was held in the lordship of the Carrillo family.[21] Neither, due to the loss of its early church archives, is there a record of his parents' marriage, nor whether they had any other children. An agricultural region, renowned for its wheat, olives and wine, Pinto had for centuries formed part of Toledo's north-easterly defence, its medieval tower, silhouetted in the cold Castilian winters against the backdrop of the snow-clad mountains of the Sierra de Guadaramma, was surrounded by its sombre mansions, market square and church of Santo Domingo de Silos. In a census in 1571 its population was recorded as 836 persons, nine of whom were hidalgos.[22] Mansio's companion in arms Alonso de Mesa, who had been born in Toledo, recorded that in his youth he had known Mansio's relatives, who presumably would have been the senior branch of his family who resided at court in the city: Don Sancho Díaz de Leguizamón and Don Tristán de Leguizamón.[23] Don Sancho, one of Bilbao's grandees and patron of its church of San Antón, was for several years chamberlain to the Emperor Charles V. Don Tristán, a son of a former page of King Ferdinand, would later serve as a captain of lancers in Italy, where he was awarded the knighthood of Santiago by the Emperor at Bologna the day before his coronation. Nothing, however, is known of Mansio's education or upbringing, nor of his father's relationship with his relatives. Judging by the wording of his various petitions and testimonials he possessed the rudiments of a classical education that most children of his hidalgo rank would have received. His future, nevertheless, was decided neither at

Romeria en Begoña, Sanctuary of the Virgin of Begoña. (Drawing by G.P. Villamil; Museo de Bellas Artes, Bilbao)

court nor in the farm lands of Pinto, but in the neighbouring township of Torrejón de Velasco, the lordship of which was held by the Conde de Puñonrostro, whose younger brother Don Pedro Arias Dávila was Governor of the colony of Nicaragua in the Indies.[24]

The dream of riches, inspired by the tales of the returning conquistadors of Mexico and from the islands of the Caribbean, the isthmian settlements of Castilla del Oro, at Panama and Nicaragua, had taken hold of the imagination of the entire country. Between the years 1520 and 1539 some 13,000 men and 700 women sailed for the New World: townsmen, merchants and yeomen, some of their names hispanicized to hide their converso origins, prostitutes and penniless daughters of government officials, friars of the Orders of St Dominic and Merced, driven by the zeal of their mission or charged to live out their penances in the exile of an unknown world, former criminals and conscripts of the Italian wars, peasants and hidalgos with only their black capes to hide their penury, queuing in their hundreds for their passage to the Indies and the fortunes each believed awaited them.[25] It was a dream few would ever realize. Some time before 1529, aged no more than sixteen, the future conquistador of Peru left his native township never to return.[26] It was a journey that would take him across the world and eventually to the great cordillera of the Andes, where he would live for the remainder of his life.

The Tower of Pinto. (Author)

The small flotilla of caravels in which he sailed from the Andalusian port of San Lúcar de Barrameda took a route by then well established in the crossing of the Atlantic: of some thirty days to the Canary and Windward Islands and a further twenty days to the Caribbean port of Nombre de Dios in the Isthmus of Panama. It was a route Don Pedro Arias Dávila, the Governor of Nicaragua, had himself taken when he had led an armada of 17 ships and 2,000 men in the conquest of the Isthmus 15 years previously, piloted by Juan Vespucci, nephew of the Florentine navigator Amerigo whose name would be given to the continent of the New World. The right of Spain's claim to the Indies had been established by the Valencian Pope Alexander VI in his bull *Inter Caetera*, issued in May 1493, in Castile's favour, and amended a year later to include Portuguese rights of conquest – 300 miles to the east of the Azores and the Cape Verde Islands. During his tenure as Governor of the Pacific port of Panama, whose colony he had founded in 1519 as the settlement of Our Lady of the Assumption, Arias Dávila had succeeded where most men would have failed in the exploration and conquest of its tropical terrain, and of its westerly region of Nicaragua and Veragua. A veteran of the reconquest of Granada, he had imposed his authority on a ruthless and often corrupt administration, and had been responsible for ordering the executions of the conquistadors Hernández de Córdoba and the elderly Vasco Núñez de Balboa, who was his son-in-law. Córdoba, an Andalusian, had commanded his expedition in the conquest of Nicaragua in 1523, founding its capital at León and exploring the Desaguadero River as far as the Atlantic coast. His subsequent appeal to the Crown for his recognition as governor of the territories was intercepted by Arias Dávila, who ordered his hanging on a charge of sedition. Nuñez de Balboa had met a similar fate. An Estremaduran and one of the early colonists, he had founded the township of Darién, in 1513, commanding that same year an expedition that had made the

The explorer Vasco Ñúñez de Balboa. (Herrera: BL, 783. g. 1–4)

discovery of the Pacific, and among whose sixty-seven volunteers had been the then relatively unknown slaver and future encomendero of Panama: Francisco Pizarro.

In the years of his governorship Arias Dávila had transformed what had been little more than an outpost on the borders of the great Mayan empire of Central America into one of the most lucrative settlements in the Indies. The commodity that had enabled him to achieve his ends had been neither the by then diminishing deposits of gold for which the Isthmus had earned its name, of Castilla del Oro, nor the spices its early explorers had believed existed in its hinterland, but in the human gold of slavery. In an age when scholars at the universities of Salamanca and Bologna were deliberating on the theological implications of recognizing the natives of the New World as human beings, while others were advocating the theory that they were one of the lost tribes of Israel, slavery under the guise of evangelization would become the labour force of Spain's colonial wealth.[27]

Queen Isabella had prohibited the enslavement of the Isthmians unless they were prisoners of war – a code to which her grandson Charles V would also in principle adhere – but it was a mandate that would never be implemented with any rigour, nor possess any real validity. Its irrelevance had been marked even further by the introduction of the encomienda system, which would be far more apparent in its function as a slave labour force than in the Muslim land enclosures of southern

Francisco Pizarro. (Antonio de Herrera, *Historia general de los hechos de los castellanos en las islas y tierrafirme del Mar Océano*: BL, 783. g. 1–4)

Spain, whose subject people would rise in rebellion in the later part of the century. It was a trade from which both the Crown and the colonists would acquire their principal revenue, enhanced over the years by the importation of Africans from Guinea and the Cape Verde Islands, and which would eventually dominate the society and economy of Central America and the Caribbean. The natives of the early Spanish settlements, moreover, faced an even greater threat to their survival because of their vulnerability to disease from Europe and Africa, principally smallpox.[28] Within fifty years the epidemic would kill nine-tenths of the indigenous people of Mexico and Central and Andean America. Malaria and syphilis,[29] which had been introduced to Spain by Columbus' mariners, and which had spread to King Ferdinand's army in Italy between the years 1494 and 1495, had also taken its toll on the lives of the Isthmian colonists.

The settlement at León, in the Isthmus' western region of Nicaragua, to which the young Mansio made his way, following the mule packs from the Atlantic port of Nombre de Dios, was little more than a stockade of wooden buildings. Its markets were filled with its Spanish traders, many of them barefoot and dressed in tafetta and lace, accompanied by their manacled Indian slaves, men, women and children, which they would sell to one another for the labour of their land or the solace of their sexuality. The world he would have witnessed was far removed from the austere landscape of Castile: deafened by the colour and sounds of its tropical vegetation and native markets, with its stalls of exotic fruit and cane alcohol, parrots, caged monkeys and newly arrived African slaves, who had also made the long journey across the Isthmus from the caravels that had brought them from the islands of the Spanish Main. At the time of his arrival in the township, armed possibly with little more than the letters of recommendation he carried from the Conde of Puñonrostro to his brother the governor, an expedition was being organized by Arias Dávila for the conquest of the westerly region of Veragua under the command of the captains Juan de Pánes and his treasurer the slave merchant Juan Téllez.[30] Its purpose was ostensibly to search for mineral deposits and to found further settlements, though in all likelihood it was to supplement the growing loss in numbers of Indian slaves due to the smallpox epidemic. The few facts to survive of the expedition, in which the by then seventeen-year-old Mansio had enlisted, record that its volunteers were devastated by the oppressive climate and disease. In his testimonial Mansio recalled he had 'experienced great risk' to his life and the 'loss of many pesos of gold'.[31] The hardship he undoubtedly endured in the three years he spent in Veragua was confirmed by his witness the Conquistador Nicolás de Ribera, who had first met him there: '. . . as for what [he] says of the province of Veragua, so devastated by rain and with such bad aspect, it would have been impossible for him, and for those who were with him in its conquest, not to have suffered greatly'.[32]

Ribera had two years previously returned from an expedition led by Pizarro along the equatorial coast of the southern Pacific, the lands of which an earlier explorer Pascual de Andagoya had mistakenly called Peru. It had also been three years since

Pizarro and his partner Diego de Almagro had reached an agreement with the priest Hernando de Luque to share in the conquest of the empire they knew to exist in the hinterland of its continent. It had been a contract to which Pánes, one of the commanders of the Veragua expedition, had been a signatory on behalf of the illiterate Pizarro, as recorded by Panama's notary:

> I, Don Hernando de Luque, priest and vicar of the Holy Church of Panama, and the captains Francisco Pizarro and Diego de Almagro, who are citizens of this city of Panama, declare our agreement to form a contract[33] that will forever be binding: in as much as the said captains Francisco Pizarro and Diego de Almagro, who have been granted permission by the Governor Pedro Arias Dávila to discover and conquer the lands and provinces of the kingdoms known as Peru . . .[34]

Charles V, by Eneas Vico from the title page of *The Cloister Life of the Emperor Charles V* by William Stirling.

The tales of their discovery had by now spread across the Indies, and the proofs they had brought back with them to Panama, of gold and silver artefacts, emeralds and other jewels, together with several natives, llamas and equatorial birds, Pizarro had taken with him to Spain in order to obtain the Crown's permission for the right of conquest – a request Arias Dávila had later denied the partners. Pizarro nevertheless had arrived in Spain to a hero's welcome in 1528, and had been received by the Emperor Charles V at Toledo. Awarding him the habit of Santiago and the rank of a hidalgo, the Emperor authorized his expedition of conquest, leaving the details of his decree to be finalized by his Portuguese Empress after his departure to Italy. What would be known as the *Capitulación de Conquista*, dated 26 July 1529, would carry the name of Queen Isabella's daughter Doña Juana, titular monarch of Spain and mother of the Emperor, who had spent most of her life incarcerated because of her madness. The presence at court of the conqueror of Mexico, Hernán Cortés, had possibly influenced the Council of Castile in authorizing Pizarro's sole command of the expedition: an appointment that would cause the understandable enmity of his partner Almagro who had remained in Panama. The articles of the decree stipulated that the name New Castile be given to the conquered territories, of which Pizarro would be governor and captain-general.[35] Almagro was only awarded the future governorship of the coastal settlement at Túmbez and the rank of a hidalgo. The priest Luque was awarded the bishopric of the future colony. Various

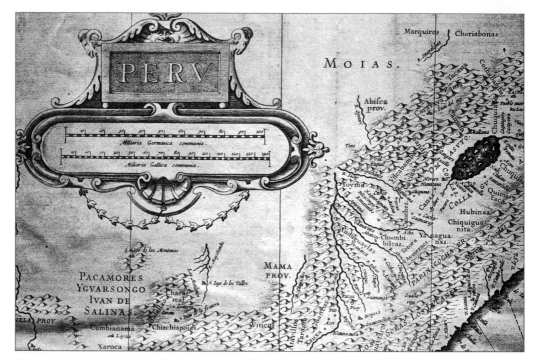

Map of Peru, engraving by Bleau. (Private Collection)

clauses were added, among them the prohibition of any conversos or moriscos enlisting in the expedition: a clause that would have been met with some incredulity by Nicaragua's colonists in view of the fact that Arias Dávila was of converso stock, and which highlights the paradox of racism in contemporary Spain.

The evangelical purpose of the expedition was emphasized by the inclusion of several Dominican friars. Provision was also made for the limited purchase of artillery in the Isthmus and the award of twenty-five horses from the island of Jamaica and of thirty African slaves from the island of Cuba. Though each of the partners was awarded an annual pension from the Crown's future revenue from the territories and booty of their conquest, they were in effect to receive no direct financial backing for its implementation other than an advance on their future incomes. Nor were they compensated for what they had already spent in out-fitting and manning their earlier voyages of exploration, as the Conquistador would recall some forty years later in an address to King Philip II:

> . . . in the desire to serve Your Majesty and to enhance the Crowns of Castile and León, the said Francisco Pizarro determined on the discovery and conquest of these realms of Peru at his own cost and mission, for which this witness neither saw, nor heard it said, that Your Majesty nor the Royal Treasury did aid him for the expense of the discovery and conquest, and that this witness, being one of the discoverers and conquistadors,

would have known had it been thus . . . for the said Francisco Pizarro set on the conquest at his own cost, and there spent the patrimony of his years of labour, for it was known to me that he was a man of wealth in the realm of Tierra Firme [Panama] . . .[36]

Pizarro, by this time middle aged, was described by his kinsman Pedro as dark featured, 'tall and spare, and having a good face and a thin beard'.[37] The illegitimate and abandoned son of a minor hidalgo from the Estremaduran township of Trujillo, he had spent his childhood in the peasant household of his mother's family before leaving to serve in Spain's army in Italy.[38] In his early years in the Isthmus he had made a name for himself as a woodsman and Indian fighter, amassing a considerable fortune as a slaver, planter and trader: the principal sources of income open to the colonist encomenderos of Panama. A man of simple tastes, who preferred the company of his Indian slave women to the social pretensions of his fellow merchants and the hidalgo wives they imported from their homeland, he appears to have possessed no wish ever to go back and live in Spain, where, whatever his achievements or wealth, he would always be regarded as little more than a peasant. On his return to Panama he brought with him his four half-brothers, who were almost half his age. The chronicler Gonzalo Fernández de Oviedo recorded that they were as 'arrogant as they were poor'.[39] The eldest was Hernando, the only legitimate son of their father, who Oviedo described as 'of great stature and girth, his lips swollen, his nose veined',[40] who of all the men who would accompany his brother in the Conquest would prove to be the catalyst of his downfall and eventual murder.

Diego de Almagro, who was from an equally humble background as Pizarro and was also illiterate, was older than him and had at one time been the foreman of his encomienda. Disfigured by the loss of an eye from an Indian javelin wound and by the facial warts that scarred the bearded features of many of the early colonists, he had been born in the township of Almagro in the Mancha of Castile, and had lived in Panama for almost as long as Pizarro. An Indian tracker by trade, it was said of him 'he could follow an Indian through the thickest forests merely by tracing his tracks, and in the event the Indian might have a league's advantage on him, yet would he catch up with him'.[41]

The partnership of the two men had, however, virtually been dissolved after Pizarro's return from Spain, and had further been hampered by the belated intervention of Arias Dávila, by then an elderly invalid, who prohibited any volunteers from Nicaragua or Veragua enlisting on their expedition.

Diego de Almagro. (Herrera: BL, 783. g. 1–4)

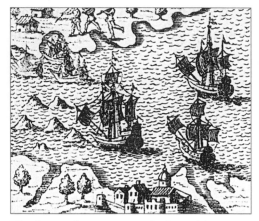

The Spaniards arriving at the Bay of San Mateo. (Herrera: BL, 783. g. 1–4)

The behaviour of Pizarro's brother Hernando, who had publicly referred to Almagro as a 'circumcized Moor',[42] had done little to improve relations between them. Almagro, who had every reason to feel defrauded by his exclusion from joint command of the expedition, after a great deal of discussion agreed to serve under Pizarro with the promise of an independent governorship in the conquered territories. Due to his ill-health, though, he decided to remain in Panama and to recruit a second expeditionary force as a reinforcement, which he would command. Most of the men who had already been enlisted, including the volunteers Pizarro had brought back with him from Spain, were in their early twenties and had never had any conventional military experience or training. Only a handful, among them Pizarro's brother Hernando, had ever served in Spain's regular army, though many of them would in their old age describe themselves as 'soldiers', as is made evident in the Conquistador's *probanza*. Each volunteer had been recruited with the promise of a share of booty, some were given captaincies because of their past experience as Indian fighters. More accustomed to labouring in the fields of their homelands than to soldiering, they presented a motley collection of unemployed slavers and die-hard adventurers, only a few of whom had taken part in the conquest of the Isthmus.

In the last week of the year 1530, a few months before Arias Dávila's death at the age of eighty in his capital at León, the first of the three caravels that would transport the 180 men and horses of the expeditionary force shed its mooring and sailed out of Panama's small harbour. Among the colonists of Nicaragua who had already been recruited for the expedition, but who had yet to sail, was the wealthy slaver Hernando de Soto, a hidalgo from Estremadura, who like Almagro had arrived in the Isthmus in Arias Dávila's armada. Though aware of Arias Dávila's opposition to the expedition, he had nevertheless accepted Pizarro's offer to command his horsemen also with the promise of a governorship, and had agreed to provide him with two of his slave ships for his expeditionary force, which he would join the following year after the departure of Sebastián de Benalcázar, another of the Nicaragua colonists. Six months after Soto had sailed from Nicaragua, Almagro and the witness Ribera entered the province of Veragua to enlist more men to supplement their reinforcements. Among the volunteers they recruited was the eighteen-year-old Mansio, who records in his testimonial he brought with him his own 'horses, armour and servants'.[43] Almost two years after Pizarro's departure, the small armada of caravels, carrying some 150 volunteers and a small contingent of Negro and Isthmian slaves and 50 horses, finally set sail from the port of Panama.[44] It was December 1532.

2

THE REALM OF THE HUMMINGBIRD

I was born as a flower of the field,
As a flower I was cherished in my youth.
I came to full age, I grew old;
Now I am withered and die.

Inca memory poem[1]

The Inca empire of Tahuantinsuyo, containing some 7 million people, comprising the Andean regions of the present day republics of Peru, Bolivia, Ecuador, northern Chile and southern Colombia, had been established by military conquest in less than a hundred years.[2] It was a society ruled by an hereditary nobility of the Quéchua tribe, known as Inca, which by their prowess had dominated the central Andean cordillera, instilling in their conquered tribes a cult of sun worship, from whom they claimed they derived their divine origin.[3] The chronicler Agustín de Zárate recorded that at Cajamarca the Inca Atahualpa told the Dominican Friar Vicente de Valverde that he believed in the deities of the sun, the Pachamama, earth mother, and Pachacámac, the creator.[4] Three Indian elders, in a testimonial on behalf of the descendants of their royal house, recorded of their rulers:

> The Incas of the eleven ayllu [clans of the dead emperors] never laboured for any one, for they were served by the Indians of all Peru . . . and they were lords who commanded all others . . . for none of their caste and tribe, poor or rich, nor any other who was a descendant of the Incas of the eleven ayllu were servitors in any manner, for they were served in all the four provinces of this realm . . . their sole office being to assist in the court of the Inca [emperor] where he resided, to eat and walk and to accompany him, and to discharge his commissions in war and peace, and to inspect the lands as great lords with their many servants . . .[5]

The civilizations whose distant vestiges the Incas had inherited had left only the remnants of their monuments and artwork to mark their existence: the Chavín of the central Andes (1200–400 BC), the image of whose puma god ornamented their pottery

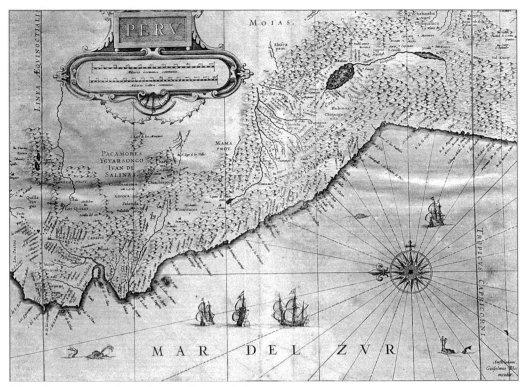

Map of Peru, engraving by Bleau. (Private Collection)

and masonry; the Nazca of the mid Pacific coast lands (400 BC–1000 AD), who portrayed their religious iconography in the giant linear earth – carvings of sacred animals, insects and birds; and the Tiahuanacu of the highland plateau on the southern shores of Lake Titicaca (AD 400–1000), whose monolith building and monuments had been erected some thousand years before the advent of the Incas. Of all the ancient Andean cultures the Tiahuanacu, a military religious community, had held the greatest influence in the evolution of their people. All that remains of Tiahuanacu's former lake city, part of which lies under the colonial township of that name, near La Paz, are its ruined wall enclosures and giant stone figures and Gateway of the Sun.

The lake of Titicaca, situated 12,725 ft above sea level and covering an area of some 3,500 square miles, bordering Peru and Bolivia, had been the spiritual epicentre of Tiahuanacu and was held sacred by the Incas as the birthplace of the progenitors of their dynasty. It was also the region from where their bards, that the Spaniards interviewed, recorded the existence in their legends of white-bearded gods, known to them as Viracocha, and because of which they had at first believed the conquistadors to have themselves been gods. The chronicler Pedro de Cieza de León recalled that when he had visited the ruins at Tiahuanacu he had asked the Indians there whether the lake city had been built during the time of the Incas, 'but that they had laughed at him, saying they had been told by their forebears it had been constructed overnight from one day to the other, and that they had seen bearded white men on one of the islands of Titicaca'.[6] The Spanish missionaries were to capitalize on the legend by equating Viracocha, also known as Thunupa, with a bearded Andean Christ, and even St Thomas, the apostle of India: an iconography still evident in the colonial mestizo church carvings and paintings of the Cuzco and Titicaca region. The myth of the white man was also evident in the northern Andean region of the Chachapoyas, whose tribesmen various chroniclers recorded were as white as any Spaniard, and which may possibly prove a far earlier connection between Andean America and the Caucasian world.[7]

Archaeology has established the traces of Inca government in the Huatanay valley at Cuzco in the central Andes in about AD 1200, and which would later expand across the southern and northern cordillera, introducing to their subject tribes a totalitarian government and a social structure of communal wealth. Though possessing neither the wheel nor the written word, by their mastery of masonry and engineering, their road

Viracocha, silverwork, late nineteenth century, Potosí School. (Private Collection)

Statue at Tiahuanacu. (Author)

building and collective system of farming, their craftsmanship of metal, textiles and pottery, their understanding of astronomy and medicine, and in the oral traditions of their poetry, they created one of the greatest civilizations in the Americas. It was a regime as enlightened in its social welfare as it was despotic in its totalitarian adherence to its ruling Inca nobility and Emperor, *Sapa Inca*. It also shared with other Amerindian civilizations, such as the Maya of Central America and the Aztec of Mexico, the practice of human sacrifice, which the few surviving elderly conquistadors, among them Mansio Serra de Leguizamón, would recall at an enquiry held in Cuzco almost half a century after the conquest: '[The Incas] instructed them [their subject tribes] in the veneration of their idols of the sun and of the stars, teaching them how to make sacrifices in the mountains and holy places of each province . . . forcing them to kill their sons and daughters to this effect . . . and to sacrifice their women and servants, so that they could serve them in the afterlife . . .'.[8]

Tiahuanacu figure. (Author)

The Inca practice of human sacrifice, as in pre-Christian Europe, was in effect a ritual worship of nature and part of a code of a religion governing every aspect of their lives. It also affected the laws by which they lived, as recorded by the Jesuit mestizo chronicler Blas Valera: '. . . from the detailed instructions given to each province's need of supplying artisans and agricultural workers for its sustenance, to the distribution of its land, to the punishments inflicted on adulterers, rapists and thieves, punishable in most cases by death'.[9] It was an image of a morality the Conquistador would depict in his last will and testament, which he addressed to his sovereign King Philip II.[10]

It was a society integrally linked to the spiritual life of its people and its belief in the supernatural: a world with which they communicated in their worship of nature and venerated in their huacas, holy places, of their mountains and valleys, and which brought them in communion with an invisible world. The mystical pre-eminence of their capital at Cuzco, cacooned in a valley 10,500 ft above the level of the sea, was reflected in the person of their Emperor, and maintained in the afterlife by the panacas, houses of the dead, of each Emperor, the living shrine to his immortality. Each Emperor in his life time established his panaca in one of the city's palaces, numbering some thousand of his relatives and attendants, to oversee his personal wealth and lands after his death. At the time of the Conquest eleven panacas were venerated at Cuzco, to which all the princes

Mansio's Will. (Patronato 107, AGI, Seville)

and higher nobility belonged through their maternal or paternal descent, entitling them to privileges and a prestige among the Quéchua and their subject tribes that the Conquistador compared to the nobility of his homeland:

> They were people of great importance, great lords and sons of kings, who governed this realm. And as such they ruled at the time I entered in the discovery of this kingdom and witnessed the Incas command and govern this land . . . for the term Inca is what we would call in Spain lords of vassals, dukes and counts, and other such gentlemen of that kind . . . and being as they were absolute rulers they ordered and received tribute, and this is known and is publicly held, and which this witness himself knows, for it is what I saw with my own eyes . . . for they were persons of great knowledge and by the government they held, though possessing no written word, they ruled like the Romans in ancient times.[11]

The subject tribes and communities possessed also a similar government of their ayllus, clans, and in the veneration of their ancestors: spirits whom they believed would appear as sparks in the fires of their hearths, or in their huacas, guarded by the nature spirits of the mountains, trees, water and stones. Even in death it was a society governed by order and contained by an earthly structure that bound the supernatural to the living world. The Inca lords, who the conquistadors would call orejones because of the gold ear ornaments they wore, and who resided in the city's 3,000 to 4,000 stone wall dwellings, were trained as administrators or as commanders of the imperial army either to expand the borders of the empire or to suppress the various tribal rebellions that would continue unabated even after the arrival of the Spaniards. Along Cuzco's lower valley and river of the Huatanay were housed the yanacona, the nomadic caste of servant labourers, responsible for the cleaning of the city's streets and the maintenance of its buildings. Also populating the lower valley were the mitimae, communities of subject tribes, who lived under the rule of their caciques, and who in their thousands had been brought to Cuzco from their tribal lands, and in a rotary system of tributary labour, known as mita, would serve in the four suyos, regions, of the empire: in either agriculture, mining or as warriors. An example of their service was given by the grandson of the great warrior chief Cariapasa, Lord of the Lupaca, from the north-western shores of Lake Titicaca,[12] who recorded that some 5,000 warriors of his nation had died under his grandfather's leadership in the army of the Emperor Huayna Cápac in the northern region of Tumibamba. As tribute, he declared, his people's children had been sacrificed in the Inca huacas, the daughters of their chiefs taken for their concubines and the men of the tribe forced to serve as mitimae.

The lesser blood tie of Inca lords, among them tribal leaders from other nations, who were granted the privilege and status of Incas, were the administrators of the general government of the suyos, supervising the maintenance of its roads which covered an area of some 14,000 miles.[13] They were also responsible for overseeing its tambos, rest houses, fortresses and toll bridges, and the distribution of the empire's tribute: the crops, minerals, materials and clothing stored in the warehouses, and accounted for by the quipucamayoc, recorders, on their quipu, coloured string chords, which were used for numeration and also to record astronomical and magical formulae. The Conquistador recalled that their usage had been handed down from father to son for some 300 years, and that they also chronicled the Inca genealogies and historical events, the quantity of crops and every article that was transported or stored in the warehouses, and even the measurements of the construction of buildings, 'something that merits great admiration and is difficult to believe for those who have not

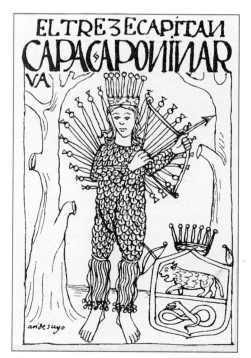

The cacique Cápac Apo Ninarua, of Antisuyo. (Felipe Guaman Poma de Ayala, *Nueva Corónica y Buen Gobierno*)

The cacique Mallca Castilla Pari, of
Collasuyo. (Felipe Guaman Poma de Ayala,
Nueva Corónica y Buen Gobierno)

examined them, or witnessed their usage'.[14] Trains
of llamas transported the empire's produce on the
four principal stone paved roads that led from its
provinces to Cuzco, the Chinchasuyo to the north,
the Cuntisuyo to the west, the Antisuyo to the east
and the Collasuyo to the south. All told some
200,000 people, in an area of some 40 square
miles, helped sustain the life flow of the Inca
capital[15] and the administration of its provinces, as
recorded by an anonymous conquistador who had
settled in the Collasuyo region of Bolivia:

In each of their provinces the Incas had
governors, ruling with great account and order
. . . there were others of lesser rank who were
known as sayapayas: inspectors who gathered
the ordinances of the Inca and of the realm,
visiting the storehouses and herds [of llamas]
that belonged to the sun and to the Inca. And
they would also inspect the mamacuna [virgins
of the sun] and the veneration and sacrifices
they would offer the sun and to the huacas, which were the idols they worshipped.
In each village were located storehouses of every item and produce . . . for laziness
and vagabondage were severely punished, and all laboured in the produce of these
goods; and in the lands where maize was unable to grow, storehouses of chuño
[dehydrated potatoes] were kept, as were other produce from each region, none of
which were consumed unless in times of war or need: then they would be
distributed with great order . . . the Inca [lords] who would visit the governors of
the provinces would be received with great honour, as if they were the Inca
[Emperor] himself, and they would be informed of all the labour commanded of the
people . . . and those [caciques] who had served the Incas well would be rewarded
with women and servants, livestock and fine clothing, and be granted the privilege
of being carried in litters or hammocks, and be given yanaconas for that purpose;
they would also be given the right to use parasols and be served with bowls and
plates of gold and silver: something no one could make use of without the authority
of the Inca . . . these privileges would also be granted them when they came to
Cuzco each year with their tribute from as far as Chile or the Charcas . . . in the
month and moon of May, which was known as Aymorayquilla, all the principal
caciques from the different suyos would assemble before the emperor in the great
square of Cuzco with their tribute of gold, silver, clothing, livestock . . . and also

their tribute of women . . . after which they would hold their feasting and perform their ceremonies and sacrifices . . .[16]

The various descriptions of Cuzco recorded by the Spaniards depict its masonry and the decorative artwork of its buildings as beyond anything they had ever witnessed in the Indies, and its great temple fortress of Sacsahuaman, constructed with stone blocks of some 12 ft in height, dominating its northern approach, as equal in grandeur and size to any such building in Spain. Laid out in the shape of a puma, the ancient deity of the Chavín civilization of the central Andes, the city's main square of Aucaypata was paved in stone and lined with sand brought from the beaches of the Pacific,[17] flanked by the palaces of its living and dead emperors.

Amarucancha, one of its four great palaces, possessed an entrance façade of white and coloured marble, its outer walls protected by two great separate cylindrical towers. Its stone chambers were hung with sheets of gold and silver and its

The cacique Cápac Apo Guaman Chaua, of Chinchasuyo. (Felipe Guaman Poma de Ayala, *Nueva Corónica y Buen Gobierno*)

interior niches were decorated with gold jewelled sculptures. Though no examples of painting and wall murals have survived, there is no reason to believe they did not exist, but were destroyed by the Spaniards because of their indigenous themes. Forty years after the Conquest the Viceroy Don Francisco de Toledo commissioned painted genealogies of the Incas on materials to be sent to Spain, and which also depicted Inca history.

An image of the palace of Amarucancha's size can be envisaged when compared to an adjoining building of a lesser structure, known as the Acclahuasi, the residence of the virgins of the sun, the mamacuna, who numbered some 1,500 women chosen for their beauty from each of the suyos of the empire as concubines for the royal harem. Casana, the palace Pizarro was to requisition for himself, contained a hall enclosure that could hold 3,000 people.[18] Across the great central square the Yacha Huasi, the house of learning, the school of its princes and Inca lords, presided over by the amauta, elders and poet bards, on the foundations of which the Conquistador built his mansion, had been constructed like all the other stone palaces with several courtyards and stockades, containing livestock of llamas, alpacas and vicuñas.

In death, as in life, the Quéchua celebrated the divine ancestry of their rulers in the religious ceremonies of their capital when the mummies of their dead emperors would be

Inca genealogy, late eighteenth century, Cuzco School. (Formerly in Private Collection)

paraded in throne litters in front of thousands of their people and carried in procession to Coricancha, the city's Temple of the Sun. Preserved with ointments and aromatic herbs and bound with white linen in an ovular shape, their faces masked in beaten gold, the mummies would be symbolically fed by their attendants with chicha, maize wine, and leaves of coca, a plant sacred to the panaca, and entertained through the speech of mediums. In a ritual that acclaimed the divinity of the Inca, the royal concubines and sister-wives of the Emperor and his daughters would play-act a theatre of the dead, miming the yuyaycucuy: the timeless frozen past of their people. Nothing today remains of Coricancha other than its foundation walling, nor of the other great sun temples founded at Pachacámac, south of Lima, Tumibamba, in Ecuador, and Copacabana, on the south-

The cacique Mallco Mullo, of Cuntisuyo, Felipe Guaman Poma de Ayala. (*Nueva Corónica y Buen Gobierno*)

eastern shore of Titicaca in Bolivia, on the site of which was built a great pilgrimage shrine in the seventeenth century in honour of the Virgin. The chronicler Pedro de Cieza de León recorded Coricancha's appearance, based on the evidence given him by Cuzco's surviving Inca princes and the few remaining veterans of Cajamarca who had seen the temple before its conversion into the convent of Santo Domingo, where the Conquistador's son Jerónimo would spend most of his adult life as a friar:

Its circumference is some four hundred paces, surrounded by a high wall of the finest masonry and precision . . . in all Spain I have not seen anything to compare to these walls, nor the placement of their stones, other than the tower known as Calahorra, by the bridge of Córdoba, and another edifice I saw in Toledo when I went to present the first part of my chronicle to the prince Don Felipe [the future King Philip II], which is the hospital the Archbishop Tavera commissioned to be built . . .[19] The stone is somewhat black in colour, rough, yet excellently cut. There are many doors and their arches are of a fine construction; at mid height of the walls runs a band of gold, of some seventeen inches in width and two in depth. The doors and arches are also embossed with sheets of this metal. Within the enclosure are four houses, not very large but of similar construction, the interior and exterior walls which are adorned with sheets of the same metal, and their ceilings are of thatch. Built into the inner walls of these houses are two stone benches, illuminated by shafts of sunlight and decorated with precious stones and emeralds. On these benches sat the emperors, and if any person

Machu Picchu. (Alexander Stirling)

would have done the same he would have been condemned to death . . . at each of the entrances were porters who guarded the virgins, of whom there were many, being the daughters of the principal lords and chosen for their great beauty, and who would remain in the temple until old age; and if any would have had dealings with men they would have been killed or buried alive, as would also be the man's punishment. These women were called mamacuna, who knew no other role than to sew and to paint the woollen garments for service in the temple, and in the making of chicha, which is a [maize] wine they make, and of which containers were filled in ample quantity . . . in one of these houses, the grandest of all, was the figure of the sun, of great size and made of gold, and encased with precious stones. There also were placed the mummies of the Incas who had reigned in Cuzco, each surrounded by a great quantity of treasure . . . around the temple house were a number of smaller buildings, which were the dwellings of the Indians who served in the temple, and an enclosure where they kept the white llamas and the children and men they would sacrifice. There was also a garden, the earth and grass of which was of fine gold and where artificial maize grew, also of gold, as were their stems and ears, and so well planted that even in a strong wind they would stand. As well, there were twenty llamas of gold with their lambs, and shepherds with their stone slings and staffs, all of the same metal . . .[20]

These images of a people at the height of their civilization would all but disappear within ten years of their conquest, the treasures of their gold and silver metal work melted into ingots, the stone masonry of their palaces used to buttress the foundations of the mansions and churches of their conquerors. At an enquiry held at Cuzco by the Viceroy Toledo in March 1572, he instructed the four surviving conquistadors in the city to give evidence of what they knew of the Inca lineage. Their words he recorded in a letter to the Council of the Indies and to King Philip II:

> What they have always heard told by the older Indians concerning the lineage of the Incas, and by others, is that from the first [Inca] until Huáscar, who was the last, there were twelve in number . . . and they have heard it said that Túpac Inca Yupanqui, father of Huayna Cápac, was the first who by force of arms made himself lord of the whole of Peru, from Chile to Pastu [Colombia], retaking various provinces in the vicinity of Cuzco which his father Pachacuti Inca had conquered,

and which had rebelled . . . and that Huayna Cápac, his son, inherited his sovereignty and conquered further lands, but because of his death Huáscar, his legitimate son, succeeded him; and while the realm was at war between Huáscar and Atahualpa, his bastard brother, Don Francisco Pizarro by order of His Majesty came to these kingdoms, and with him the said witnesses Alonso de Mesa, Mansio Serra de Leguizamón, Pedro Alonso Carrasco and Juan de Pancorbo.[21]

The chronology and accounts of the reign of the Emperor Huayna Cápac and of the subsequent wars of succession to his empire are full of ambiguity and contradiction in the early Spanish chronicles, none of whose authors were witnesses to the events they recorded. All their accounts were dependent on the testimony of the amauta bards and quipucamayoc they each in turn interviewed over the years at Cuzco. The evidence of their informants appears to vary depending on their allegiance to the rival panacas of Huayna Cápac's sons. The prominence given to

Incas of Peru, engraving. (Private Collection)

The Coya Rahua Ocllo. (Felipe Guaman Poma de Ayala, *Nueva Corónica y Buen Gobierno*)

Atahualpa's illegitimacy by the Spaniards was possibly more the work of the chroniclers themselves in portraying a European sense of morality, and in somehow justifying the legality of Atahualpa's killing at Cajamarca. The portrayal of Huáscar as a corrupt tyrannical weakling by a number of chroniclers also adds to the justification of the Conquest. Possibly neither representation was accurate, other than in the sense of demonstrating their respective ambition to occupy their father's throne. God and man to his people, the Emperor Huayna Cápac had brought his dynasty to the pinnacle of its power.[22] Though raised in Cuzco he had been born at Tumibamba and had spent much of his life campaigning to expand and secure the frontiers of his empire. Only in the latter part of his reign did he move his court from Cuzco to Quito, north of his retreat of Tumibamba, which he had named in honour of his panaca. Each of the early chronicles records that the succession to his throne had remained unresolved. Though neither primogeniture nor legitimacy in the European sense of the word was an established requisite among the Quéchua, the purity of the Emperor's blood line, and by a tradition established by Huayna Cápac's parents, of royal incest, favoured the succession of the son of a sister-queen.[23]

It was a succession that depended also on the sanction of the High Priest of the Sun, the Villac-Umu, a shaman from the ayllu of Tarpuntay, and on the allegiance of the imperial panacas of Cuzco. On the death of his sister-queen the Coya Cusi Rimay, who was probably the mother of his son Ninancuyochi, the Emperor married their younger sister the Coya* Rahua Ocllo, who for many years had been his concubine.[24] Reputed for her exceptional beauty and the magnificence of the court over which she presided, she was said to have been accompanied by a thousand musicians during her travels across the empire.[25] The eldest of their sons was Topa Cusi Huallpa, known as Huáscar, the Hummingbird, whom the Emperor had appointed Governor of Cuzco and of his southern domains.[26] The youngest of their daughters was the Coya Quispiquipi Huaylla, who after her baptism would be known as Doña Beatriz Yupanqui,[27] and who was the mother of the Conquistador's son Juan:

---

* Coya was the title of the sister-queen of the Emperor, or of their daughter.

As is publicly known of Huayna Cápac Yupanqui,* once king and lord of these realms of Peru, and of its mountains and valleys . . . that among his many children born to him was my mother Doña Beatriz Yupanqui. And that at the time of her birth at Surampalli in his domain of Tumibamba, he gave her for her guardian and service the cacique Cariapasa, principal lord of the Lupaca, for being his legitimate daughter of his queen, mother of Huáscar Inca, who was to succeed him as king and lord . . .²⁸

The Emperor Huayna Cápac. (Herrera: BL, 783. g. 1–4)

The Indians and Inca lords who were witnesses to her son's testimonial thirty years after the Conquest record that great feasting was held throughout the empire at her birth which lasted for 'ten days and ten nights'.† The palace compound of Surampalli where the Coya Doña Beatriz was born was identified by the archaeologist Max Uhle in 1923, in the valley of Yunguilla, lying south of Tumibamba.²⁹ As her son recalls, at her birth she was awarded to the guardianship of the Cacique Cariapasa, Lord of the Lupaca nation, one of her father's great warrior chiefs. As the daughter of the Emperor she was also given lands in Huayna Cápac's personal fiefdom of the Sacred Valley at Yucay, north of Cuzco, at Huaylla, from which she took her territorial title, and which would later form part of the rich encomienda of Callanga of her Spanish lover.

The palaces and temples of Tumibamba, the ruins of which lie buried in the neighbourhood of the Ecuadorian city of Cuenca, had been built on the site of the former capital of the Cañari people by the Coya's father and grandfather at the time of their separate conquests of the northern Andes.

They are among the finest and richest [palaces] to be found in all Peru, situated at the crossing of two small rivers in a plain having a circumference of twelve leagues. It is a chilly land, abounding in game such as deer, rabbits and partridges, turtledoves and other birds. The Temple of the Sun was of stone put together with the subtlest skill, some stones are large, black and rough, and others seem of jasper . . . the façades of many of the buildings are beautiful and decorated, some had been set with precious gems and emeralds, and inside, the walls of the temple and the palaces of the Inca

---

* Yupanqui was the Quéchua title denoting royalty.
† See Appendix 3.

lords, had been covered with sheets of the finest gold and embossed with many statues, all of this metal . . .[30]

Among the hundreds of other sons and daughters born to the Emperor was Atahualpa, the great Turkey Cock, whose mother was his cousin and who was regarded as the Emperor's favourite son.[31] Three other sons, also from different mothers, whose names feature in the history of the Conquest, were the Incas Túpac Huallpa, Manco and Paullu. What each chronicler records is that in the last years of Huayna Cápac's life his empire was devastated by a plague, probably smallpox, which had spread from the northern borders of his realms to as far south as Cuzco. The chroniclers record that the epidemic was believed by his shamen to have been the retribution of the god Viracocha, and for whose appeasement the human sacrifice of thousands of children was ordered throughout the empire. The Jesuit Bernabé Cobo wrote that in an act of penitence the Emperor had gone into seclusion and had fasted to bring an end to the suffering of his people, and that during his fast he had seen the ghosts of three dwarfs enter his chamber which he interpreted as a sign of his impending death. The chronicler Sarmiento de Gamboa also describes in some detail how the Emperor then summoned his diviners to guide him in his choice of successor. The carcass of a young llama was brought to his presence and its entrails were read by the High Priest, the Villac-Umu, who informed him that the auspices for the succession of his son Ninancuyochi were unfavourable. The carcass of a second llama was brought to him, and again the same auspices were predicted for the succession of his son Huáscar. It was a divination that would never be repeated.

In the year 1530 of the Christian calendar, the Inca Emperor was dead.[32] A thousand servants from his household were killed in sacrifice to serve him in the afterlife,[33] and for ten days the tribes of Quito mourned his passing in the traditional weeping before his body was taken to Tumibamba to be mummified, where the Cañari people who worshipped the moon deity would mourn their sovereign for the length of an entire moon.[34] At Tumibamba the High Priest offered the throne to Ninancuyochi, but within a few days he too was dead, either poisoned or stricken by smallpox. The little that can be surmised from all the conflicting accounts is that the widowed Coya Rahua Ocllo was instrumental in the High Priest's subsequent proclamation of her son Huáscar as Emperor: an election welcomed by the panacas of Cuzco who over the years, and to their detriment, had witnessed the growing pre-eminence of their northern empire. Among the dead Emperor's sons only Atahualpa, who had the support of his

The Emperor Húascar. (Herrera: BL, 783. g. 1–4)

father's northern warrior armies, and who was then possibly twenty-seven years old, five years older than Huáscar,[35] would excuse himself from travelling south to Cuzco to pay homage to his brother.

Within a few weeks the cortège of the Emperor's mummified body began its 1,200-mile journey south to Cuzco. Bound in white cloth, it was carried on a throne litter by his principal lords and accompanied by the litters of the Coya Rahua Ocllo and her retinue. The procession travelled on the great Chinchasuyo road that separated the coastal plains and the cordillera, from where its progress was reported to the new Emperor by the chasqui, relays of runners, who could cover the entire distance the cortège would travel in less than five days. To the traditional wailing of women mourners, their breasts exposed in demonstration of their grief, the caravan of litters and armed warriors with their baggage train of yanacona porters and llamas made its ascent into the cordillera along its stone terraced roads and canyon valleys. At the mountain rest house of Limatambo, where it had encamped for several days, the Coya Rahua Ocllo was summoned by her son to travel ahead to Cuzco. Some time after her departure the retinue of Inca princes and lords was massacred. It was an act she would never forgive her son, and a reprisal for what he had believed had been his relatives' complicity in Atahualpa's refusal to render him homage. The massacre, chronicled by most of the early Spanish accounts, would also add to the resentment they recorded that was felt by the lords of Cuzco to their new Emperor's decision to appropriate the panaca lands and wealth, and which would unite many of them in siding with Atahualpa's eventual rebellion.[36]

Within a year the Inca realm of Tahuantinsuyo was torn in a civil war which would result in the killing of tens of thousands of its people and witness the sacking of the city of Tumibamba by Atahualpa's armies and the massacre of its Cañari inhabitants, among them some 2,000 Lupaca warriors of the Coya Doña Beatriz's guardian.[37] The war of the two brothers was finally brought to an end by the capture of the young Emperor on the outskirts of Cuzco. Imprisoned in a wooden cage, he was forced to watch the killing of nearly all the members of his panaca and of his young sister-queen, whose bodies were impaled on the northern road to what had once been his imperial capital. The only members of his immediate family to survive were his full-blooded sisters the coyas Doña Beatriz and Marca Chimbo, who after her baptism would be known as Doña Juana, then possibly twelve and thirteen years old. The chronicler Juan de Betanzos recorded that they were spared because of their youth and because, unlike their other sisters, 'they had known no man'.[38] The skin of his shoulders threaded by ropes, Huáscar was taken by the warrior chiefs Quisquis and Chalcuchima to the mountain hamlet of Andamarca, south of Cajamarca. There, above the waters of a river, together with his mother, the Hummingbird, the last God Emperor of the Sun, was killed. In less than two years the Inca realm of Tahuantinsuyo had virtually dismembered itself, and through the fate of circumstance had laid itself open to its final and inevitable destruction by the small army of Pizarro's conquistadors who had disembarked on its northern shore.

3

THE KILLING OF THE
GREAT TURKEY COCK

Atahualpa was a man of some thirty years of age, of fine appearance and disposition, somewhat stocky, his face imposing, beautiful and ferocious, his eyes bloodshot.

Francisco López de Jerez
Verdadera Relación de la Conquista del Perú

The arrival of the white-skinned, bearded strangers had been heralded by various portents the shaman of the imperial court had interpreted as announcing the fall of Tahuantinsuyo: an eagle had been seen being attacked by condors above the main square of Cuzco; comets were sighted across the Andes; and a blood-red circle had been witnessed enveloping the moon.[1] The triumph of the Inca Atahualpa's warrior chiefs Quisquis and Chalcuchima in their capture of Cuzco had also coincided with the first sighting of the strangers. The presence of the small contingent of conquistadors on the north-western coast was relayed to the Inca, who in the closing months of 1532 was making his triumphal progress south from Quito towards Cuzco.

There are innumerable theories as to why Pizarro's men were allowed to found a settlement on the coast, and then to march unhindered into the heartland of the Inca realm. Some chroniclers claimed it was simply because of the fear the equatorial Indians had of them, believing them to be gods, and their horses, arquebus and cannon to be demon spirits. There is, however, no evidence that the Inca Atahualpa believed in the divinity of the Spaniards. At the time of their landing his armies were engaged in a full-scale war against his brother the Emperor Huáscar in the central Andes and Cuzco region, a campaign that would last until the arrival of Almagro's reinforcements almost two years later. Atahualpa's reaction towards the Spaniards, other than curiosity, was more probably based on his desire to avoid their alliance with the armies of his brother, by then in retreat, and may well have been the reason he sent them guides to lead them to the township of Cajamarca, where he could see them for himself, and where he had halted his triumphal progress to Cuzco. His scouts and messengers, moreover, would

Pizarro's arrival at Túmbez.
(Herrera: BL, 783. g. 1–4)

have informed him of every detail of the Spaniards and of their movements: from their constant enquiries and search for gold, to the mortality of their horses and number of the camp women and porters who accompanied them, among them Isthmian and Negro slaves, their foreheads branded with the letter R, for rey, king, the mark of their bondage to their Spanish emperor.[2] He would also have been informed of their rape of some 500 mamacuna virgins of the sun temple, who the Spaniards had rounded up in the main square of the township of Cajas, north of Cajamarca.

Pizarro's contingent of 168 volunteers had only begun their trek into the foothills of the great cordillera of the Andes some twelve months after they had sailed from Panama, having first awaited the arrival of the ships of Sebastián de Benalcázar and the slaver Hernando de Soto from Nicaragua. The horsemen were commanded by the thirty-year-old Soto and captained by Benalcázar, who was some ten years older, and one of the few veterans of the conquest of Honduras. Pizarro commanded the main body of foot soldiers, which included the two small cannon of the Greek Pedro de Candía, a former sailor and native of Crete who had accompanied him to the court at Toledo. Another of his captains was his thirty-year-old brother Hernando, and in whose squadron rode his other half-brothers Juan and Gonzalo, both in their early twenties.[3] The only priest to accompany the contingent was the thirty-year-old Dominican Vicente de Valverde, the

The conquistadors fighting the tribesmen of Túmbez. (Herrera: BL, 783. g. 1–4)

sole survivor of the six friars of his Order, appointed by the Crown to act as chaplains to the expedition, after their superior Reginaldo de Pedraza had abandoned the march and returned to the Isthmus, 'taking with him,' in the words of the foot soldier Diego de Trujillo, 'some hundred emeralds he had sewn into his garments'.[4] For almost eight weeks they made their way through the mountain passes of the Andes, finally reaching the great valley and township of Cajamarca, on the outskirts of which the Inca and his court were encamped. It was a confrontation that would decide the future course of Andean American history. Forty years later the illiterate Estremaduran Trujillo recalled the events that followed their entry into the township:

> That day the governor [Pizarro] sent the captain de Soto with twenty horsemen to visit Atahualpa and entered the lodging where he was camped, staying there until very late. And as he did not return and suspecting that he may have been killed, the governor ordered Hernando Pizarro to take with him horsemen and foot soldiers, and I among them, to discover what had taken place. When we reached his camp we found the captain de Soto with the men he had taken, and Hernando Pizarro said to him: 'Your Grace, what is happening?' And he replied: 'As you can see, we are still waiting,' and then saying: 'soon Atahualpa will come out' – who was still in his lodging – 'but until now he has not.' Hernando Pizarro shouted at the interpreter: 'Tell him to come out!'

The man returned and said: 'Wait, he will see you shortly.' And Hernando Pizarro said to him: 'Tell the dog to come out immediately!' . . . and then Atahualpa came out of his lodging, holding two small gold cups in his hands that were filled with chicha, and gave one to Hernando Pizarro and the other he drank. And Hernando Pizarro said to the interpreter: 'Tell Atahualpa that there is no difference in rank between myself and the captain de Soto, for we are both captains of the king, and in his service we have left our homelands to come and instruct him in the Faith.' And then it was agreed that Atahualpa would come the following day, which was a Saturday, to Cajamarca. Guarding his camp were more than forty thousand Indian warriors in their squadrons, and many principal lords of the land. And on departing Hernando de Soto reared the legs of his horse, near to where were positioned the first of these squadrons, and the Indians of the squadron fled, falling over each other. And when we returned to Cajamarca Atahualpa ordered three hundred of them to be killed because they had shown fear and fled, and this we discovered another day when we found their bodies. The following day Atahualpa came with all his people in procession to Cajamarca, and the league they travelled took them until almost half an hour before sunset. Six hundred Indians in white and black livery, as if pieces of a chess board, came ahead of him, sweeping the road of stones and branches. And the governor, seeing they were taking such a great time, sent Hernando de Aldana who spoke their language to ask him to come before it was too dark.[5] And Aldana spoke to him, and only then did they begin to move at a walking pace. In Cajamarca there are ten streets that lead from the square. And in each of these the governor placed eight men, and in some, fewer number, because of the few men we had, and the horsemen he positioned in three companies: one with Hernando Pizarro, one with Hernando de Soto with his own men, and one with Sebastián de Benalcázar with his, and all with bells attached to their bridles, and the governor positioned himself in the fortress with twenty-four of his guards; for in all we were a hundred and sixty: sixty horsemen and a hundred on foot . . . as Atahualpa entered the square of Cajamarca, and as he saw no Christians he asked the Inca [one of the Inca lords] who had been with us: 'What has become of these bearded ones?' And the Inca replied: 'They are hidden.' And he asked him to climb down from his throne litter on which he sat, but he refused. And then the Friar Vicente de Valverde made himself seen

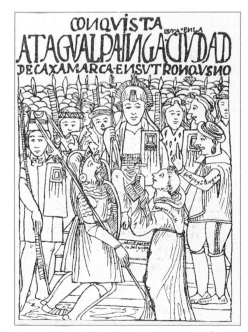

The Inca Atahualpa at Cajamarca. (Felipe Guaman Poma de Ayala, *Nueva Corónica y Buen Gobierno*)

and attempted to inform him of the reason why we had come on the orders of the pope and of one of his sons, a Christian leader who was the emperor, our lord. And speaking of his words of the Holy Gospel Atahualpa said to him: 'Whose words are these?' And he replied: 'The words of God.' And Atahualpa said: 'How is this possible?' And the friar Vicente told him: 'See, here it is written.' And he showed him a breviary which he opened, and Atahualpa demanded to be given it and took it, and after looking at it he threw it on the ground and ordered: 'Let none of them escape!' And the Indians gave a great cry, shouting: 'Inca, let it be so!' And the shouting made us very frightened. And the friar Vicente returned and climbed to the wall where the governor was and said to him: 'Your Excellency, what will you do? Atahualpa is like Lucifer.' And then the governor climbed down and armed himself with a shield and sword and put on his helmet, and with the twenty-four men who were with him, and I among them, we went directly to Atahualpa's litter, pushing our way through the crowd of Indians, and as we tried to pull him off his litter the horsemen charged to the great sound that was made from their bridle bells, and entered the fighting . . . and there in the square fell so many people, one on top of the other, that many were suffocated, and of the eight thousand Indians who died, over half died in this manner. The killing of those who fled continued for half a league and into the night . . .[6]

The chronicler Pedro Pizarro would also recall that he had been told that some of the conquistadors when they had first seen Atahualpa's retinue enter Cajamarca had urinated in their armour out of sheer fear. For the majority of Pizarro's volunteers it had been the first time they had ever fought in their lives. Their victory and the slaughter that ensued they owed more to the terror that their small cannon and horses had inflicted on the Inca's mainly unarmed attendants. No explanation, however, is given by any of the chroniclers as to why Atahualpa had not been accompanied by his squadrons of warriors when he entered the township. What is apparent was his desire to demonstrate to both the Spaniards and his own people his sovereignty and courage, which some of his warriors had lacked when challenged by Soto's horsemanship.

Atahualpa's capture would virtually paralyse his empire, denigrating him in the eyes of his subjects to the level of his brother the Emperor Huáscar, whose public humiliation and torture was witnessed at Cuzco. Nor was his treatment of his brother any less cruel than what he had himself experienced during his own brief imprisonment at the outbreak of his rebellion. The great imperial panacas of Cuzco and their lords, divided by their rivalries, were soon to find themselves not only facing the open desertion of many of their subject tribesmen, but the retribution of Atahualpa's northern warrior chiefs, men who were neither of Quéchua or Inca royal blood, but who had risen from the ranks of the imperial armies, and who had little regard for their princely order. The almost total breakdown of Inca rule, and what was becoming the virtual dismemberment of their sovereignty, indicated by the caciques who are recorded to have entered the encampment to offer the Spaniards their allegiance, possibly more than anything else influenced Pizarro's later decision to execute Atahualpa.

Manacled and kept prisoner in one of the township's stone lodgings, the Inca offered Pizarro tribute for his release, an act which in itself would have been regarded by his people as a symbol of his vassalage. The tribute, which would also have included the lordship of the subject tribes, their herds of llamas and women, was recorded by the horseman Cristóbal de Mena:

> The cacique [Atahualpa] said that he would summon ten thousand Indians and that they would fill a chamber with silver,* and that all this he would give him if he freed him. This the governor promised him, as long as he did not deceive him . . . [some time later] we discovered the cacique had imprisoned another lord, called Cuzco† who was a greater lord and his brother, though not a son of his mother; and that Cuzco, who was being brought hither, knew that the Christians had taken his brother prisoner . . . and fearing the Christians would kill him [Atahualpa] and recognize his brother Cuzco as lord, ordered that he [Huáscar] be killed . . .[7]

For five months Pizarro tenuously secured the survival of his men by holding the Inca hostage on the promise of his payment of tribute, to which only he and his men would hold sole right once it had been collected. Three separate armies of Atahualpa's northern warrior chiefs were camped within days' and weeks' marches of the township: the chiefs Rumiñavi to the north, Chalcuchima to the south and Quisquis guarding Cuzco, numbering some hundred thousand warriors. Their reluctance to attack the Spaniards was due solely to their desire to prevent Atahualpa being killed, and because of which they were to comply with his order for the gathering of the tribute.

On 14 April 1533, Almagro's reinforcements, having only just heard of Atahualpa's capture and the location of Pizarro's men at San Miguel,[8] finally entered the valley of Cajamarca after a march from the coast of almost twelve weeks. It was a sight that brought as much rejoicing to Pizarro's beleaguered men, as it did dismay to the imprisoned Inca and his small retinue of attendants, including women from his harem who Pizarro had allowed to accompany him. Luis Sánchez, a foot soldier in Almagro's army, recorded: '. . . all those who marched with the Adelantado suffered greatly in the fighting, hunger and deprivations, for the land was at war, and in the crossing of many mountains, ravines and rivers'.[9] Weighed down by their armour and plagued by the intense heat of the equator and the contrasting cold of the cordillera, where horses and men in single file had crossed the giant hanging reed

---

* Silver – the Spanish word *plata*, silver, also meant treasure or money, as it still does to this day in certain Andean regions.
† Cuzco was one of the titles of the Emperor Huáscar, who was killed at Andamarca, south of Cajamarca.

bridges of its rivers and ravines, it had been a march that had cost the lives of thirty of Almagro's men. The Conquistador Nicolás de Ribera recalled they had experienced: 'much hardship and lack of provisions until we reached Cajamarca, where the governor Don Francisco Pizarro was encamped. And though he had made Atahualpa his prisoner he was greatly overjoyed by our arrival, for we had arrived at a time when he had great need of our assistance because of Atahualpa's imprisonment and the threat from the multitude of his warriors . . .'.[10]

The township that Almagro's army entered resembled little more than an armed encampment, guarded by Candía's cannon and by mounted and foot sentries. The rudiments of a small church had been erected in its square, where the following morning the Friar Valverde celebrated Easter Mass. The celebrations of Almagro's weary men were, however, soon dampened by their realization that they would not be entitled to the vast hoard of treasure still being gathered for the Inca's tribute, and which was being brought daily to the township in caravans of llamas from the neighbouring regions.

Pizarro's refusal to share the tribute equally with Almagro and his men created a hostility between the two groups of conquistadors, which only added to the already fragile relationship of the two former Isthmian slavers. It would inevitably ferment the armed confrontation of the conquistadors years later on the windswept plains of Salinas, south of Cuzco, and of Chupas, near Ayacucho, where more of them were to be killed than at any time during the Conquest, and which would bring about the bloody deaths of both Almagro and Pizarro. The repercussions of their differences, if not their status in later years, would manifest itself in the title given Pizarro's men of 'first conquerors', for taking part in Atahualpa's capture, and the less imposing one of 'second conquerors' to Almagro's volunteers. Few of Almagro's men would recognize this label, among them Mansio Serra de Leguizamón, who would always describe himself as a 'first conqueror and discoverer'.[11]

An outward appearance of begrudging cordiality was nevertheless maintained in the encampment by both groups, conscious of the fact that strength in numbers was their only hope of fighting their way out of Cajamarca and seizing the imperial capital of Cuzco, where they believed the greatest amount of treasure was stored, and where Pizarro had sent three of his men and a Negro slave, accompanied by the Inca's guides. Billeted in the tents they had brought with them from the Isthmus and in the stone wall and thatch-roof houses of the township, the men were provided with food by their Indian women and lived off a diet of potato, then unknown in Europe, maize, guinea pig, fowl, llama meat and chicha maize. Many of the women had followed them from the coast, others were natives of the township or had belonged to the Inca's retinue, among them his sister the Ñusta Quispe Sisa* who he had given Pizarro for his concubine, and who after her baptism would

---

* Ñusta meant niece or daughter of the Emperor, though one whose mother was not a coya.

be known as Doña Inés.[12] According to the foot soldier Trujillo, among the contingent Hernando de Soto had brought with him from Nicaragua had been the first Spanish woman to set foot on the southern continent, Juana Hernández, though her presence, possibly because she was a prostitute, is not mentioned by any of the official chroniclers.

Nothing, however, appears to have lessened the Spaniards' continual fear of attack by the Inca's armies in a bid to free him. It was a fear expressed by the horseman Miguel de Estete: 'The Inca let it be known what he planned to do with us, for it was his intention to take our horses and mares, which was what impressed him most, for breeding, and to castrate some of us for his service to guard his women, as was their custom, the rest he would sacrifice to the sun.'[13] The eighteen-year-old Pedro Pizarro, who had arrived with Almagro's reinforcements from San Miguel de Piura, where he had formed part of Pizarro's earlier settlement, left a vivid portrait of the Inca's captivity:

> . . . many caciques served him, though they always remained outside in the courtyard, and when ever he called one of them he would enter bare-foot and carrying in homage a burden on his back . . . on his head he [the Inca] wore a llautu, which are braids of coloured wool, half a finger thick and a finger in width, in the manner of a crown . . . on his forehead he wore a fringe attached to the llautu, made of fine scarlet wool, evenly cut and adorned with small gold strings. His hair, like that of all his lords, he wore cut short . . . one day when he was being fed by his sisters and when he raised some food to his mouth, a particle fell on his clothing, and giving his hand to one of the women he stood up and went into his chamber to put on new clothing, and when he came back he wore a shirt and a dark brown mantle. I felt the mantle which was smoother than silk and I said to him: 'Inca, of what is this cloth made?' And he said to me: 'It is made of birds who fly by night [vampire bats] in Puerto Viejo and Túmbez and who bite my people.' And on my asking him what he kept in his chests, he showed me they contained the clothing he had worn and all the garments that had touched his skin. And I asked him: 'For what purpose do you have these garments here?' He answered that it was in order to burn them, for what had been touched by the sons of the Sun must be burnt to ashes, which none was allowed to handle, and scattered to the wind . . .[14]

Several thousand subject tribesmen and their caciques and women, among them Cañaris, Chachapoyas and Huanca warriors who had sought shelter with the Spaniards, were by then camped in the valley. A number of Inca lords from Huáscar's defeated armies were also camped outside the walls of the township, adding to the general confusion of divided loyalties witnessed by the Inca and his retinue from his stone cell. For the next 4 months the combined company of some 330 conquistadors were to remain in the township, awaiting the arrival of further caravans of the tribute treasure. Deposited in its square, the thousands of gold and silver artefacts were taken to a chamber, of some 22 ft in length and 17 ft in width, which would eventually be filled with gold to a height of 8 ft, and filled twice over in its entirety with silver.[15] The conquistadors Diego de Trujillo, Bernabé Picón and Serra de Leguizamón were later to claim that the original chamber in which the treasure had been kept had burned down.[16]

Eleven days after the arrival of Almagro's men, Hernando Pizarro and a small squadron of horse returned to Cajamarca after an absence of almost three months in search of treasure, in an expedition the Inca had sanctioned to the Temple of Pachacámac, south of Lima. Though finding little treasure, Hernando had brought with him as his prisoner Atahualpa's warrior chief Chalcuchima. Wishing to meet with his master, he had agreed to accompany Hernando to the encampment, giving him some 5,000 pesos of gold and ordering his servants to shoe his horses with silver. Within hours of his audience with the Inca he was tied to a stake and partially burned by Hernando de Soto to reveal the whereabouts of treasure he believed he had ordered buried near the township. The brutality exhibited by Soto, who had often shown the imprisoned Inca great kindness and had taught him to play chess, is demonstrative of the psychology of the men of the Indies, none of whom, including Almagro and Pizarro, would have thought twice about meting out a similar punishment, nor believed that they would have shared a more humane fate at the hands of the Inca, who had proudly showed them the shrunken head of one of his brothers he used as a drinking vessel. The Indian Tancara, in evidence he gave to an enquiry in 1607, recorded that Hernando Pizarro had burned his grandfather to death and other caciques in the province of Omasuyos. Another Indian testimonial revealed that he had burned some 600 Lupaca tribesmen.[17] Torture and killing were to become for the Spaniards a way of life. No prisoners were taken. No quarter was given.

Some four weeks after Almagro's reinforcements had reached Cajamarca, Pizarro ordered the smelting of what had been accumulated of the tribute, in nine separate forges. For seven days and nights 11 tons of gold and silver artefacts were fed into the furnaces, yielding some 13,420 lbs of 22.5 carat gold in ingots and 26,000 lbs in silver. A few days after the smelting had been completed, one of the three foot soldiers[18] who had been sent to Cuzco under the protection of the Inca's guides to supervise the collection of the city's tribute, returned to the township accompanied by a caravan of llamas, bringing some of the 700 sheets of gold which had been stripped from the Temple of Coricancha. A month later Hernando Pizarro left Cajamarca for the Isthmus, taking with him the Crown's share of the Inca's tribute – the Royal Fifth – of some 100,000 pesos of gold and various artefacts, among them a life-size gold statue of a boy. In the following days the two other foot soldiers returned from Cuzco, carried in litters by their Indian porters and followed by a train of 255 llamas with more sheets of the temple's gold.

The distribution of the tribute treasure would take a whole month to complete. A document, signed by Pizarro, recorded that the full amount of treasure smelted at Cajamarca amounted to 1,326,539 pesos of gold and 51,610 marks of silver.[19] Neither of these figures would include the gold and silver artefacts and jewels that the Spaniards took as personal booty, nor Atahualpa's gold throne litter chair which Pizarro appropriated for himself. Hernando de Soto on his eventual return to Spain a few years later took with him a personal fortune of some 100,000 pesos of gold, a far greater figure than he is recorded as having been awarded by Pizarro. The gold had been smelted in ingots of 8¾ lbs in weight – some 1,000 pesos. Each of Pizarro's horsemen were awarded approximately 8,800 pesos of gold and 362 marks of silver, each of his foot soldiers 4,440 pesos of gold and 181 marks of silver. For these men, most of whom had known nothing but poverty, it was a fortune that would transform their lives. Pizarro's own share in gold was 57,220 pesos. The awards in gold to his three half-brothers were indicative of their influence in his small council of captains, and also of Soto's initial investment in the expedition: Hernando Pizarro – 31,080 pesos; Hernando de Soto – 17,740 pesos; Juan Pizarro – 11,100 pesos; Sebastián de Benalcázar, Pedro de Candía, Gonzalo Pizarro – 9,009 pesos each. The Friar Valverde because of his vows of poverty received no award. The few men who had stayed behind at San Miguel, and who had formed part of Pizarro's expeditionary force, were awarded 15,000 pesos between them. Though Almagro and his men had no claim to the tribute, Pizarro awarded them 20,000 pesos. It was a gesture that did little to alter their feeling of resentment and only increased their demand to leave Cajamarca and to continue their march to Cuzco, the sacking of which they saw as their only hope of enriching themselves.

Mansio Serra de Leguizamón, though not even a captain, was awarded 2,000 pesos of gold by Pizarro.[20] It was an award none of Almagro's men would receive individually with the exception of Nicolás de Ribera, who had been one of Pizarro's oldest companions, and which was possibly indicative of Pizarro's regard for him. An encomendero of Lima would record that some five years after the events at Cajamarca, veterans could still be seen wearing the jewels they had taken there as booty. Most of them would dissipate their fortunes, gambling them away at the toss of a card in the months they had stayed in the encampment, or in their reckless spending on the few available goods to be found which they paid for in bars of gold and silver. The notary Francisco López de Jerez recorded that a jug of wine cost 60 pesos of gold; a pair of boots or breeches: from 30 to 40 pesos; a cape: 125 pesos; a clove of garlic: ½ peso; a sword: 50 pesos; a sheet of vellum paper: 10 pesos.[21] The foot soldier Melchor Verdugo is recorded as having purchased a horse, an Isthmian Indian and a woman, described as marked with a facial scar, and twenty chickens for 2,000 pesos from the priest Asencio. A horse in poor condition was valued at 94 pesos, and one in good condition at

3,000 pesos. Negro slaves, depending on their age and physique, were sold for between 300 and 600 pesos. Juan Pantiel de Salinas, one of the farriers, is recorded as having spent days shoeing horses with silver.[22]

The distribution of Atahualpa's tribute inevitably sealed his fate. Pizarro's notary López de Jerez recorded that at the time the Inca had informed a number of his captors that he had seen a ball of fire illuminate the night sky, and that he knew it was an omen of his own death.[23] Legend has created an almost theatrical image of the events that led to his supposed trial and execution based on the alleged evidence of the Indian interpreter Felipillo,[24] who was said to have overheard Atahualpa ordering an attack on the township – a story originating some twenty years after the Inca's death. Even though various eyewitnesses record that both Almagro and the treasurer Alonso de Riquelme had demanded his execution and that Pizarro had only reluctantly agreed to their request, it seems implausible that he would have been swayed in his decision by anyone's demands. Pizarro's brother Hernando, who would later claim to disapprove of his action because it lacked the Crown's authority, was already in the Isthmus and about to sail for Spain. Hernando de Soto, who had offered to take the Inca to Spain – ostensibly for the same reason, but in reality to further his own influence at court – was also absent from Cajamarca on a scouting sortie to investigate a report of the approach of an army commanded by the chief Rumiñavi. It was a report that proved to be without foundation, but which had enabled Pizarro to justify his decision to his men. There appears to be no real evidence that Pizarro was opposed by anyone in his action.

On the evening of 26 July 1533, his neck, arms and feet manacled in chains, the Inca was brought out of the chamber that had been his prison for almost eight months into the township's square, where he was tied to a stake and made to sit on a stool in front of the entire assembly of conquistadors. He was then addressed through an interpreter by the Friar Valverde and urged to accept baptism, but he made no reply until a Cañari tribesman who Pizarro had appointed his executioner approached him. It was then, the foot soldier Lucas Martínez Vegazo recorded, that the Inca began to cry out, entreating Valverde, as if he were agreeing with what had been demanded of him, and Valverde baptized him, giving him Pizarro's name of Francisco, and telling him that because of his repentance he would not be burnt alive as had been decreed. He once more began to cry out, gesturing with his hands and indicating the height of his children who he said were very young, and pleading with Valverde to commend their safety to Pizarro. 'He wept and spoke to the tongue [interpreter]', recalled Mansio Serra de Leguizamón, 'and again he asked the Marqués to care for his two sons and daughter he had left in Quito.' Many of the Inca lords and his women who had accompanied him in his imprisonment began to wail and prostrated themselves on the ground, but by then the Cañari had been given the signal he had been waiting for, and with one wrench of each end of the rope he had tied around the Inca's neck, garrotted him. All that night his body remained in the square, seated on the stool and tied to the stake, his head slumped to one side, and his arms and legs covered in his blood.

The events at Cajamarca were recorded by eight conquistadors.[25] They were men neither schooled as historians nor possessed of any literary pretensions, but who were among the few of Pizarro's volunteers able to read and write. In a letter to the Audiencia of the island of Santo Domingo, where he had stayed for a brief period while on his return to Spain, Hernando Pizarro had described only the principal events of his brother's march to Cajamarca, the first account of these matters to reach Spain. A copy of his letter was made by the chronicler and genealogist Gonzalo Fernández de Oviedo, which he incorporated in his *Historia General y Natural de las Indias*, written in about 1550, in the fortress of Santo Domingo, of which he was warden. The Castilian hidalgo Cristóbal de Mena, a former encomendero of Nicaragua, who because of his disaffection with

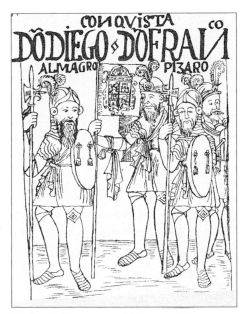

Diego de Almagro and Francisco Pizarro. (Felipe Guaman Poma de Ayala, *Nueva Corónica y Buen Gobierno*)

Pizarro had returned to Spain immediately after the distribution of the Inca's tribute, shortly afterwards published his chronicle *Conquista del Perú, llamada la Nueva Castilla*, one of the few accounts highly critical of Pizarro. Other than a meeting he is recorded to have had with one of Almagro's agents in Spain in 1536, nothing else is known of his life.

Mena's controversial story was followed by the publication at Seville of *Verdadera Relación de la Conquista del Perú* by Pizarro's notary Francisco López de Jerez, and written partly as a refutation of Mena's chronicle. It has always been assumed that because of a leg wound he had suffered during the capture of the Inca, López de Jerez had been forced to return to Spain directly from the township, arriving at the port of Seville, as he affirms in his chronicle in June 1534. The few surviving records show that after his wife's death he married the daughter of a hidalgo family from Seville, and that in 1554, signing himself solely Francisco López, he was granted permission to return to Peru as notary to the Audiencia of Lima.[26] It was a post historians have always believed he never filled, and that he remained in Spain until his death, the place and date of which is unknown. His presence as notary to the Audiencia of Lima between the years 1559 and 1565, however, can be established by the words added to the final page of Mansio Serra de Leguizamón's probanza, and published here for the first time: '. . . inscribing my signature Francisco López, who had been among the men who had gone immediately afterwards [from Cajamarca] to place Cuzco under the royal jurisdiction, in the company of the reserves of the captain Hernando de Soto and Mansio Serra and

Martínez Vegazo as they marched southward from Vilcasbamba to Cuzco, all of which he witnessed . . .'.[27] The only other person at Cajamarca of the same name was an illiterate surgeon barber who served on the later march to Cuzco, but only as far as Jauja, and who returned to Spain in 1535.[28]

The foot soldier Pedro Sancho de la Hoz replaced López de Jerez as Pizarro's notary and was the author of *Relación del Descubrimiento y Conquista del Perú*, dated 1534, which he sent to the Emperor Charles V, the original manuscript of which was lost. A copy, translated into Italian, is dated 1550. Sancho left for Spain two years after writing his account, but like so many of the returning conquistadors he soon dissipated his share of the Cajamarca treasure, and was given permission to return to Peru in 1539. Eight years later, during the settlement of Chile he was executed by one of the Conquistador Pedro de Valdivia's captains on a charge of sedition, his head displayed in the main square of its capital at Santiago.

Miguel de Estete, a Riojano from Santo Domingo de la Calzada, had been one of the men Hernando de Soto had brought with him from Nicaragua. During Atahualpa's imprisonment he had accompanied Hernando Pizarro to the coastal temple at Pachacámac, his description of which López de Jerez incorporated in his chronicle. On his return to Spain in 1534 he settled at Valladolid, where he possibly wrote his account *Noticia del Perú*. The date and place of his death are unknown. Juan Ruiz de Arce, an Estremaduran who had lived in Jamaica and in Honduras, returned to Spain a year after Cajamarca, where he was received at court. He was one of the few conquistadors not to have squandered his fortune, retiring to his native township of Alburquerque. His manuscript, of seventeen folio pages, remained unknown until its discovery and publication in 1933. Pedro Pizarro and Diego de Trujillo were among the few veterans still alive at the time the Viceroy Don Francisco de Toledo asked them to dictate their memoirs. Pedro Pizarro, who died in 1587 at Arequipa, sent his memoir, dated 7 February 1571, the following year to Spain, and which was subsequently lost. In the early seventeenth century a copy of his manuscript was acquired from one of his descendants by the Jesuit chronicler Bernabé Cobo. Trujillo, who was probably completely illiterate, unlike Pedro Pizarro had been present at the capture of Atahualpa. A year after Cajamarca he left Cuzco for Spain with his share of booty, and lived in the township of his name in Estremadura before returning to Peru. His manuscript was discovered in 1934 in the library of the Royal Palace in Madrid.

Few of these accounts make any mention of the undoubted pillage, rape and brutality that ensued. It was an omission also prevalent in their discrepancies, and in the partiality to which each, other than Mena, was indebted to Pizarro for patronage and honours, as is evident in their portrayal of his reluctance to execute the Inca. This act had in effect temporarily united the two rival factions of conquistadors, and would guarantee them the collaboration of the remnants of the Emperor Huáscar's depleted armies, and in practice determine the future of the Conquest.

THE CITY OF THE SUN GOD

He it was who took from the Temple of Cuzco as booty the sun of gold the Incas adored, and which he staked one night in a game of gambling and lost before dawn; and which is why there exists to this day in Peru a common refrain among gamblers when they encourage one another in their gaming by exclaiming: Gamble the sun before the dawn!

The Friar Antonio de la Calancha
Corónica Moralizada del Orden de San Agustín

Sixteen days after the killing of the Inca the combined contingents of conquistadors began their march south towards the imperial city of Cuzco. The horsemen and foot soldiers were joined by several thousand warriors and women, who acted as their porters.[1] In the cortège of litters that followed the Indian columns was the young Inca Prince Túpac Huallpa who had sworn fealty to Pizarro, accompanied by his sister-wife Azarpay and Atahualpa's warrior chief Chalcuchima, in chains and guarded by twenty foot soldiers. The vanguard of cavalry and their bannerman, holding aloft the Royal Standard, emblazoned with the scarlet and gold arms of Castile and León, were commanded by Almagro and Hernando de Soto: the plumed morrión helmeted horsemen, in full armour and riding in battle formation, their lances sloped across their shoulders. Marching behind them were the infantry led by Pizarro and the Friar Valverde, the wooden cross he had brought with him from the Isthmus strapped to a mule.* A small company of arquebusiers followed them, led by the Greek Candía and his Indian handlers, pulling the two small cannon. At some distance a reserve squadron of horsemen commanded by the treasurer Riquelme escorted the baggage train laden with the crown and the men's share of the Cajamarca treasure. The columns of conquistadors and their Indian auxiliaries slowly advanced towards the southern cordillera, its snow-clad peaks almost hidden by mist and cloud, their ranks by now

* The Cross of the Conquest is enshrined at Cuzco's church of El Triunfo.

The Apurímac River, engraving by
Champin, from François Castelnau,
*Expedition dans les Parties Centrales de
l'Amerique de Sud*, 3rd Part, 1852.
(National Arts Library, V&A Museum)

depleted of the men Benalcázar had escorted to the settlement at San Miguel de Piura, and those Pizarro had given permission to return to Spain. For almost two months they followed the stone roads and trails through which their Indians scouts led them, dwarfed by the vast cordillera of the Andes, until they eventually entered the valley and township of Jauja, lying on the banks of the Mantaro River. Lucas Martínez Vegazo in his evidence to Mansio Serra de Leguizamón's probanza recalled: '. . . in the same valley of Jauja Mayta Yupanqui, Atahualpa's warrior chief, in command of a great multitude of warriors, attacked us Spaniards and we fought the Indians until we broke and dispersed their squadrons, pursuing them and killing them for some twelve leagues, and among the Spaniards was Mansio Serra, who greatly served Your Majesty, and this I know, for it is what I saw'.[2] The warriors had been massed on the far bank of the township's bridges which they had burned, and Almagro's cavalry, fording the river, had charged them several times before dispersing them. It was the first engagement the Spaniards had faced against Atahualpa's army, the success of which had depended on their cavalry and the Indian auxiliaries that had followed them.

For two weeks they remained encamped in the township awaiting the arrival of Riquelme's baggage train, and where Pizarro founded the first Spanish municipality of the conquered territory. Within days of Riquelme's arrival the Inca Túpac Huallpa died. Conscious of the effect his death might have on the auxiliaries he had brought with him, who regarded him as their emperor, Pizarro ordered the men to break camp. 'In the advance to Cuzco,' recorded Mansio, 'the captain Hernando de Soto went ahead with seventy hand-picked soldiers, I among them, for much of the land was still at war,* and we reached the province of Vilcastambo, against whose Indians we fought . . . and I took prisoner many of their scouts after a great deal of fighting and risk'.[3] The trumpeter Pedro de Alconchel stated that Soto had taken Mansio with him for 'being young and diligent',[4] and the horseman Luis Sánchez that they went in pursuit of the warriors 'until the crest of Vilcaconga, fording and swimming across a river with much difficulty, for the natives had

---

* Evidence that fighting was still waging between the remnants of Huáscar's armies and Atahualpa's warrior chiefs.

burned its bridges, and it was winter and the rivers were in flood'.[5] It would take Soto's exhausted squadron several days to reach the Apurímac, the great river canyon of the Andes, and then to climb its great mountain ridge of Vilcaconga, some 12,000 ft in height. Mansio recalled that on reaching the crest of the mountain, some 28 miles from Cuzco, they were attacked by the chief Quisquis' warriors:

Hernando de Soto. (Herrera: BL, 783. g. 1–4)

> . . . and did battle with them, and which was with great difficulty; and in the battle many of our men were killed and wounded, as were many horses, and those that remained were wounded. And that among all the men the captain had taken with him I alone was chosen to return along the route we had taken to show the governors where to ford the river and bring them to where we were. And in great danger I returned through the lines of the Indians who surrounded us, and I was able to inform Don Diego de Almagro of what had taken place, and to show him and those who were with him the way to where the captain was besieged, and urge them there at all speed. And having informed Don Diego and those who were with him, within hours they relieved captain Soto and his men after marching a full day, and at great risk because of the multitude of Indians. On the orders of Don Diego I remained by the river in guard of it, and so as to show the governor Don Francisco Pizarro and the rear guard where to ford, and the route to take; and this I showed him, and with all speed we marched to relieve Don Diego and His Majesty's servitors, and where I helped bury our dead and cure our wounded of the royal encampment, and also bury the horses so the Indians would not discover our losses.[6]

In his memoir, written forty years later, Diego de Trujillo recorded:

> . . . that night we were in great peril, for it was snowing and many of the wounded were suffering from the cold and we were surrounded and could see fires lit on all sides . . . and at midnight from the direction of Limatambo we heard Alconchel's trumpet call which gave us much courage and inspired us to continue fighting the Indians, who had also heard his trumpet sound, and realizing that our men were coming to our aid they extinguished the fires and moved towards Cuzco . . . and it was so dark that one could not even see the glint of a coin, nothing but their sound . . .[7]

'After the killing of five Spaniards,' Lucas Martínez Vegazo stated, 'and with less than a shot left of our crossbows, and being positioned high up the crest and encircled by the

natives, the rescue arrived in the middle of the night, in groups of ten and of twenty . . .'.[8]
'. . . if that same night,' observed Pedro de Alconchel, 'the Adelantado Don Diego de Almagro and this witness and other horsemen had not come to their aid, some thirty men, more or less, not one of them would have escaped'.[9]

The relief of Vilcaconga and Alconchel's solitary clarion call announcing to the beleaguered conquistadors the arrival of Almagro's column was recalled for posterity by the historian William Prescott in his *History of the Conquest of Peru*, and was the single most important battle fought since their departure from Cajamarca. Five of their best horsemen had been killed and numerous men wounded. Soto's decision to ride forward without waiting for Almagro at Vilcas was seen by Pizarro as an act of insubordination, which could well have led to the massacre of the entire contingent of men. On reaching Vilcaconga, Pizarro ordered the men to re-group in the neighbouring village of Jaquijahuana, where they were joined by the Inca Manco, a sixteen-year-old half-brother of the Emperor Huáscar. 'I saw him meet us between Jaquijahuana and the mountain of Vilcaconga,' recalled Mansio, 'and greet the Marqués* Pizarro and all those who were with him in the conquest of this land, and to whom he swore fealty, and from that time he was acknowledged [by Pizarro] as lord of this realm . . .'.[10] Juan de Pancorbo recorded:

> . . . he gave the Marqués an account of the treachery of Chalcuchima, Atahualpa's chief, who we had brought with us as our prisoner, and of the instructions he had given against us to messengers he had sent to Quisquis, another of Atahualpa's chiefs, who was in command of Cuzco and of its outlying regions; for he [Manco Inca] had brought with him these messengers who he had had captured on the road and who he handed over to the Marqués. And this witness heard them tell how they had been sent by Chalcuchima to inform Quisquis that we were mortal and had difficulty climbing the mountain passes, and that we gave our lances to our yanacona who came behind us, and that our horses tired easily, and how they could be attacked in such passes . . . information they had placed in their coloured string cords [quipu] . . . and the Marqués, seeing it was so, said to Chalcuchima: 'Dog, is this what you have kept from me? How could you deceive me?' And he began to deny this and Manco Inca said to him: 'Here are the three messengers and their quipu, how can you deny this?' The messengers were questioned and said that it was the truth and Chalcuchima who was being carried in a litter fell from it, and it seemed to this witness that it was as if he were dead, and that same day the Marqués ordered he be burnt in the square of Jaquijahuana, and this witness saw him being burnt and shout aloud, and the little I could understand of what he said, it appeared to me he was

---

* Pizarro was created a marqués in October 1537.

invoking Pachacámac and Huanacauri, his principal huacas, and calling for Quisquis to avenge his death . . .[11]

The brutal killing of Atahualpa's warrior chief in front of the entire company of men by Pizarro was a warning to his Indian auxiliaries that he would not tolerate their betrayal. It would also make the young Inca prince, who had survived Quisquis' retribution against the imperial panacas, only too conscious of his own precarious role accorded him by Pizarro as his puppet ruler. Within the hour of their advance on Cuzco the conquistadors were to see the massed squadrons of Quisquis' warriors, who had positioned themselves in front of the approach to the city. Though Mansio and his witnesses varied in their estimates of their numbers, from 100,000 to 50,000, their gross exaggeration was possibly more out of ignorance, having never before seen such multitudes, which probably numbered about 10,000 men. 'The governors began their advance on the city,' stated Juan Pantiel de Salinas, '. . . half a league away Quisquis with a great number of men, which as far as I could tell were some eighty thousand in number, came out in its defence, and with whom we fought all day until almost nightfall when they retreated, leaving many Spaniards and horses wounded . . .'.[12] Mansio recorded that after their battle '. . . some two hundred Incas came to offer their allegiance to Don Francisco Pizarro . . .'.[13] The following morning in battle order the conquistadors entered the city. '. . . in all, we were no more than one hundred and twenty,' Bernabé Picón recalled.[14]

On the morning Pizarro recorded in a letter to the cabildo of Panama as Saturday 15 November 1533,[15] Hernando de Soto's vanguard of horsemen descended over the brow of the Carmenca and galloped two abreast into the city's narrow cobbled streets that led to its great square of Aucaypata, and in Mansio's words 'took possession of its strongholds'.[16] The city was virtually deserted and most of its palaces and public buildings had been set on fire by Quisquis' retreating army. Amid the smoke of its smouldering buildings and watched by its few frightened inhabitants, Soto's bearded and weary horsemen, among them Mansio, positioned themselves at either end of the square, their lances raised in salute. And to their cries of *Santiago y Castilla!* echoing across the vast quadrangle Pizarro led his infantry in battle order. An emotionless man, none of the chroniclers describe him as having shown any expression of particular joy at his victory, nor of having marched his small army across the cordillera of the Andes and captured one of the greatest cities of the Americas: a feat that would prove him to have been one of the most remarkable military leaders and exponents of what has come to be termed guerrilla warfare.

Within hours the order was given for the sacking of the city.[17] Its palaces and temple of Coricancha, already partly denuded by the pillaging of Quisquis' warriors and by what had already been taken for Atahualpa's tribute, were stripped of their remaining treasure. For days on end, in an orgy of vandalism and destruction, with their swords,

Francisco Pizarro, engraving. (Hulton Getty Picture Collection)

poniards and lances, the conquistadors hacked and stripped every artefact they could find from the walls and alcoves of its buildings, sheets of gold and silver, emeralds and pearls, carvings and sculptures. Overnight the city was transformed into a garrison of marauding soldiers, their armour and helmets adorned with the jewels they freely looted, intoxicated by the euphoria of their victory and by the Indian chicha they drank, which only added to the ferocity of their behaviour and rape of the city's women, old and young alike: a brutality only alluded to by the chroniclers.

In an age that had witnessed the looting of Rome by the army of their Emperor, and which within ten years would see the pillage of the medieval cathedrals and monasteries of a Catholic England, the sacking of Cuzco needs to be seen in the context of the time, and the brutality that ensued as equal to any in contemporary Europe. Both Spaniard and Inca had traditionally rewarded their soldiers and warriors with the booty of battle: gold, silver, women and male slaves. The fall of Cuzco could be no exception. The chronicler Cieza de León wrote that Quisquis, who had taken with him most of the city's mamacuna as concubines for his warriors, had also looted a great quantity of treasure. For Pizarro and Almagro, as at Cajamarca, the treasure would be the means of repaying the loans made them by a number of the conquistadors who had supplied them with ships and arms, as in the case of Hernando de Soto, and also their investors in Panama, merchants and Crown officials. It was to be several months before Pizarro would allow the official distribution of the booty, melted into ingots and said to have been half the amount in gold and four times in silver of the Cajamarca tribute, and which possibly represented almost three-quarters of the entire artistic heritage of Inca civilization. As Mansio recalled in his will, his share amounted to 8,000 pesos of gold and also included the Punchao, the gold Inca image of the sun: ' . . . which was of gold and which the Incas kept in the house of the sun [Coricancha], which is now the convent of Santo Domingo, where they practised their idolatries, and which I believe was worth some two thousand pesos of gold . . .'. It is more than probable that the gold image he referred to, if not only because of the relatively low value he placed on it, was a smaller sun disc of the temple's sanctuary which he may have either looted for himself or been awarded by Pizarro, and which he lost in a night of gambling: an act of such wanton abandon it would be commemorated in the Indies for years to come. Among the later chroniclers who recorded the event was the Indian Juan de Santa Cruz Pachacuti who drew an image in his manuscript of the inner sanctuary of the temple, which he inscribed in the margin with the words: 'Of this sheet of gold, it is said it was gambled and lost by a Spaniard in Cuzco, or so it is related by those of that place . . .'.[18] Well could the young hidalgo some forty years later somewhat arrogantly remind his sovereign King Philip II of the wealth of the Indies, of which the Spanish Crown had been the principal beneficiary:

From these realms has been taken such an infinity of gold and silver and pearls and riches to the realms of Spain, and which are daily sent to Your Majesty and his

Punchao, engraving. (Private Collection)

kingdom; all of which has been made possible by the conquest, discovery and pacification of these realms by the Marqués Don Francisco Pizarro and those who accompanied him, and the greatest service ever recorded in either ancient or modern history any vassals have rendered their monarch; all at their own cost and endeavour and without any expenditure of the Majesty of the King Don Carlos, our emperor and lord, as is well known, and for which the crowns of Castile and León have been so greatly endowed . . .[19]

Other than the principal Punchao of the temple, the Spaniards failed to find the Inca war huaca, a square stone of great size encased in gold and jewels, and the Muru Urco, a giant gold chain in the shape of a snake with the head of an anaconda, which the Emperor Huayna Cápac had commissioned to mark the birth of his son Huáscar. The chain had been used during the religious festivals at Cuzco and had stretched the entire length of the city's square. For years to come Peru's colonists would attempt to discover its supposed location in the waters of the lake at Urcos, south-east of Cuzco. And like the great treasures from the Inca Temple of Copacabana, at Lake Titicaca, not a trace has ever been found of the undoubted booty taken by Quisquis' warriors. Only after the distribution of the city's treasure did Pizarro, on 23 March 1534, found Cuzco as a municipality in words that convey the psychology of men who, regardless of their ignorance and blatant immorality, saw themselves as the evangelical heirs of the reconquest of Muslim Spain:

I, Francisco Pizarro, knight of the Order of Santiago, servant and vassal of His Majesty the Emperor King Don Carlos, our lord and gentleman of Spain, adelantado in his name, captain-general and governor of these kingdoms of New Castile, wishing to follow the custom of our ancestors and the order they possessed, and of those who His Majesty commanded for such great service of God, Our Lord, to augment our Holy Catholic Faith and the good conversion of the natives we have defeated in these remote lands, separated from the knowledge of the Holy Faith, and whom by its word were deemed servitors and brothers of ours and descendants of our first father, I wish to continue the settlement of these kingdoms which I have already commenced, in the name of Their Majesties. And wishing to thus continue by founding in this great city, the headship of all the land and sovereignty of the people who there live, and where I am, and at present reside, a town settlement of Spaniards, of those who accompanied me in the conquest of all these lands and of this city, having risked great hardship to their persons and lives and loss of estate in the name of Your Majesty; and thus

Detail of the door and wall of Mansio Serra de Leguizamón's mansion, Cuzco. (Nicholas du Chastel)

Mansio's mansion, Cuzco. (Nicholas du Chastel)

convene to the service of God, Our Lord, and distribute among them the lands they have won in compensation and satisfaction of their endeavours . . .[20]

Shortly after his proclamation Pizarro appointed eighty-eight encomenderos to his municipality. 'In recognition of the service I rendered Your Majesty,' Mansio recorded in his probanza, 'and the great expenditure I had incurred, I was among those when the land was divided to be awarded two distributions as a person of merit and for my service, and for which I was given seals.'[21] Mansio's statement adds credence to the fact that he was possibly one of the wealthiest of Almagro's volunteers, resources he could have either acquired in the years of his service in Veragua as a slaver, or from the gift of his rich relatives at court. 'I saw that the Marqués was always conscious of those who served him well in the war,' recalled Pedro de Alconchel, 'and because he was also so greatly fond of Mansio Serra for being so diligent and deserving he made him an encomendero of Cuzco and gave him a distribution of Indians.'[22] Mansio's award far exceeded that of any other conquistador of his age and relatively junior military rank, other than Pizarro's youngest brother Gonzalo, and was possibly a reward for the courage he had displayed at Vilcaconga. The *repartamientos*, distributions, of encomiendas were in effect primarily allocations of Indians from various subject tribes encamped in the Cuzco region as mitimae, tributary labourers, of the Inca lords. As Pedro Pizarro recorded it was Pizarro's intention to award a cacique to each of his encomenderos.[23] The tribal lands of the caciques would also form part of their encomiendas at a later time when the conquistadors had been able to inspect them for themselves, and to subdue any resistance to their authority with the aid of their caciques who formed part of their personal retinue. Mansio was awarded Indians of the lands of Catanga and Callanga in the Yucay valley, and of Alca in the Cuntisuyo, numbering in all several thousand Quéchua, Aymara and Manarí tribesmen and their caciques.[24] He was also given by Pizarro a section of the Yacha Huasi, the former Inca house of learning, the adjoining area of which was called Amaru Cata, the slope of the serpent. Here he would build his mansion which would be known as the Casa de Sierpes, the House of the Serpents, and whose carved images of snakes can be seen to this day on its Inca stonework.

Building by building the city witnessed the eviction of its lords and their families. Pizarro, who had awarded himself almost the entire neighbouring valley and Indians of the Yucay, once the personal fiefdom of the Emperor Huayna Cápac, also requisitioned for himself the palace of Casana, dominating the central square of Aucaypata. The Friar Valverde, who would become the city's first bishop, was given for the site of his church the palace of Suntur Huasi. Almagro was awarded the Emperor Huáscar's palace of Colcampata, overlooking the northern approach to the city. Pizarro's brother Hernando and Hernando de Soto were given equal share of the palace of Amarucancha, which had belonged to the Emperor Huayna Cápac's panaca of Tumibamba. The Temple of Coricancha was for a time left in the possession of the Inca Manco before it was eventually requisitioned by Pizarro's brother Juan.

Other than treasure and land, the most prized awards – of which no record was ever made – were the persons of the Inca princesses, daughters and nieces of the Emperor Huayna Cápac, who became the concubines of the more prominent conquistadors. Among them were the two full-blooded sisters of the Emperor Huáscar, the coyas Quispiquipi Huaylla (Doña Beatriz) and Marca Chimbo (Doña Juana), who were then probably thirteen and fourteen years old and who the foot soldier Juan de Pancorbo stated he had first seen in Cuzco within a few days of the capture of the city.[25] Almagro took the eldest princess, Marca Chimbo, for his concubine, the youngest Pizarro awarded Mansio, together with her lands and Indian yanaconas in the valley of Callanga in the Yucay which she had been given by her father.

The complicity of the Inca Manco in the concubinage of his half-sisters and in the bondage of his subject tribes would, however, earn him little gratitude from Pizarro, who Mansio recalled denied him the right to any share of the city's palaces or of his ancestral lands: 'All the land, houses, cattle [llamas] of this city and valley, was divided and given to those who conquered this city and kingdom . . . and it is known to me that the Inca Manco was neither given nor awarded any lands of encomiendas of Indians so that he

The Inca Manco. (Felipe Guaman Poma de Ayala, *Nueva Corónica y Buen Gobierno*)

could maintain himself in accordance with his rank and lordship, for had anything been given him it would have been known to me'.[26] In fear for his life, and ignoring the advice of his amauta elders and of his shaman the High Priest, the Villac-Umu, to refuse his collaboration, the Inca Manco ordered the killing of several of his half-brothers who he saw as potential rivals to his throne. His authority diminishing every day in the small court he was allowed to keep, many of the principal caciques no longer recognized his sovereignty and regarded the Spaniards as their liberators from their past bondage. The chiefs of the great nations of Cañari, Chachapoyas and Huanca had all pledged their allegiance solely to Pizarro.[27] Even the Coya Doña Beatriz's guardian Cariapasa, Lord of the Lupaca, who had lost several thousand of his warriors fighting on behalf of the Emperor Huáscar, refused to render the Inca the service of his people: 'When Don Francisco Pizarro entered Cuzco there came to the city the principal lord of the province of Chuquito called Cari [Cariapasa] an elderly Indian who was governor of that province, and he arrived at the village of Muina where his tribesmen were bondaged, and said to them: "My brothers, we are no longer living in the time of the Inca, for each and every one of you can go home to your lands . . ."'.[28]

Pizarro, nevertheless, was aware that the capture of Cuzco had only delayed what would be a decisive confrontation with the army of the chief Quisquis, which had retreated into the Cuntisuyo, to the west of the city. Also an even greater force commanded by Atahualpa's other warrior chief, Rumiñavi, was encamped between Cajamarca and Quito. Pizarro realized that not only would he have to mobilize all his scattered force, from Cuzco and the settlements of Jauja and San Miguel, commanded by Riquelme and Benalcázar, but also raise a far larger army of Indian auxiliaries. For this purpose he offered formally to recognize the Inca as native ruler and authorized his coronation according to Inca rites. The crowning of the sixteen-year-old prince with the *mascapaicha*, the traditional headdress and forehead tassel of the Inca sovereign, was witnessed by the entire company of conquistadors in the by then denuded Temple of Coricancha. The ceremony was followed by a procession in the city's great square, where all the mummies of the emperors were displayed before the thousands of people who had gathered from the outlying regions. The Inca and his brothers and sisters, among them Mansio's child concubine, dressed in all the splendour of the imperial panacas, their faces masked in beaten gold, were carried in litters to make their final sacrifice to the sun outside the city's walls. It was a ritual that a year later would be seen for the last time by the priest Cristóbal de Molina, and which would symbolize the last vestige of Cuzco's grandeur:

> In a plain on the outskirts of Cuzco where the sun rises, they would take all the mummies of the temple and of their rulers under richly adorned canopies, and would make of this encampment a pathway . . . along which would parade all the lords of Cuzco, who were orejones and richly dressed with shawls and shirts embroidered in gold or silver, wearing bracelets and patens in their head-wear of very fine gold that shone with a brilliance, comprising of two rows of persons, each of three hundred lords; in procession and in silence they awaited the sunrise and even before its appearance they began to chant in great unity, their voices rising in tone with the rising of the sun . . . the Inca was seated in a mound nearby, in a tent and on a throne of great splendour, and as the chanting increased he rose with much authority and walked towards the centre of the two rows of lords, and he himself began to chant, a chant that was imitated by all the lords . . . and by mid-day their voices had increased in strength, as had the sun, all during which time many sacrifices were made of llamas and of meat which was burnt . . . at eight of the afternoon more than two hundred young women came from Cuzco, each carrying a pitcher of chicha . . . which they offered to the sun, and also a plant they chew in their mouths which is called coca . . . and when the sun set they demonstrated great sorrow and in the darkness adored its passing with great humility . . . and each returned to the city as did the mummies of their past rulers, each one attended by their mamacuna and servants who would fan them with plumes of birds' feathers . . .[29]

5

THE FALL OF TAHUANTINSUYO

Many chroniclers and people recall that in the various battles the Spaniards had with the natives of the New Spain, a knight with sword in hand and mounted on a white horse was seen fighting on the side of the Spaniards, who was none other than the Apostle Santiago, and who is venerated throughout the Indies.

José de Acosta
Historia Natural y Moral de las Indias

Within a few days of Cuzco's capture Pizarro had sent a squadron of his best horse in search of Quisquis' army. Mansio Serra de Leguizamón recorded:

As the city of Cuzco had been won the governor Don Francisco Pizarro commanded the captain Soto to go to the province of Cuntisuyo with fifty horsemen and also some footmen in pursuit of Atahualpa's warrior chiefs, and I was among those who served there for more than two months, punishing them and fighting them, and working in the most rugged of country, suffering great hunger, until we found their chiefs in the midst of their many warriors, and we fought them, defeating them and capturing some of them. The governor then ordered us to return to Cuzco, for he feared our enemies would attack us; and we returned to where he and the rest of the men were in guard of the city, and which the Indians had surrounded, putting our lives in much danger because of their numbers and the hungers and necessities from which we suffered.[1]

It would be several weeks, however, before Soto's horse would again leave the city, accompanied by the Inca Manco and 5,000 auxiliaries. Lucas Martínez Vegazo stated: '. . . the Marqués once more sent him [Soto] in pursuit of the warriors, and the Adelantado Don Diego de Almagro went with him, and in order to relieve Jauja where the Marqués had left some of the Spaniards in guard of the gold and silver of His Majesty, and which had been gathered after Hernando Pizarro had left for Spain; and we Spaniards experienced great risk to our lives and hardship, and which also Mansio Serra experienced, for I witnessed part of the expedition . . .'.[2]

The conquistadors and their Indian auxiliaries, who were led by the Inca Manco, reached Jauja three weeks after the commander of its settlement Alonso de Riquelme had successfully fought off Quisquis' attack. The great chief's engagements against Almagro and Soto's horsemen, who continued their pursuit, were limited to defending his warriors' march north to their townships and hamlets in the mountain regions of Quito. However, within days of his army's departure from Jauja, Pizarro was informed of the landing at Puerto Viejo on the northern equatorial coast of an armada of some 500 Spaniards from the Isthmus under the command of Don Pedro de Alvarado, a veteran of the conquest of Guatemala. The arrival of so large an army of adventurers and freebooters, attracted by the news of the vast riches of Peru, was seen by Pizarro as a threat not only to his authority but to the Cajamarca treasure, most of which was still at Jauja. With the dual purpose of defending the township and preventing Alvarado from taking possession of his equatorial settlements, he ordered Almagro to take the main body of his men to the northern coast, leaving a small detachment to garrison Jauja and Cuzco, as Mansio records:[3]

I was one of the forty soldiers chosen to remain in the city of Cuzco in its defence in the company of the captain Beltrán de Castro, which was when the governors had gone to meet with Don Pedro de Alvarado who had come from Guatemala with his men. While on guard of this city it was learned the Incas planned to kill us all and recapture Cuzco, bringing with them as their chief Villac-Umu [High Priest of the Sun]. In order to forestall their purpose, I and a number of my companions disguised ourselves as Indians, and taking with us our arms we went on foot to where Villac-Umu was encamped with a great number of his warriors. And taking heart I was the first to seize him and we brought him as our prisoner to Cuzco and handed him over to the captain Beltrán de Castro . . .[3]

Diego Camacho recalled that Mansio had set out to the Villac-Umu's camp in the Cuntisuyo with nine or ten other soldiers, among them his friend the encomendero Francisco de Villafuerte. Pedro de Alconchel was at Jauja with Pizarro at the time he received the news of the High Priest's imprisonment in Cuzco and of the ransom that had been given for his release. Pizarro appears to have been infuriated by their action, which he knew would only antagonize the Inca. Mansio, because of his resentment at being deprived of his share of the ransom, grossly exaggerates its value, claiming it to have been worth more than 200,000 pesos of gold. Luis Sánchez describes its value as 34,000 pesos of gold and 36,000 marks of silver.[4] Whatever the discrepancy, all forty of Cuzco's encomenderos were signatories to a donation by the city's cabildo, dated 4 August 1534, of 30,000 pesos of gold and 300,000 marks of silver.[5] 'And we soldiers, who had been responsible for his capture,' Mansio commented in his probanza, 'refused any share of the ransom which was sent to His Majesty and his royal officials.' The

Meeting of Almagro and Don
Pedro de Alvarado. (Herrera: BL,
783. g. 1–4)

ransom in fact was dispatched to Pizarro at Jauja, and supposedly kept by him regardless
of the means by which it had been acquired. Whether Almagro was to use part of the
treasure in his payment some weeks later, of 100,000 pesos of gold, to Alvarado for the
disbandment of his armada remains a mystery.

The threat of the Guatemalan invasion had dominated Pizarro's mind for several
weeks, and he instructed Almagro to engage Alvarado's soldiers if necessary. With no
more than 250 men and a vast quantity of gold at his disposal, Almagro had been
able to bribe the conqueror of Guatemala to disband his army, whose men had
ravaged the northern territory of the Inca empire in a genocide unequalled by any of
Pizarro's veterans. With the eventual defeat some months later of the chiefs Quisquis
and Rumiñavi, whose depleted armies of warriors had made their last stand against
Almagro and Benalcázar's combined forces near Quito, Pizarro was to secure the
conquest of the northern Inca empire. In August 1534, the city of San Francisco de
Quito was founded, and five months later on the lands of the cacique Taulichusco at
Lima, Pizarro founded his capital of Los Reyes, the City of the Kings, named in honour
of the Feast of the Epiphany.[6]

On the return of the army to Cuzco, increased in number by the disbanded veterans of Alvarado's armada, Almagro took charge of the city's governorship in the absence of Pizarro, who had remained at his settlement at Lima. The relationship between the two men, though cordial, was to deteriorate over the months due to Almagro's claim to Cuzco as forming part of the territories Pizarro had promised him, and which he had petitioned the Crown to award him. Pizarro's brothers Juan and Gonzalo and their followers vigorously opposed the claim, creating an open confrontation between the opposing partisans, among them Soto, who supported Almagro. There is no record of Mansio's role in the dispute, though Almagro's later hostility towards him possibly demonstrates his allegiance. Pizarro's subsequent arrival in the city was to prevent further confrontation between the two factions. His offer to Almagro of the conquest of the southern Inca empire of Chile finally brought the dispute to an end. Soto, however, was refused permission by Almagro to join the expedition, even after offering to pay 200,000 pesos of gold for a share of its command, an amount symbolic of the vast sum of unaccounted treasure the veterans of Cajamarca and Cuzco had acquired for themselves.[7] Disillusioned by what he saw as his last chance of establishing his own independent fiefdom, and by an increasingly acrimonious relationship with Pizarro's brothers, Soto decided to return to Spain. Taking with him a caravan of several hundred llamas and Indian porters, carrying his vast fortune, he began a journey that would see his reception at court at Valladolid. Here he was feted and honoured by the Empress and awarded the knighthood of Santiago, embarking shortly afterwards on his conquest of Florida, where he was to die six years later on the banks of the Mississippi River.

Towards the end of June 1535, the first of Almagro's contingent under the command of Juan de Saavedra left the city on the southern Inca road to the Collasuyo. On 3 July, Almagro followed Saavedra with 50 horse and infantry to Lake Titicaca where he was met by his advance party, his army by now numbering in all some 570 Spaniards.[8] The Inca Manco, who had remained at Cuzco, had authorized his half-brother Paullu and the High Priest of the Sun to accompany Almagro with 12,000 Indian auxiliaries. Among the expedition's missionaries was the chronicler Cristóbal de Molina, author of *Conquista y Población del Perú*. His words more than any other portray the singular inhumanity of his countrymen, in a march that would witness the death of almost half of the expedition's Indian auxiliaries in the crossing of the southern cordillera of the Andes:

The Spaniards took with them from the region of Cuzco for the conquest a great number of llamas, clothing and Indians; those who had not wished to accompany them willingly, in chains and tied to ropes, and each night they would be put in harsh imprisonment, and in the day they would work as porters and almost die of hunger . . . and in each of the villages they took more Indians who they placed in chains . . . and also the women who were of fine appearance they took for their service, and if they injured themselves they would make them carry them in hammocks and litters . . .

and in such manner also they imposed their authority on their Indian retainers and on their Negroes, who were great pillagers and robbers, and those of whom were the greater were esteemed . . . I have written these things I witnessed with my eyes, of those, who because of my sins, I did accompany, so that they who read this will understand of what I speak, and of the cruel manner was made this journey and discovery of Chile . . .[9]

With the departure of Almagro's expedition Pizarro appointed his 26-year-old half-brother Juan as Governor of Cuzco. No more than 200 Spaniards had remained in the city, among them most of its founding encomenderos and a number of artisans, notaries and merchants who had recently arrived from the Isthmus.[10] It was possibly at this time, as he records in his probanza, Mansio took part in an expedition with Juan and Gonzalo Pizarro to the Bolivian highland region of the Collasuyo: '. . . and served there, pacifying and conquering the land after many engagements with the natives who were in considerable numbers, and we Spaniards few, ill fed and with a great many tasks to perform . . .'.[11] A year previously his fourteen-year-old mistress the Coya Doña Beatriz had given birth to their son Juan. 'I witnessed,' the Indian Mazma of Mayo recorded of the princess, 'Indians of all the regions and nations show her their obedience and respect . . .'.[12] Nothing is known of the Coya's appearance, though both her mother the Empress Rahua Ocllo and her sister Doña Juana were recorded as being exceptionally beautiful.[13] Her sister Doña Juana, however, was to suffer the humiliation of being abandoned by Almagro, to whom she had given a large quantity of gold, and was later repeatedly raped.[14] It was an abuse from which not even their half-brother the Inca Manco would be immune with the abduction and rape of his wife by Gonzalo Pizarro, towards the end of 1535, and which would eventually precipitate his flight from the city. Captured within days by a squadron of Gonzalo's horse, he was brought back to Cuzco in chains. A letter written some four years afterwards by the Vizcayan Pedro de Oñate and Juan Gómez de Malaver to the Emperor Charles V gives an account of the ill-treatment he received at the hands of his captors:

We have been commissioned to write the enclosed, in order that Your Majesty may learn the truth of what weighs on our conscience, and what we owe to the loyalty and service to His Majesty, of what we were informed by Manco Inca Yupanqui, who is the Inca at present in rebellion, and who was at the time some seven leagues from Cuzco at a village known as Tambo [Ollantaytambo] . . . the Inca received us well and listened to our words and made the following reply: 'How is it that the great Apu [lord] of Castile ordered that I and my women be imprisoned with iron rings to our necks, and that I be urinated and excreted in my face? And that Gonzalo Pizarro, brother of the principal lord, would take my wife, and who he still holds with him? And that Diego Maldonado would torture me so as to demand from me gold, telling me that he was also a great lord?' He also protested that Pedro del Barco and Gómez de Mazuelas, who are encomenderos of this city, and Alonso de Toro and Pantiel [de Salinas], Alonso de Mesa, Pedro Pizarro [the future chronicler] and Solares, all encomenderos of this city, urinated on him when he was being held captive, and that with a lighted candle they burnt his eyelashes . . .[15]

Nor was the young hidalgo Serra de Leguizamón untainted by the cruelty shown the Inca prince. For weeks the Inca Manco suffered the abuse of his captors, chained to a stake in the main square of the city, a spectacle that outraged his subjects, however tainted their loyalty, and led to the killing of several encomenderos in the outlying regions of the city. The immediate retribution of the Spaniards was recorded by Diego Camacho, whose brother was one of the victims:

Because of the killings by the Indians in the province of Cuntisuyo of an encomendero by the name of Pedro Martín [de Moguer] and another encomendero called Simón Suárez, I saw the captain Juan Pizarro and Gonzalo Pizarro, and Mansio Serra among them, leave the city with other soldiers to exert reprisal of the province; and being as I was in the city of Cuzco I heard it said the reprisal had been carried out at the capture of the mountain fortress of Ancocagua, where more than eight thousand Indian warriors had taken refuge, and that a great deal of fighting took place . . .'.[16]

The chronicler Cieza de León wrote that Mansio and three other conquistadors, Juan Flores, Francisco de Villafuerte and Pedro del Barco, volunteered to gain entry to the fortress by shaving their beards and disguising themselves as Indians, and that they made their ascent of the mountain crag at 2 in the morning, accompanied by an Inca lord:

The Spaniards were fearful, believing they had been betrayed and cursed the orejón [Inca lord] who appeared to have closed the gate behind him, but throwing back his robe he took out his battle axe and shouted: 'Viracochas, come quickly!* and which they did, though some Indians had injured the orejón: many now came shouting they had been betrayed and wounding the orejón, who they killed and who begged the Spaniards to avenge his death. The four men with their swords in hand fought alone against the entire encampment of Indians, their lives being saved solely by the darkness of the night. Juan Pizarro with the rest of his men then came to their aid, and as dawn was breaking the Indians could see their great number that had gained

---

* Viracocha was the name by which the Spaniards were first known because of the Incas' initial belief that they were the spirit warriors of their god of that name.

entry into their fortress, nor could their enemies lightly ignore the clamour of shouting of their men, women and children, and those who could see the steel of their swords many decided to take their own lives, throwing themselves over the cliffs on to the crags and rocks below, where the blood of their brains coloured the snow . . . without restraint the Spaniards wounded and killed, cutting arms and legs, letting none survive: the yanacona did the same, and the greater their clamour the greater the killing . . . and those who were not killed, with their women and children, whose eyes they shielded, threw themselves over the cliffs to their deaths . . .[17]

When Juan Pizarro and his squadron returned to Cuzco he was to find the city under the control of his elder brother Hernando, whom Pizarro had appointed governor, an action demonstrative of the rigid order of seniority among Pizarro's captains. After an absence of three years he had returned to Peru laden with honours from the court at Toledo where he had taken the Crown's share of the Cajamarca treasure, and where he had been made a knight of Santiago. He had brought back with him 4 white women slaves for his brother Pizarro, and had also obtained permission to import 100 Negro slaves for both himself and his brother, which only confirms the conqueror of Peru's former trade as a slaver.[18] Aware of the ill-feeling the Inca's imprisonment and the killings at Ancocagua had created among the natives of the city, he ordered the Inca Manco's release and restored some of his privileges. As a further act of reconciliation he granted the Inca permission to leave Cuzco to officiate at a ceremony in the neighbouring valley of the Yucay in the company of the High Priest the Villac-Umu, who had deserted Almagro's expedition to Chile. It was a gesture influenced in part by the Inca's promise to bring him a quantity of gold from the valley and a life-size gold statue of his father Huayna Cápac. Unbeknown to the Spaniards, the Inca had been planning to make his escape from Cuzco and head an uprising organized by the Villac-Umu, who had spent months travelling across the Bolivian altiplano, highland region, recruiting men and arms. The Conquistador Bernabé Picón recorded that the planned rebellion was betrayed to the Spaniards by the Coya Doña Beatriz, possibly out of love for Mansio: 'At the time the Villac-Umu, who had deserted the expedition for the discovery of Chile of the Adelantado Don Diego de Almagro, returned to Cuzco, I heard it said that Doña Beatriz warned her master Mansio Serra, with whom she was not married, that the Villac-Umu had come to take the Inca with him who wished to flee the city, and that he made this publicly known and informed Hernando Pizarro.'[19]

On the eve of Easter Sunday word finally reached the city of the mass uprising throughout the four suyos.

More or less three years after the conquest [Mansio recalled] this city of Cuzco was besieged in a general uprising led by Manco Inca . . . in whose defence I served . . . and the said Manco Inca attacked the city with a great number of warriors, of more than two

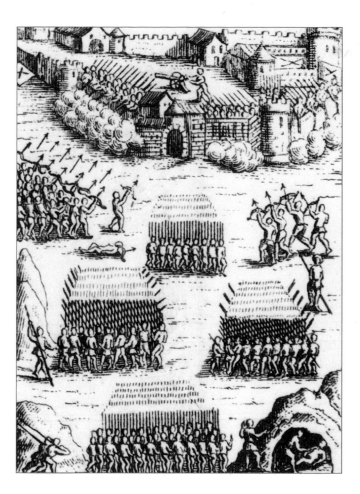

The Inca Manco's siege of Cuzco. (Herrera: BL, 783. g. 1–4)

hundred thousand Indians, and besieged and captured much of the city and setting it on fire, and those who remained in its defence, I among them, barricaded ourselves in one of its fortresses which in the Indian language is called Hatuncancha; and Manco Inca sent a great number of Indians against the city of Los Reyes where the Marqués Pizarro was at the time, and against other settlements of Spaniards . . . from as far as Chile to Popayán and Pastu, a distance of some seven hundred leagues . . . and there were many in this city who attempted to flee to the ports of Lima and Arequipa to escape by sea, but who were detained by Hernando Pizarro and Juan Pizarro and Gonzalo Pizarro, the Marqués Pizarro's brothers, who defended this city, and who I accompanied in that defence . . . and it was known that the Marqués had sent word from these realms to Guatemala and to Tierra Firme [Panama] asking them for their help.[20]

In the first few days of the siege the garrison had retreated to the two fortress palaces of Suntur Huasi and Hatuncancha, to the north-east of the square of Aucaypata, where they barricaded themselves, and from where day and night they led sorties of cavalry and infantry to face the onslaught of warriors who had set fire to the city's buildings. Of the Spaniards, 30 lay dead and most of the company of under 200 men were wounded in the initial days of fighting. The chronicler Garcilaso de la Vega records that at night the surrounding hills were lit by thousands of fires, and that in the day nothing but the massing of warriors could be seen.

Within a week the Inca Manco's squadrons of Quéchua and subject tribes, which had marched undetected to Cuzco from all the suyos of the empire, had taken control of most of the city. Their renewed loyalty to their former Inca lords was due primarily to the brutality shown them by their encomenderos and sexual abuse of their women, in either their encomienda lands or settlements. In all probability Manco's army numbered between 100,000 and 200,000 warriors and yanacona porters. In the fortress of Hatuncancha, amid the cries of the wounded and stench of unburied bodies, three friars heard the confessions of the 200 men as they prepared for their deaths. Several hundred of their Indian auxiliaries and their Negro and Isthmian slaves were also barricaded inside the fortress, together with Indian concubines and children, among them the Coya Doña Beatriz and her two-year-old son. Francisco de Illescas recalled that the Coya had also been accompanied by the Inca's two young daughters, whom she had taken to live with her after he had fled the city: 'and because of which I heard it said it was the reason many dangers the Indians had intended were avoided . . .'.[21] In the stockades of the

The Miracle of Santiago. (Felipe Guaman Poma de Ayala, *Nueva Corónica y Buen Gobierno*)

fortress the Spaniards had stabled what had survived of their horses and mules, some eighty animals. Pedro Pizarro wrote that in one of the many forays the horsemen made into the square Mansio had been unseated from his horse, escaping with his life, and had seen his mount speared and hacked to death. In another sortie, which had prevented the burning of the thatch roof of the fortress tower of Suntur Huasi, some of the besieged men and women, invoking the intercession of God for their deliverance, claimed to have seen the apparition of the Virgin – an event that would be commemorated years later by the construction on its site of Cuzco's church of the Triunfo. Another miraculous apparition – known as the Miracle of Santiago – that the beleaguered garrison claimed had been seen at the height of the siege, and which would also be represented in the religious art of the colony, was of Spain's patron saint, as recorded by the chronicler Friar Martín de Murúa:

Sacsahuaman. (Alexander Stirling)

I wish to refer to what I have heard told by Spaniards and Indians, who swear to the truth of what they say, and who recall that in the most difficult time of the fighting a Spaniard appeared mounted on a white horse and killing many Indians, and many of the Spaniards believed him to have been Mansio Serra de Leguizamón, one of the leading conquistadors of Cuzço; yet later, when they enquired about this they discovered that he had not been fighting there, but in another part of the city, even though there was no other among the Spaniards who possessed a white horse other than he. It was understood by many that it had been the Apostle Santiago, patron and defender of Spain, who had appeared there.[22]

The Inca had established his principal encampment overlooking the city on a hill known to the Quéchua as the Speckled Hawk, in the massive stone fortress Temple of Sacsahuaman, from where with impunity he commanded the daily assault. Built by the Emperor Huayna Cápac's grandfather, the fortress, comprising three great stone defensive towers, ringed by a wall whose foundation stones were of some 12 ft in height, had been completed by the Emperor Huáscar to guard Cuzco's northern approach. A description of the stronghold was left by the chronicler Pedro Sancho de la Hoz:

A fortress of earth and stone of great beauty, with windows that look out on to the city and which give it an aspect of much attraction. Within the fortress are many chambers and a principal tower, of cylindrical shape, with four or five smaller towers, one above the other: the chambers and halls within are small, though their walls are of fine workmanship, and so well assembled, their stone joinery in perfect order like that which can be seen in Spain, one against the other, though without any evidence of sand, and so smooth that they appear as if polished. It possesses so many adjacent towers and courtyards that a person would be unable to inspect them all in one day: and many Spaniards who have travelled in Lombardy and other foreign realms say that they have never seen the like of such a fortress or castle. It could garrison five thousand Spaniards: neither can it be besieged by battering ram, nor can it be mined from underground, because of its mountainous position . . .[23]

Diego Camacho recalled that the siege lasted for fourteen months in all, and that Mansio served there all that time:

. . . with his arms and horses, in the day and at night time, taking part in the engagements and battles of each day with the natives, in which we all ran great risk and fought with much difficulty: for we were surrounded by more than three hundred thousand Indian warriors, and they had put us under such duress that they burned the greater part of the city; and seeing this, and realizing the danger, the captain Juan Pizarro decided that we had to capture the fortress where a great number of warriors had fortified themselves; and so it was decided, and among those who went up there was this witness and Mansio Serra, and some seventy soldiers in all; and for some days we had the fortress besieged and one night Mansio Serra and a few others voluntéered to gain entry through a small opening they had seen, and thus they entered, and all the others after them, and we captured the surrounding area to the fortress at great peril and much fighting, and that night Juan Pizarro was killed. Hernando Pizarro, who had remained in the city, then came up and we held to the siege until the fortress was captured: scaling its walls with ladders, and in all this, as in the earlier siege of the city, Mansio Serra's service was of principal importance . . .[24]

Lucas Martínez Vegazo stated that twelve conquistadors climbed up into the fortress: '. . . killing and wounding the natives and shouting "España! España!"'[25] Mansio himself claimed he had been the first to enter and cry victory, though wounded in the stomach.[26] It was said that the killing had been so intense that for days hundreds of condors could be seen swooping down on the fortress' bloody walls to eat the flesh of its dead warriors. The capture of Sacsahuaman would form part of the legends of the Indies, recounted in the taverns and gaming houses of Spain, and commemorated by the coat of arms awarded Cuzco by the Cardinal of Seville: 'A castle of gold in a field of red, in recognition that the said city and its fortress were conquered by force of arms in the royal service; and for a border eight condors in a field of gold, which are large birds like vultures of the province of Peru, in recognition that at the time the city was won they flew down to eat the flesh of the dead . . .'.[27]

The fall of the great fortress, whose giant stone foundations can still be seen above Cuzco, marked a turning point in the siege of the city and had gained Hernando Pizarro's weary and half-starved soldiers a period of respite, though their victory had been marred by the death from his wounds of Hernando's brother Juan. In the following days, several sorties were ordered into the surrounding countryside to forage for food and llamas, before Hernando Pizarro himself led a squadron of horse into the northern valley of Ollantaytambo. Beyond what is known as the Sacred Valley of the Incas, Ollantaytambo and its river of Urubamba are dominated by surrounding mountains, in the far extremity of which lies the ruins of its giant stone terraced fortress where the Inca had positioned the bulk of his army. The small squadron of horse finally entered the valley and slowly made their way up towards the fortress, the massive walls of which were manned by archers from the Amazon subject tribes. The horseman Diego Camacho recalled the failure of the expedition:

In the company of Mansio Serra this witness and seventy horsemen went to the said province and fortress, which we attacked on the day of our arrival. The Indian warriors, having ventured out of the fortress, a great battle took place until that night, in which many Spaniards were killed and wounded; and abandoning our encampment and tents we were forced to flee to Cuzco that very night, losing everything we had taken with us; for had we remained until morning not one of us would have returned alive because of the great numbers of warriors and the ruggedness of the land.[28]

Their retreat from the valley would within a short time lead to a further siege of the city, and though its garrison by now had sufficient food supplies it would be several months before one of the two armies marching to its relief would reach the vicinity of Cuzco.

Pizarro, having himself successfully withstood the attack on his small settlement at Lima, had raised a force of some 350 men under the command of Alonso de Alvarado, which would later be reinforced by a further 200 men from the Isthmus. However, it was Almagro's dishevelled army, which had found neither gold nor riches on its ill-fated expedition to Chile, that was the first to reach the city, having marched across its vast and desolate northern desert. The chronicler López de Gómora recorded:

There is a desert from Atacama, the last town in Peru, to Copayapú, the first in Chile, a distance of some eighty leagues [280 miles] . . . as the water was not sufficient to supply the whole army, Almagro ordered the horsemen to cross the desert in bands of five or six . . . Jerónimo de Alderete, who was governor of Chile many years later, was once in Copayapú, and seeing that there was not much snow on the passes went to see whether he and his company could find any trace of the losses Almagro's army had suffered . . . they found a Negro leaning against the rocks in a standing position and also a horse standing as if carved of wood, with its reins now rotted in his hands . . .[29]

The news of Almagro's successful crossing of the Atacama, of some 500 men and what remained of his Indian auxiliaries, and their arrival at the settlement of Arequipa had been relayed to the Inca, who had once more withdrawn his forces to Ollantaytambo but had suffered the desertion of a great number of his warriors from the subject tribes. On reaching the township of Urcos, 25 miles south-east of Cuzco, Almagro sent emissaries to Hernando Pizarro informing him of his intention to take possession of the city as forming part of his governorship, the Crown's award of which he had only received during his expedition to Chile. He also dispatched two of his captains, Pedro de Oñate and Juan Gómez de Malaver, to the valley of the Yucay in an attempt to negotiate a peace settlement with the Inca – an interview also recorded in their letter to the Emperor Charles V:

. . . finally, he [the Inca Manco] ended our meeting, saying: 'Ask my father Almagro if it is true what he says and that you are not lying, that I will be allowed to leave in peace and enter the city together, he, with his men, and I, with mine; and that he will leave me to kill all those Christians who have harmed me: then shall I know

whether what he says is the truth.' And while we were still with him an Indian brought from Cuzco a letter Hernando Pizarro had sent him, which he showed us, telling him that he should not go in peace with Almagro because he was planning to burn him alive and make his brother Paullu Inca, who he had brought with him from his discovery of Chile; he then told us that the letter had been read to him by a Christian who was his captive . . .[30]

The failure of the emissaries to persuade the Inca to accept a peaceful settlement only hardened Almagro's resolve to press his claim to the governorship of Cuzco by force of arms, and he ordered his army to break camp. In the bitter cold of the Andean winter his troops entered Cuzco under cover of darkness. His men and auxiliaries, led by the Inca Paullu, took

Machu Picchu. (Alexander Stirling)

possession of the city's buildings, setting fire to

the lodging where Hernando Pizarro and his brother Gonzalo had barricaded themselves. Most of the survivors of the siege, exhausted by their suffering and fearful for their lives, willingly surrendered to his troops. The few men who refused, among them Mansio Serra de Leguizamón, were put in irons and imprisoned with Hernando and Gonzalo Pizarro, their Indian women and children left to the mercy of Almagro's soldiers, who had little to show for their long and arduous march other than their hatred for the Pizarros.

Diego de Almagro's occupation of Cuzco would finally bring to an end any hope the Inca Manco might have held of defeating the Spaniards, even though the conquistadors had suffered the loss of a thousand men throughout their various settlements. For a further two years his depleted armies would continue to wage their struggle until they were finally defeated by superior arms and cavalry. Accompanied by a few remaining squadrons of his warriors, the Inca Manco retreated from the Yucay to face his exile in the mountain fastness of the forests of Vilcabamba. There, he built a fortified township, which would be known as the 'lost city of the Incas', and whose ruins possibly lie buried in the sub-tropical forests of Espíritu Pampa, north-east of Cuzco, and not far from the great Inca mountain Temple of Machu Picchu, which would remain unknown to the conquistadors and to the world until its chance discovery by the young American archaeological student Hiram Bingham in 1911.[31]

6

THE WARS OF THE VIRACOCHAS

Though their wars were long, and of great occurrence, never before in the history
of the world did a people of a nation so cruelly pursue them, ignoring death and
their own lives in order to avenge their passions and hatred of one another . . .

Pedro de Cieza de León
Las Guerras Civiles del Perú

The morning after his entry into Cuzco the 64-year-old Adelantado Almagro,
accompanied by his Isthmian mestizo son Diego and his principal captains, proclaimed
himself ruler of the southern territories of the Inca empire. Hernando and Gonzalo
Pizarro, together with several of their supporters, among them Mansio Serra de
Leguizamón, were at first imprisoned in the house of Diego Núñez de Mercado, and then
in what had been the Temple of Coricancha.[1] The Imperial city was a charred ruin as
the Friar Bishop Valverde would recall a year later on his return from Spain, bringing
with him some fifty servants and relatives:[2] '. . . most is tumbled down and burned . . .
and few stones of its fortress standing. It is a wonder when one finds any house in the
environs with more than walls.'[3]

The retribution of Almagro's landless and impoverished soldiers was relentless in their
search for the hidden caches of gold and silver of their prisoners and in the rape of their
women. Within days, however, Almagro ordered his men to resume their march to
confront the approaching army of Alonso de Alvarado which Pizarro had sent from
Lima. As Alvarado rested his troops by a river at Abancay, north of the city, Almagro's
horsemen attacked them. Led by Rodrigo de Orgóñez, a veteran of the Spanish imperial
army that had sacked Rome 10 years previously, the rebels routed Alvarado's contingent
of 500 men. The humiliation that Alvarado and his men endured during their long
march to Cuzco, chained in columns and many of them barefoot, was a sight that
brought even greater alarm to the imprisoned loyalists of the city. Most of them by now
believed they would be killed or spend the rest of their days rotting in the improvised
cells of the fortress of Sacsahuaman, the site of their past victory against the Inca
Manco. For almost twelve months they would remain prisoners, though a number of
them escaped, including Alvarado and Gonzalo Pizarro. The wealthiest among them,

mostly veterans of Cajamarca, were tortured by Almagro's men to reveal the whereabouts of their gold and silver, hidden mainly in the gardens or walls, tapados, of their lodgings. Their Indian women were to suffer a similar fate. Nearly all were raped, the most important of whom, such as the coyas Doña Beatriz and Doña Juana, were made concubines of Almagro's captains. It was a fate probably also shared by one of Pizarro's women, the Ñusta Cuxirimay Ocllo, known as Doña Angelina.[4] Though Pizarro sent various emissaries to Almagro, and was himself to meet his former partner under a flag of truce, he failed to reach an accord with him. Almagro's subsequent decision – against the advice of all his captains – to release Hernando Pizarro, as a gesture of goodwill, was however to enable Pizarro to order the army he had recruited at Lima to make its advance on Cuzco.

At dawn on 26 April 1538, within sight of the city's walls at a plain known as Salinas, the two armies eventually faced one another on either side of a river. Almagro's troops, numbering 500 men, half of whom were horsemen, were commanded by Orgóñez and supported by 10,000 Indian auxiliaries led by the Inca Paullu with 6 small canon. Hernando Pizarro, his huge figure in full armour and dressed in orange livery, commanded the loyalist forces of 700 men, and advanced his infantry across the river. Reminiscent of a medieval battle, the conquistadors, accompanied by their armed Indian retainers and watched by their camp women from the safety of their tents, slowly advanced towards one another, their pennants adorned with the arms awarded them by their distant Emperor in whose name they fought, loyalist and rebel alike. Orgóñez's pikemen also made their advance, assisted by two columns of cavalry which were ordered to begin their attack: at full gallop, their lances breaking on impact, a desperate and bloody hand-to-hand fight ensued, leaving 150 Spaniards dead. Almagro, who was too ill to take part in the fighting, observed the battle from a hillock and witnessed the slaughter of his wounded men at the hands of his own Indian auxiliaries, who at the last moment changed their allegiance. He stayed there for almost two hours before mounting his mule and making his escape to Cuzco. The dead were looted of their armour and weapons, and what had not been stripped from their corpses by their countrymen was pillaged by the Indians. In the ruins of the fortress of Sacsahuaman Almagro was captured and taken manacled to the Temple of Coricancha.

For three months the elderly adelantado would remain a prisoner. Sickly and broken in spirit Almagro presented a pitiful sight, pleading his age and his past service to the Crown. His words, however, were lost on Hernando Pizarro, who would neither forgive nor forget his own imprisonment and past humiliation, and who ordered Almagro's execution. On 8 July the great square of the city was lined by a squadron of arquebusiers as a priest and Almagro's executioner headed the small column of men from the Temple of Coricancha, behind which his garroted corpse was carried to a podium. To the sound of a drummer his head was struck off and placed at the end of a

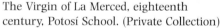

The Virgin of La Merced, eighteenth
century, Potosí School. (Private Collection)

pike, his one eye open, and his bearded and blood-smeared features were paraded before
the silent throng of Spaniards and Indians and Negroes. Wrapped in a shroud, his
headless and naked corpse was taken by his African slave to be buried in the monastery
of La Merced. The Jesuit chronicler Blas Valera recorded that half a century later an
elderly conquistador, who because of the year he mentions and his hidalgo rank in all
probability was either Mansio Serra de Leguizamón or Alonso de Mesa, was to witness
the ghosts of the men who had fallen at Salinas, among them Pedro de Leguizamón, one
of the conquistador's cousins who had fought in the ranks of Almagro's army:

> There is on the battlefield a church dedicated to St Lazurus, where the bodies of those
> who died there were buried. A noble and pious Spaniard, who had been one of the
> conquistadors, often went there to pray for the souls of the dead. It happened that
> while praying one day he heard groans and weeping in the church, and one of his
> friends who had fought and died in the battle appeared to him . . . and at his
> suggestion the mestizos, the sons of those Spaniards by Indian women, moved their
> fathers' bones to the city of Cuzco in 1581 . . . and many Masses were said . . . and
> the vision then ceased to appear.[5]

At the time of Almagro's execution Mansio Serra de Leguizamón was twenty-six years old. Nothing is known of his appearance or of his intimate character. Other than referring to his parents with affection in one of his wills and in his probanza, testimonial, he makes no mention of any of his courtly relatives. It was as though he had closed the door on his past for ever. Nor will it ever be known whether he had loved the young Coya, the mother of his son Juan, whom he named after his father. Her undoubted rape by Almagro's soldiers and her concubinage to one of his captains would have been a humiliation his hidalgo pride would have been unable to accept, and it seems probable it was during this period of time that he abandoned her. It was a price he had paid for his loyalty to the Pizarros.

Almagro's defeated veterans, deprived of their booty, faced a life of abject poverty; some, it was said, shared their cloaks for want of clothing. Almagro's 22-year-old son Diego was sent to Lima under guard, where he lived under house arrest in a penury equal to any of his father's supporters. The effects of the rebellion had furthermore created a scarcity of goods and a price inflation throughout the colony. It was a situation from which a number of conquistadors were to enhance their fortunes by trading as merchants. A letter of the period records that Hernando Pizarro imported into Cuzco from the Isthmus: '176 bottles of wine; sixty shirts of Holland lace; 26 pairs of velvet hoses; 71 pairs of shoes and velvet slippers; 18 spectacles; 56 pairs of leather gloves from Córdoba; 12 habits of the Order of Santiago; 80 hats; 6 jars of anchovies; and 386 packs of playing cards.'[6] 'A coat-of-mail and a helmet,' Mansio complained, 'cost 2,000 pesos of gold, and the rest of one's armament and horse some 2,000 to 3,000 gold pesos.'[7] In order to counter the growing discontent, especially among the landless volunteers from the Isthmus who had served at Salinas, Pizarro ordered a number of expeditions of conquest, which also enabled him to create more encomiendas.

One such expedition to the Cuntisuyo was led by Nicolás de Heredia and captained by Mansio, whose encomienda of Alca was in the province, who took with him forty of his Indian retainers. The horseman Rodrigo López Bernal recalled the Conquistador's prowess as an Indian fighter among the squadron of a hundred Spaniards:

I saw Mansio Serra serving there as a captain and caudillo . . . and much was risked for there were few of us Spaniards in comparison to the great number of Indians who attacked us and surrounded us in very barren terrain, making it impossible for us to reach a river [Cotahuasi] for the water we needed to drink; and that night in the tambo fortress of Alca, Mansio Serra and the Indians in his service left our encampment in order to break the siege, entering the fortress from the high ground of a slope, passing their sentries and putting them to the sword so that they could not warn their warriors; and in this manner in the middle of the night they climbed to the upper villages where the great multitude of warriors were camped, and catching them asleep they killed many of them, and then gave the Spaniards who had remained below the signal to climb up and follow them . . .[8]

The conquest of the western Cuntisuyo was shortly followed by an expedition led by Hernando Pizarro and the Inca Paullu, who had been pardoned for his past disloyalty at Salinas, to the Collasuyo and the Desaguadero River on the southern shores of Lake Titicaca. This route would eventually take them to the Bolivian valley of Cochabamba, where they would engage the remnants of the Inca Manco's southern armies, and then further south to the Charcas region and the future settlement at Chuquisaca (later known as La Plata because of its silver), the Bolivian capital of Sucre. It was a campaign that had not only established Chuquisaca and its neighbouring mines of Porco as a Pizarro fiefdom, but had seen the annihilation of Inca resistance in the southern part of the empire. It had also witnessed the virtual destruction at Titicaca of the Lupaca nation, whose elderly cacique Cariapasa[9] was forced to abandon his lands and flee to the coastal region of Tacna, where he was to spend the rest of his days as a baptized Christian, taking the name of Juan, in bondage to the encomendero Lucas Martínez Vegazo. It was a pitiful end to the life of one of the Emperor Huayna Cápac's greatest warrior chiefs and former guardian of his daughter the Coya Doña Beatriz. The expedition's return to Cuzco would also mark Hernando Pizarro's departure for Spain, together with one of the largest shipments of bullion and treasure. Unlike Soto's reception at court, Hernando would be indicted for Almagro's execution: a charge for which he would spend his remaining years under house arrest in resplendent luxury in the castle fortress of La Mota at Medina del Campo.

Pizarro's campaign in the Collasuyo was followed by the invasion of Vilcabamba, the Inca Manco's refuge in the sub-tropical Andean forests. The Indian auxiliaries in the campaign were commanded by the Inca's brother, Paullu, who, taking advantage of the role he would play in the invasion, petitioned Pizarro to award him an encomienda of various lands in the Cuntisuyo and Antisuyo, including Mansio Serra de Leguizamón's rich fiefdom in the valley of Callanga in the Yucay.[10] Pizarro agreed to his request and promised to recompense the encomenderos for their loss. It was a promise he would never be able to fulfil, as the Conquistador's younger son Francisco arrogantly reminded the Council of the Indies some fifty years later:

Of the said services of my father they were not honoured with sufficient dignity; for though the Marqués Don Francisco Pizarro at the beginning of the Conquest and settlement gave to my father the encomiendas of Cuntisuyo [Alca] and Antisuyo [Catanga and Callanga], which was worthy of his honour, Paullu Inca, a son of Huayna Cápac, having placed himself in the royal service, petitioned for the said provinces of Antisuyo as they had been the hereditary lands of his father and ancestors, and as the Marqués felt the matter to be of such importance for the benefit of the Crown he awarded him the encomiendas of Antisuyo which were of great value, of [annual] rent of more than twenty thousand pesos . . . and even though the Marqués Pizarro promised my father that he would give him an encomienda of equal value, he was never able to do so because of his death . . .[11]

In April 1539, the army assembled at Cuzco – 300 Spaniards and 1,000 Indian auxiliaries – under the command of Gonzalo Pizarro. The road they took was retraced four centuries later by the American Hiram Bingham in his search for Vilcabamba. Mansio, who captained a squadron of cavalry, recorded that he was in the vanguard of the fighting and that he captured the Inca's wife and his brother Cusi Rimache.[12] He also recorded that Manco, who had made his escape across a river, cried out to him in quéchua: '. . . that he was not such a coward as they thought him, and that his warriors had killed some two thousand Spaniards since and before his rising, and that he intended to kill them all'.[13] Titu Cusi Yupanqui, one of Manco's sons, claimed that on the expedition's return to Cuzco it halted for a short while at the mountain hamlet of Pampaconas, where many of its soldiers attempted to rape the captured Coya Cura Ocllo, who defended herself by defiling her body with her excrement. Some four months later Pizarro brought the Coya to the township of Ollantay in the Yucay valley, from where he sent Manco some gifts in the hope of negotiating a peace. Incensed that his messengers, a Negro and two Indians, had been killed, Pizarro ordered what was one of the most pitiful and brutal acts recorded of his person. Stripped of her clothes and tied to a pole and whipped by his Cañari auxiliaries, the Coya was ordered by Pizarro to be shot dead with arrows. Her mutilated body was then placed in a canoe and let loose to float down the Yucay River. On his return to Cuzco Pizarro implemented a further reprisal in the city and in the Yucay with the burning of a number of Inca lords and caciques, among them the shaman Villac-Umu, who had been captured in the Cuntisuyo. These acts would forever taint his name with ignominy in the eyes of a by now defeated and almost defenceless people, and whose plight and abject poverty are only chronicled in the few surviving records in the Archives of the Indies, at Seville.

At the time of the Vilcabamba campaign there were possibly as many as 4,000 Spaniards living within Pizarro's governorship of settlements and encomiendas, probably 200 of whom were women.[14] One of the encomiendas Pizarro had awarded in the Cuntisuyo, near to Mansio's lands, was to the Irishman Thomas Farrell – possibly one of the many Catholic exiles who had fled to Spain after the Reformation.[15] In 1540 there were 274 encomiendas recorded in the various regions of the colony: 86 at Cuzco; 22 at Huamanga; 34 at Huánaco; 37 at Arequipa; 45 at Lima; 45 at Trujillo; and 5 at Chachapoyas.[16] The colony's missionary Orders of Dominicans and Mercedarians, who perhaps numbered no more than a hundred throughout the various settlements, over the years acquired some of the largest encomiendas in Peru. Only later did the Franciscan Order, which held a small mission in the Quito region, and the Augustinian Order establish themselves in Cuzco and in the southern provinces of the Collasuyo.[17] The end of Inca resistance also enhanced the colony's appeal to a large number of immigrants from both the Isthmus and Spain, and who began to populate the settlements at Arequipa, Sucre and Huamanga: mostly peasant farmers and Basque and Sevillian merchants, attracted by the 200 per cent profit on the goods they imported.

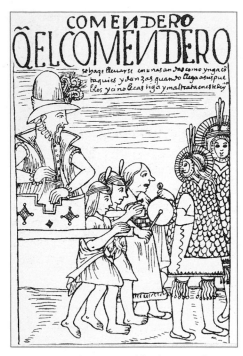

An encomendero carried by his vassal Indians. (Felipe Guaman Poma de Ayala, *Nueva Corónica y Buen Gobierno*)

Artisans and architects were also among the new arrivals, and who with the aid of Indian craftsmen began transforming the former Inca palaces of Cuzco into the monasteries, churches and mansion houses of its conquistadors, pre-Colombian foundations visible underneath their sombre walls and façades reminiscent of Toledo.

The Indian chronicler Poma de Ayala described Cuzco's encomenderos as wearing 'thick doublets, flat scarlet hats with plumes, tight fitting breeches, and short capes with long sleeves'.[18] It was a far cry from the morrión helmets and armour they now only wore in their expeditions, or the virtual rags most of them possessed when they had left Panama only a decade previously. Their ear lobes, clothes and armour, bejewelled with precious stones, the veterans of Cajamarca presented an extraordinary and exotic spectacle to the Isthmian arrivals, as did the rich livery of their horses and Negro slaves, and escorted on their travels by their Indian caciques and warriors from their encomiendas. The horses they rode were mostly of part Arab stock from Andalusia, small in height, hardy and intelligent, and comparable to the wild North American Palomino the Spaniards had taken there. Their mules, which were favoured by many of the conquistadors because of their strength and ability to carry heavy armour, were imported from as far afield as the island of Mallorca, reputed to breed the finest animals.

Pizarro further extended the frontiers of the colony by authorizing the conquest of Chile under Pedro de Valdivia, who founded its settlement of Santiago. Three years previously a small settlement had also been established from Spain at Our Lady of Buenos Aires, the future capital of Argentina, and which later moved across the río de la Plata to Asunción, also named after the Virgin. Another expedition, which Pizarro's brother Gonzalo commanded, was to the north-equatorial Amazon basin in search of the legendary kingdom of *el Dorado*, the Golden one. This place was so named because of a legend of a tribal chief who it was said covered his naked body with gold dust, which he would wash away by bathing in the waters of the Lake of Guatavitá as an offering to his people's gods. The expedition, however, discovered neither *el Dorado* nor any of his tribe's fabled treasure, though some of its volunteers explored the Amazon as far south as the Napo River, where they first learned of the existence of a tribe of women warriors, known as Amazonians.

There are, however, few descriptions left of Pizarro. Mansio Serra de Leguizamón considered him to be one of the bravest men he had ever known.[19] A man of the Indies, who had spent less than a third of his life in his native Spain, the conqueror of Peru was never understood by his own King or countrymen. Nor were the methods he employed found acceptable by a Castilian court. Neither was his execution of Atahualpa condoned. That the conquest of the Inca empire would have been achieved sooner or later by a European power was inevitable. That any other conqueror would have been more humane is debatable. A simple man of simple tastes, though ennobled after the siege of Cuzco, he exhibited none of the ostentation of his veteran soldiers, dressed habitually in a black smock. It was said of him that he gambled a little and played bowls.[20] Like most of the Cajamarca veterans he lived with his Indian women, mothers

The licentiate Don Cristóbal Vaca de Castro. (Herrera: BL, 783. g. 1–4)

of his four children, at Lima: a settlement whose coastal climate and wooden buildings resembled the homeland of many of its Sevillian merchants. There, amid the peace and relative prosperity of the colonists of his capital, an event took place that once more brought Peru to civil war. On the morning of Sunday 26 July 1541, a group of armed men made their way into his mansion. Hearing the disturbance caused by their entry, Pizarro attempted to strap on his armour, and accompanied by his half-brother Pedro de Alcántara and two pages, sword in hand, he confronted the intruders whom he recognized to be veterans of Almagro's defeated army. In a few minutes he lay dead, his face and body mutilated by the sword and poniard wounds of his assailants. He was sixty-five years old and was buried like a common criminal in an unmarked grave.* Within hours of his death Almagro's son by his Isthmian Indian mistress Ana Martínez was proclaimed by his supporters to be ruler of Peru.

Diego de Almagro, known as el mozo, the younger, had arrived in the colony two years after the capture of Cuzco. Though he had been pardoned by Pizarro for his part in his father's rebellion, he had nevertheless appealed to the Crown for the restitution of his governorship. His petition influenced the Council of the Indies to send the licentiate Don Cristóbal Vaca de Castro to the colony as arbitrator of his father's long-standing dispute, and also to hear in person the charges that had been levelled against Pizarro of complicity in his execution. The rebellion spread throughout the settlements, forcing many of the encomenderos to flee to the coast or to the northern Andes, where loyalist

---

* Pizarro's supposed remains are buried under the high altar of Lima's cathedral.

contingents later mustered to await the arrival of the licentiate, who would assume the governorship of the colony. Mansio recalled:

> I left Cuzco for the coast, in order to take a caravel in search of the licentiate Vaca de Castro, accompanied by eight friends, all well armed, mounted and provisioned; and because Almagro, the younger, had been informed that I had gone in search of the licentiate, he took from me my house in Cuzco and my Indians; and I and my friends were captured by García de Alvarado, his captain, who dispossessed us of our arms, horses and Negro slaves, all of which were worth some eight thousand pesos of gold, and having robbed us and hung one of our companions he brought us to Cuzco as his prisoners.[21]

Mansio was taken prisoner in the Cuntisuyo by a rebel squadron of Almagro's commander García de Alvarado, who had executed in Arequipa's main square Mansio's comrade in arms Francisco de Montenegro, who he hanged. His partially built mansion in the city and his encomienda of Alca were looted and stripped of all their possessions and appropriated by Martín de Bilbao, one of Pizarro's assassins. Among the few loyalists who had managed to flee Cuzco was the Friar Bishop Valverde, the veteran of Cajamarca, who on reaching the equatorial coast was killed by Indians in the estuary of Guayaquil. Others, who at the time were on various expeditions of conquest, as in the case of Gonzalo Pizarro in the Amazon basin, were to remain ignorant of the rebellion and of Pizarro's death.

In the closing days of 1541 the licentiate Vaca de Castro landed on the northern coast. On reaching Quito he sent dispatches to all the principal municipalities and settlements, calling for their surrender and offering the rebel army that had assembled in strength at Lima and at Cuzco a pardon if they laid down their arms. It was an offer that was ignored not only by Almagro, but by the majority of the cabildos, many of whose officials had requisitioned the encomiendas in their regions. However, it was several months before he could assemble an army, of under a thousand men, many of them from the Isthmus, to march south and relieve Lima. For eleven months the city of Cuzco remained in the hands of Almagro and his captains, supported by the Indian auxiliaries of the Inca Paullu, who once more sided with a rebel army. Weapons of every kind, coat armour and gunpowder were manufactured in the city's armouries, most of whose smiths were Greeks and employed by their fellow countryman Pedro de Candía, one of the few disaffected veterans of Cajamarca who had thrown in his lot with the rebels. Mastiffs, originally brought from the Isthmus for their use against Indians, were trained as attack dogs to head the vanguard of the cavalry. In the first days of September 1542, the rebel army left Cuzco on its march north to the central Andean settlement at Huamanga. Like many other conquistadors, Alonso de Mesa, who had also managed to flee Cuzco before its capture, fearing he would be killed in the coming battle, dictated his will shortly before the rebel army reached the mountain ridge of Chupas. Among his

Battle of Chupas between Almagro and the loyalist army of Vaca de Castro. (Herrera: BL, 783. g. 1–4)

various bequests he ordered that in the event of his death a gaming debt owed him by Mansio be repaid. He ends his will by listing the possessions he had taken with him to battle: 'a dark brown stallion, and one which is black called Gaspar, and a black mare called Fernanda, together with my arms and my spurs . . .'.[22] On the mountain ridge of Chupas, the two armies met in an encounter as bloody as that of Salinas, described in part by Lucas Martínez Vegazo and several other encomenderos of Arequipa in a letter to the Emperor Charles V:

> The rebels began their advance across the mountain ridge to almost a league in distance of our troops as their horsemen scouts rode out to inspect our positions. The governor [Vaca de Castro] then ordered one of his captains and fifty arquebusiers to move forward and take possession of the nearest ridge, and also another captain with equal number of lancers, which they succeeded in doing; seeing this, our enemies, who were still some three quarters of a league in distance from us, began to move in search of a position to engage us, and this they did, placing their artillery in line and their squadrons of cavalry who were some two hundred and thirty horse, accompanied by some fifty foot soldiers; their infantry consisted of two hundred

arquebusiers and a hundred and fifty pikemen, all so well armed that not even troops from Milan could match them in their armour and weapons; their artillery consisted of six guns, of ten and twelve feet in length, and capable of shooting a ball the size of an orange; they also had six other smaller guns and great quantities of munitions and powder . . . the governor then ordered our advance, and we marched to within reach of their arquebusiers' shot, advancing further still, until we engaged them with our lances, pikes and swords in a battle that lasted for almost an entire hour; and never was witnessed such a cruel and brutal fighting, in which neither brother, relative nor friend, spared each others' lives . . .[23]

Pedro de Candía, who had commanded the rebel artillery and had been reluctant to fire on the loyalist army, was within the hour lanced to death by Almagro. It was a betrayal that had effectively cost the rebels their victory, even though they had been urged to continue fighting by their young commander who promised them the Indian women of the loyalist captains for their booty.[24] As at Salinas, the Inca Paullu and his auxiliaries, seeing the battle gaining in the loyalists' favour, changed allegiance and Paullu turned on his former allies, slaughtering them without mercy. As night fell the dead and wounded could be counted in their hundreds, their bodies stripped of their clothing by the Indians as booty and left to be mauled by the packs of mastiffs. Among the dead were Vaca de Castro's commander Alvarez Holguín and the rebel captain Martín de Bilbao, who had been awarded by Almagro Mansio's encomienda and mansion at Cuzco, and who before the battle had harangued the loyalists by boasting that he had killed Pizarro. Almagro's commander Juan Balsa, whose concubine the Coya Doña Juana had accompanied him to the battlefield, had managed to flee, only to be captured by his own Indian retainers who beat him to death. The news of the defeat of the rebel army and the summary executions of some hundred rebels at Huamanga within days reached Cuzco and resulted in the release of the loyalist prisoners, including Mansio. Almagro, who had fled to the Yucay valley, was eventually captured and brought to Cuzco where Vaca de Castro ordered his execution in the city's main square. Honouring his last request, his headless body was taken to the convent of La Merced where it was buried beside his father, the head placed at the feet as the mark of a traitor.

The rebellions of the conquistadors, however, had overshadowed what every new immigrant would soon realize was the transformation of the former Inca empire into little more than a human factory of slave labour for the benefit of its colonists, rich and poor alike. Even a humble Spanish barber or a barefooted immigrant was able to rent from an encomendero Indians for his personal service, who were little more than slaves. The Indian Poma de Ayala, in various of the pen-and-ink sketches he made for his chronicle, depicted the poorer Spaniards carried on the backs of their Indian servants, and the encomenderos on throne chairs, as had been the custom of the Inca emperors.

The Friar Vicente de Valverde, first Bishop of Cuzco, engraving by Champin, from Castelnau. (National Arts Library, V&A Museum)

Though responsible for the appalling treatment of the Indians by authorizing their bondage, the Spanish Crown, however, had always envisaged that their welfare would have been supervised by the missionary Orders in charge of their conversion. Very little is known of the Church's early role in the Conquest, principally because it was neither politic for any chronicler openly to criticize its missionaries, and because most of the history of its evangelization was written by its members.

From the earliest days of the Conquest and of Cajamarca, the Dominican friar and future Bishop of Cuzco Valverde appears to have had little influence over the behaviour of Pizarro's men. The sexual needs of the conquistadors and their open relationships with their Indian women were possibly ignored by him. It was a stance from which few of the other missionary Orders would vary other than from appearances, especially as Pizarro himself had lived openly with his Indian mistresses. Only the Indian chronicler Poma de Ayala, born shortly after the Conquest, and whose manuscript was discovered in the Royal Library at Copenhagen in 1908, directly censured the rampant immorality of the colony's missionaries in the sexual abuse of their charges. Like all institutions, among its sinners were also its saints, principally the Dominicans Bartolomé de las

Casas and Domingo de Santo Tomás, a future Bishop of Sucre and author of a dictionary of quéchua published at Valladolid in 1560, and who had represented the rights of the Indian caciques at court in their failed attempt to purchase their freedom. More than any other Order the Dominicans dominated the religious life of the colony until the arrival of the Jesuits some forty years after the Conquest. Casas, who held considerable influence at court, was a former encomendero of the island of Hispaniola and the most vocal critic of Indian bondage. Though he had never been to Peru, and accepted the slavery of Negroes as morally justifiable, his writings had by then become the singular most important condemnation of the conquest of the New World, and of colonialism in general.

Over the years the Council of the Indies had been informed of the state of Indian affairs. Several testimonies are to be found in the Archives of the Indies of Indians protesting to their local missionaries of their maltreatment at the hands of their encomenderos. One such appeal was presented to Bishop Valverde in Cuzco by an Indian who had taken the name of Juan de Vegines, and who he later ordered to be freed from his bondage: 'who complained to his Grace of the treatment he had received from his master the encomendero Alonso de Luque, who whipped him repeatedly and kept him tied by a chain, and gave him little to eat . . .'.[25] There was little in fact that Valverde or the few missionaries who opposed such treatment could do, other than to appeal to the Crown.

It was in this atmosphere of reform, purveyed in the Spanish court and in the Council of the Indies, that the licentiate Vaca de Castro, a native of León and knight of Santiago, had been ordered to Peru with a mandate not only to implement changes to the existing laws governing Indian welfare, but drastically to curtail the power of the conquistadors. Sooner rather than later, however, his mandate became apparent to the victorious encomenderos of Chupas by his refusal to award them any further land grants of Indians, an act that they viewed as a direct threat to their feudal privileges which they had won by the sword. Equally, his corrupt nature was also to manifest itself in the various awards he was to make to merchants, from whom it was later claimed he had received bribes, and to the religious Orders. Martel Santoyo in a letter to the Spanish court wrote: 'All the monasteries of the Dominicans and Mercederians hold encomiendas. Not one of them has doctrined or converted one single Indian. They attempt to extract from them [their encomiendas] what they can, working them to the utmost; with this and their collections of charity they enrich themselves. A bad example. It would be better that those who come are diligent in their morals and doctrines . . .'[26]

Irrespective of his own moral failings, and ignoring the more apparent abuse of the encomienda Indians that he had been charged to eradicate, the licentiate Vaca de Castro would nevertheless be responsible for alleviating the poverty to which the Inca royal family had fallen, and which had been condemned by the Council of the Indies. Several years previously Bishop Valverde, referring to the poverty and degradation of the women

Inca noble and arms of Paullu Inca,
engraving by Champin, from Castelnau.
(National Arts Library, V&A Museum)

of Inca nobility, many of whom had reverted to prostitution, wrote to the Emperor: 'Your
Majesty has the obligation to grant them the means to eat, for they wander this city
abandoned, and which is a great shame to witness: and what I feel is that the women,
after being instructed, will become Christians, for there will be no lack of men who would
wish to marry them if Your Majesty were to reward them . . .'.[27] Another letter, written
by Luis de Morales in 1540, records: 'There are many who have nothing to eat and who
die of hunger, and who, from house to house, beg for food in the name of God and of his
Holy Mother . . .'.[28] A letter he wrote a year later refers to the poverty of the Inca
princesses, and in particular that of Mansio's former mistress the nineteen-year-old Coya
Doña Beatriz, who had married an impecunious Vizcayan hidalgo, Pedro de Bustinza:

> . . . In the said province of Peru there are many princesses, especially in the city of
> Cuzco, daughters of Huayna Cápac, who many a fine hidalgo would marry, for some
> demand them; though for lack of their dowries they refuse to betroth them, especially
> as all of them previously possessed dowries and much land that was left them by their

The Inca Paullu's palace of Colcampata, engraving by Champin, from Castelnau. (National Arts Library, V&A Museum)

father: Your Majesty: I beg that because of your own respect for their lineage you order they be given dowries and lands so that they may live decently and marry, and so they will be secure to live honestly and in the service of God . . . there is a citizen of Cuzco, a poor hidalgo, who has married a daughter of Huayna Cápac, sister of Paullu Inca, who is called Doña Beatriz, and who by the grace of God has children and who lives in great poverty: I beg Your Majesty that you grant them an encomienda so that they may be able to sustain themselves, and, in so doing, render God great service, and by which much joy will be given the natives . . .[29]

It was a degradation from which only the Inca Paullu would be immune. Then aged twenty-four, a few months older than his half-brother Manco, his mother, the daughter of a tribal chief from Huayllas, had been a concubine of the Emperor Huayna Cápac. Though possessing neither the purity of royal Inca blood of his half-sisters Doña Beatriz and Doña Juana, he had established himself as puppet ruler at Cuzco, ingratiating himself with his people's conquerors and receiving the begrudging obedience of the Inca lords, by then virtually reduced to begging for a living. Exempt from sharing the bondage of their former subject tribes, the Incas of the city by now represented an almost pathetic spectacle in their ceremonies held by Paullu in the palace of Colcampata, which Pizarro had awarded him, and which had previously belonged to

Almagro. His treatment by the city's encomenderos was little better than that of his relatives: 'Paullu Inca, lord and natural brother of Atahualpa, sons of Huayna Cápac, is a man of little caution unlike the Spaniards, and each day they cheat him, and take from him what he owns, either by force or deception, obliging him to sign documents and papers he can neither read nor understand . . . and Your Majesty should see he be not maltreated, so that such maltreatment be not witnessed by his caciques who visit him to render him homage . . . '.[30]

Paullu appealed to the Crown for justice, informing the Council of the Indies of his wish to become a Christian and relating his service on behalf of the Spaniards, and boasting that he had served them 'on horseback and on foot with crossbow and musket . . . '.[31] The Council not only upheld his title to an encomienda, but prohibited any Spaniard from entering his palace at Cuzco without his permission. The royal decree was also to award him a coat of arms and the rank of a hidalgo – an honour that later influenced his adoption of Spanish court dress, though he never learnt to speak Castilian. Vaca de Castro was also instructed by the Council to award a number of encomiendas to the other principal members of the Inca royal family. The Coya Doña Beatriz, mother of Mansio's eight-year-old son Juan and of her Spanish husband's two sons, Pedro and Martín, was awarded the encomienda of Urcos, lying to the south-east of Cuzco.[32] Her sister Doña Juana, who had been the concubine of the rebel commander Juan Balsa and mother of his son Juan, was also awarded an encomienda, but forced to marry the Conquistador Francisco de Villacastín. The favour shown the two princesses was also aimed at persuading them to abandon their religion. In 1543, at a ceremony in the principal church of Cuzco, imitating the pomp and ritual of the Castilian court, the licentiate presided at the baptism of both princesses, in which they were given their Spanish names and hidalgo title. Paullu, for whom Vaca de Castro stood as godfather, was given the name and title of Don Cristóbal. It was an occasion, however, that would be marred by the Inca Paullu's gift to the Spanish governor of the mummy of his father the Emperor Huayna Cápac, and which to the consternation of the two princesses he later exhibited privately in one of the city's mansions, charging the Indians of Cuzco for the privilege of seeing it. Only the intervention of the Dominican Friar Tomás de San Martín, who threatened to excommunicate him, led him to order the mummy's removal, though he refused to surrender the gold he had obtained.[33]

Another of the Crown's recommendations made to Vaca de Castro had been to obtain a record of Inca history. In a series of interviews with quipucamayoc at Quito and at Cuzco, a report was made of the Inca dynasties and of their history, most of which has been lost.[34] The testimonies of the quipucamayoc at Cuzco were gathered by Pedro de Escalante, an Indian interpreter, and by the Coya Doña Juana's husband Villacastín, who the chronicler Garcilaso de la Vega recorded had two front teeth missing, the result of a stone having been thrown at him by a monkey.[35] Villacastín was accompanied by the clerk and future chronicler Juan de Betanzos, also married to an Inca princess and who made a living as an interpreter. Much of the surviving evidence given by the four quipucamayoc interviewed at Cuzco was influenced by their dependence on the Inca Paullu, whose intention to discredit any rival claims to his leadership is more than evident in his pretence to have been the only legitimate heir to the Inca throne, stating somewhat imperiously that the royal coyas Doña Beatriz and Doña Juana had 'already received enough to eat from the guardians of this realm'.[36] The evidence was also rewritten in part years later by a friar in order to add weight to Paullu's grandson's future petitions.

Equally important to the reforms the Crown had wished to implement was an accord with the Inca Manco, who was still in rebellion in the forests of the Andes, and who was offered a rich encomienda by Vaca de Castro in exchange for his fealty.[37] The interview of his emissaries with the Inca was recorded in a letter he sent to the Emperor, in which he describes the velvet brocade he sent Manco and the parrots he received from him in return. The Inca Don Martín Napti Yupanqui, who like other baptized members of the royal house had been granted hidalgo rank, recalled the failure of the mission: 'In the presence of this witness the said governor Vaca de Castro sent from this city many Indians and orejones and other Indian servants with messages to the Inca Manco so that he would leave in peace with his people, but this he refused to do . . .'.[38] Two years later the Inca Manco was dead, murdered by an Almagrist rebel who he had given shelter at Vitcos, near Vilcabamba. He was twenty-eight years old: a sad and often ignored figure in the history and tragedy of the Conquest.

Though the licentiate Vaca de Castro would prove to be the first of a long line of colonial administrators who were to regard their office as a means of enriching themselves and the coterie of relatives they each brought with them to Peru, in the two years of his administration he was to oversee the greatest economic prosperity the colony had ever witnessed. This was due principally to the mining of gold and silver in the Charcas region of Bolivia, near Sucre, and an increase in trade with the Isthmus. It was a period that also witnessed Spain's dominion extended into the northern Argentine region of Tucumán. The final year of his governorship was, however, dominated by the news that reached Peru of a decree announced by the Crown in the city of Barcelona, known as the New Laws, governing the treatment of the natives of the Indies. Its author in part was Bartolomé de las Casas. Though excluding from its statutes Negro and Moorish slaves, its purpose was the reform of the encomienda system of tributary labour and the introduction of a legal framework to protect the Indians from the abuses inflicted on them by the colonists. It prohibited their labour as slaves and granted them the right of judicial redress to the Crown. It also denied the encomenderos' heirs the right of succession to their encomiendas. The decree, moreover, entitled the Crown to obtain the entire tribute of the encomiendas at the expense of its encomenderos, who were only to be allowed a small share of their revenues in the form of a life pension, more than doubling the Crown's income. In the most contentious article of its statutes with regard to Peru, all encomenderos who had taken part in the Battle of Salinas, whether under the banner of the Crown or in the ranks of the elder Almagro's rebel army, were to forfeit their encomiendas: a ruling that not only demonstrated the Crown's censure of the elder Almagro's rebellion and of his execution without royal approval, but which in effect would have left every veteran of the Conquest in ruin.

On 10 January 1544, the official chosen to introduce the new legislation to the colony arrived in the Isthmus of Panama. Don Blasco Núñez Vela, a former inspector of Castile's garrison, who had been appointed to replace Vaca de Castro as the first Viceroy of Peru, was accompanied by several lawyers and a large retinue of clerical administrators. Though warned by the Audiencia of Lima of the folly of attempting to bring into effect such drastic reforms, the elderly Viceroy ignored the advice and proceeded to introduce the decrees in his lengthy progress from Túmbez to Lima. His entry into the capital did little to ingratiate him with its encomendero nobility, whose vast wealth and social pretensions he openly ridiculed, describing those of them who claimed hidalgo rank to have been little more than 'tailors and cobblers'.[39] Vaca de Castro, who had voiced his misgivings of the New Laws, was arrested and imprisoned on a charge of sedition and corruption. Also arrested in Lima was an official whose loyalty the Viceroy had questioned, and whose killing he inadvertently ordered. Imprisoned by his own soldiers, the Viceroy eventually fled to Quito, leaving in ruins the Crown's authority. The fate of the licentiate would be no less ignominious. Freed from captivity, he returned to Spain and faced trial on charges of appropriating funds from the sale of encomiendas and embezzlement – charges he would vehemently deny, pleading poverty and penury which his correspondence with his wife in Spain during the years of his governorship did little to substantiate: '. . . all I have sent you and will also send you, you must treat with great secrecy, even among the servants, for the less the king knows, the more reward he will show me . . . and not a straw must be purchased in my name, so it is known that neither you nor I possess a single maravedí.'*[40] For over a year he was imprisoned at the royal fortress of Simancas, and then lived under house arrest in the Castilian township of Pinto where Mansio Serra de Leguizamón had spent his childhood, before being exonerated of all charges. This was far removed from the anarchy and rebellion that had taken hold of the land he had left behind, and of a governorship to which his heirs, among them his son Don Pedro Vaca de Castro, the future Archbishop of Seville, would owe their fortune.

* A peso of gold was worth approximately 470 maravedís.

7

THE DEVIL ON MULEBACK

> . . . let us pray to God with all our hearts he be content
> with these few crumbs we offer him.
>
> Francisco de Carbajal,
> after hanging four prisoners

Shortly before the flight of the Viceroy Núñez Vela from Lima, an elderly and portly hooded figure could be seen making his way on muleback across the arid landscape of the Cuntisuyo towards Cuzco. Francisco López Gascón, who as a young man had studied for the priesthood in his native Castile and had adopted the name of his former patron Cardinal Bernardino de Carbajal, had been on the point of returning to the Isthmus, and had been unable to find a ship at Arequipa.[1] Several years previously he had arrived in the colony from Mexico accompanied by a Portuguese woman, owning, as he was fond to boast, 'only the few coins he had owed a tavern in Seville'.[2] A former veteran of the Italian wars, he had commanded the licentiate Vaca de Castro's infantry at the Battle of Chupas. Exhausted by his long journey, he entered Cuzco with little more than what he possessed in his baggage and a reputation for a brutality that would within the year pervade Peru.

The object of the elderly soldier's journey was the summons he had received from Pizarro's youngest remaining brother Gonzalo, who at the head of an armed company of encomenderos from Sucre had entered the city two months previously and proclaimed himself ruler of Peru, in protest against the New Laws. Tall and black-bearded like all his brothers, Gonzalo was then thirty-two years old. Neither greatly intelligent nor particularly articulate, he was said to have been a handsome man and renowned for his sexual promiscuity and the physical courage he had demonstrated in his expedition to the Amazon basin in search of *el Dorado*, from where he had returned to Quito barefoot and in rags. The chronicler Agustín de Zárate, who almost lost his life for writing a history of Gonzalo's rebellion, described Gonzalo as a 'fine horseman and musketeer, and though of little culture he spoke well, though very coarsely . . .'.[3] Gonzalo's popularity among the colonists as his brother's political heir was unrivalled by any other conquistador. His proclamation, however, was opposed by a small group of Cuzco's encomenderos, though equally opposed to the New Laws, among them Mansio Serra de Leguizamón. The retribution of Gonzalo's followers was swift: '. . . he ordered I be tortured and caused me much injury,' Mansio Serra de Leguizamón recalled, 'and he seized from me my Indians and my house, which he gave to his ally and vassal Guerrero; and he kept me prisoner and threatened to have my head cut off, which he would have done had it not been for his fear of people's reaction'.[4] Francisco de Illescas stated that no one was able to leave the city 'without being brought back a prisoner and hung, and only after Gonzalo Pizarro and his men had left Cuzco was he [Mansio] able to make his escape from his confinement and flee the city on horseback . . .'.[5]

Some twenty of the city's most influential encomenderos fled the city to Arequipa's port of Mollendo where they had hoped to find a ship that would take them to Lima, only to discover that its few remaining vessels, alarmed by the news of the impending rising, had weighed anchor, leaving them no option but to disperse.[6] Most of them made the long and arduous journey along the coast; others, including Mansio, whose encomiendas were located in the region, sought refuge among their Indians. Though their flight from Cuzco had initially caused many conquistadors assembled in the rebel encampment to the north of the city to waver in their allegiance, the future course of events was decided by the rank and file of the city's landless Spaniards, who would form the backbone of the rebel army: merchants, artisans and former conscripts of the Almagrist wars, together with various members of the religious Orders. The Friar Agustín de Zuñiga declared publicly that if the decrees of the New Laws were carried out 'they will leave my sisters and nieces with no future but the whorehouse'.[7] It was a following that owed as much to the charismatic personality of Gonzalo, as to the fears they shared with the veteran conquistadors for reforms that would deny them the labour of their Indians, on whose servitude the wealth and livelihood of each colonist, poor and rich alike, depended.

Reinforced by some 20,000 Indian porters, 12,000 of whom would act as handlers of their cannon, the rebel army Francisco de Carbajal had joined at Cuzco finally began its march north towards Lima. Only on reaching the central Andes did Gonzalo learn of the arrest of the Viceroy and of his departure from the capital on a ship bound for the Isthmus. Poised within a few hours' march of Lima, Carbajal, who had by then been appointed by Gonzalo commander of his army, taking with him a hundred arquebusiers, entered the city at night and demanded a signed decree from its officials confirming Gonzalo's governorship of the colony. In the early hours of that morning, he then led three of Cuzco's fugitive encomenderos, naked and on mules, to the outskirts of the city where he hung them from a tree, each according to their rank, selecting the highest branch for the hidalgo and conquistador Pedro del Barco.[8] It would be the first sight the 600 soldiers of the rebel army would have of the city on their march into its main square: the Indian handlers positioning their cannon facing its principal buildings, the infantry and cavalry forming their squadrons alongside, supported by arquebusiers. Flanked by Carbajal on his mule and

Sebastían de Benalcázar. (Herrera: BL, 783. g. 1–4)

by the banners emblazoned with the arms of Cuzco and of the Pizarros, Gonzalo was acclaimed caudillo of Peru. One by one, the bishops of Lima, Quito and Cuzco acknowledged his authority, followed by the judges and Crown officials and the Mayor of Lima Nicolás de Ribera. On the morning of 28 October 1544, the colony severed its allegiance to its Viceroy, and in all but name to Spain. It was an act that would be followed by the surrender of the Pacific fleet and the capitulation of the Isthmus of Panama.

Within five months of the city's seizure the rebel army once more continued its march towards the northern equatorial coast, where the Viceroy's ship had inadvertently landed him, and where he had raised a small force of loyalists, among them the Conquistador Sebastían de Benalcázar, who had brought with him a squadron of men from his fiefdom at Popayán. In a campaign that would last for almost a year the rebel forces would finally entrap the loyalist troops on the plains of Añaquito, leaving among the loyalist dead St Teresa of Avila's brother Antonio de Ahumada.[9] The elderly Castilian Núñez Vela, whose blood-stained beard and hair would be worn as adornments on the helmets of the rebel captains,[10] was stripped of his armour and clothing and left naked to the mercy of the Indian auxiliaries.

Some weeks prior to the battle Carbajal, however, had been ordered to return south to put down a loyalist rising in the Charcas region led by Diego de Centeno, an encomendero of Sucre. Entering Lima with only 12 horsemen, within days he had provisioned a force of some 200 men, each aware of the reputation of the elderly soldier, renowned not only for his brutality but for his caustic wit. The chronicler Garcilaso de la Vega, who as a young boy had met him in Cuzco, recalled that on one occasion Carbajal, coming across a new recruit he had sarcastically addressed as 'Your Grace', asked the man his name, and being told that it was 'Hurtado' (stealing), he had commented: 'Not worth finding, let alone stealing.'[11] On taking prisoner a loyalist encomendero, who pretended not to know why he was to be hung, he had said to him: 'I perceive you wish to establish a pedigree for your martyrdom, so that you can point to it as an heirloom for your descendants? So be it, and now, adíos.'[12] Most chroniclers record that his bizarre appearance only added to a reputation of sadism and cruelty which would earn him the name of *el demonio de los Andes*, the devil of the Andes:

. . . instead of a cloak he always wore a purple moorish burnoose with a hood . . . and on his head a hat of black tafetta with a plain silk band adorned with black and white

Battle of Añaquito.
(Herrera: BL, 783. g.
1–4)

chicken feathers. This ornament he told his soldiers he wore to set an example to them, for one of the things he most exhorted them to do was to wear such apparel on their helmets, for he claimed it was the mark of a true soldier and would distinguish him from the frivolity of the plumes worn by an encomendero . . .[13]

The reprisals ordered by Carbajal and the Conquistador Alonso de Toro, the rebel governor of Cuzco, and which were personally sanctioned by Gonzalo by letter, included the execution and torture of a great number of suspected loyalists. Mansio had himself been recaptured in the Cuntisuyo, possibly some six months before the Battle of Añaquito. Luis Sánchez recorded: 'At the time I was in the city of Cuzco and witnessed Alonso de Toro, lieutenant-governor of Gonzalo Pizarro, take Mansio Serra prisoner and do him injury, and it was believed that he would kill him for being his enemy . . .'.[14] In a letter to Toro, dated 21 July 1545, Carbajal had ordered that the Conquistador Diego Maldonado 'be tortured by chords and water, after being placed naked on a donkey'.[15] Maldonado, known as *el rico*, the rich, was probably the wealthiest encomendero in Peru and was reputed to have given his wife on their marriage the giant pearl known as 'La Peregrina', the pilgrim, which he had probably looted during the sacking of Cuzco and which would find its way into the hands of the Spanish royal family.* Mansio's close friend Alonso de Mesa had fared little better after his arrest some months later, having his arms broken by Toro on the rack.[16] Torture and circumstance would soon break the spirit of each of the loyalist prisoners, among them Mansio, and who finally pledged their allegiance to Gonzalo. Among the correspondence dictated by the illiterate Gonzalo is a letter he sent from Quito to Pedro de Soria, his brother Hernando's factor, who had fled the loyalist rising at Charcas and was at the time in Arequipa, dated 18 October 1545, in which he instructs him: '. . . to thank Serra and [Diego] Camacho for what they have done, and for which one day I will reward them'. He ends his letter by telling Soria to remember him to them, 'and to all my encomenderos and our friends'.[17] The only other reference to Mansio's complicity in the rebellion is recorded by the chronicler Pedro de Cieza de León. He wrote that after Carbajal's later pursuit of Centeno's loyalist forces near Lake Titicaca, Carbajal gave Mansio and two other encomenderos permission to return to Cuzco, and that after the three men left his squadron, 'he entrusted his banner to Pedro Alonso Carrasco, who he appointed his lieutenant commander'.[18] It seems likely that Mansio's desertion to the rebel cause would have earned him a prominent role among Carbajal's squadron of cavalry, though he would have been allowed little share of the booty Carbajal extracted from his victims in the various settlements of the Bolivian altiplano and Charcas where he pursued Centeno's loyalists. Centeno's eventual escape to a cave in the Cuntisuyo, where he remained hidden for almost a year, marked the last semblance of armed resistance to the rebellion.

It was probably after serving in Carbajal's squadron of cavalry and on his return to Cuzco that Mansio was allowed to repossess his encomienda and mansion. The relative penury in which he found himself, due to the loss of almost two years of tribute from his Indians and the looting of his mansion and lands, probably influenced his decision to seek a dowry in marriage and to discard the Indian mother of his daughter Doña Paula, who was probably ten years old at that time. His son Juan, then twelve years old, was living with his mother Doña Beatriz in Cuzco. The Coya's husband Pedro de Bustinza had been one of the leading supporters of the rebellion and had helped the Inca Paullu establish the allegiance of the city's Indian nobility for Gonzalo. The bride Mansio chose was Doña Lucía, the sixteen-year-old daughter of his neighbour the Conquistador Gómez de Mazuelas, who brought him a dowry of 20,000 pesos of gold.[19] The marriage took place at Cuzco, possibly towards the end of the year 1546. The little that is recorded of Doña Lucía's father is that he was born at Valdetorres, in Medellín, Estremadura, the son of Pedro de Mazuelas.[20] He is listed as having sailed for the Isthmus on 29 February

---

* La Peregrina was purchased by the actor Richard Burton from a member of the Spanish Borbón family as a wedding gift for his wife Elizabeth Taylor.

1516, and where, sometime before his departure with Almagro's reinforcements, he married a Spanish woman whose surname was Zuñiga. One of the more elderly encomenderos of Cuzco and a staunch rebel, Mazuelas had been amply rewarded by Gonzalo for his loyalty, as is evident in a letter written by a settler from the region of Titicaca: 'I recently came across a steward of Gómez de Mazuelas who was on his way to take possession of Don Gómez's Indians. Handsomely has the governor [Gonzalo] our lord, rewarded him, giving him 25,000 pesos of gold in annual rent, and what he possesses is of such value that it is worth four times what Luis de Alamo and Nuño de Chávez were awarded . . .'[21] Mazuelas' sadistic character is, however, self evident in the description left of him by Pedro de Oñate in his letter to the Emperor Charles V, in which he names him as one of the torturers of the Inca Manco during his imprisonment at the hands of Juan and Gonzalo Pizarro. As for his wife, nothing is known of her, and it is possible she may have died in the Isthmus and that he would have sent for their daughter after the younger Almagro's defeat at Chupas, where he had fought in the loyalist ranks. That it was a marriage of convenience for the by then 34-year-old hidalgo is confirmed in the letter his father-in-law wrote to Gonzalo Pizarro shortly afterwards, dated 27 February 1547:

My illustrious lord, by other letters I have sent you and which you have not answered, I have already informed your excellency of the events that have taken place here [in Cuzco]. In this letter I will only touch on what has wasted me away, with the little I possess, which is ever at your excellency's disposal and service . . . as your excellency is by now aware, Mansio Serra de Leguizamón, encomendero of this city, married my daughter, who I would have imagined would have best served your excellency in this city or in the domain of his encomienda, and if he be there, and that be the case, I breathe freely in accepting his departure . . . however, as I know him to be so obsessed with this business of his gambling, I believe he has gone to that city [of Lima] which offers him greater opportunity to be among people of that persuasion; yet not content in merely gambling what he possesses and what he does not possess, he has sold the dwelling of his mansion in this city, which has caused us all here a great deal of trouble, and being informed of this, my daughter, his wife, has petitioned the justices of this city for the tribute he receives from his Indians . . . the justices, nevertheless, have informed me that your excellency has ordered that the tribute be sent to Lima. If your excellency has no need for it in expenditure for your service, I beg it be sent to his wife, even if it be only for her food and sustenance. And this I beg as your servant, for other than it being just, I will also receive some mercy. Our lord, most illustrious excellency, may health and prosperity be yours, whose illustrious hands I kiss . . .[22]

The gaming tables of Lima, for which Mansio had abandoned his young bride, were more than any other settlement representative of the wealth of the Indies and of the ostentation of its encomendero aristocracy, evident in the richness of their dress and jewellery and beauty of their women, Spanish and Indian, some the daughters, wives and concubines of their loyalist enemies. It was a wealth derived not only from the tribute of their Indians, but from the vast quantity of silver that by then was being mined near Sucre, at a mountain known as Potosí that had recently been discovered. The trade of the colony with the rebel-held Isthmus had also enabled it to continue importing the wines, clothing and other European articles of luxury, stockpiled by Seville's merchants at Panama and the Caribbean islands, and paid for in gold and silver coin still minted with the effigy of their Habsburg Emperor. Gonzalo's government of Peru in practice differed little from that of his brother or of Vaca de Castro, and the administration of its settlements and economic prosperity remained virtually unhindered by his rebellion, and was enriched by his appropriation of the Crown's share of bullion and taxes. His naïve belief, however, that the governorship he had won by force of arms he could eventually retain as a servant of the Crown was not shared by Carbajal, well aware of the fate of Gonzalo's brother Hernando, who was still languishing in prison in Spain for ordering Almagro's execution:

> My lord, when a viceroy is killed in a pitched battle and his head is struck off and placed on a gibbet, and the battle was against the royal standard, and where there have been as many deaths and as much looting, there is no pardon to be hoped for, and no compromise to be made; even though your lordship makes ample excuses and proves himself more innocent than a suckling babe. Nor can you trust in words or promises, nor whatever assurances be given you, unless, that is, you declare yourself king; and seize the government yourself without waiting for another to offer it to you, and place the crown on your head: allocating whatever land is unoccupied among your friends and adherents; creating them dukes and marquises and counts, such as there are in all the countries of the world, so that they will defend your lordship in order to defend their own estates; . . . and pay no heed if it is said that you are a traitor to the king of Spain: you are not, for as the saying goes, no king is a traitor . . . I beg your lordship to consider carefully my words, and of what I have said about ruling the empire in perpetuity, so that all those who live here will follow you. Finally, I urge you again to crown yourself king . . . die a king. I repeat, and not a vassal . . . for who so ever accepts servitude can merit no better . . .[23]

At the time none of the rebel encomenderos and conquistadors envisaged that the Crown had either the means or the will to send a battle armada and army half way across the world to reassert its authority. Nor did they believe that the Crown would be able successfully to mobilize reinforcements for such an operation from its settlements in Mexico and Guatemala without the support of the rebel-held Isthmus and of its Pacific fleet. Also it did not seem plausible that such a task force, unfamiliar with the equatorial and Andean terrain, would have survived a campaign against an army equally well armed and supplied with munitions and gunpowder manufactured in the colony. Moreover, they were aware that their appropriation of almost two years of the Crown's revenue of silver bullion had left Spain's already precarious financial resources on the brink of bankruptcy. Though the revenue from Peru up to that time is greatly exaggerated – averaging annually the equivalent cost of a single campaign against the city of Metz[24] by the imperial army – it was a source that the Spanish Treasury relied upon, and which the Emperor had pledged his German and Italian bankers for several years to come.[25] It had also taken almost a year for the news of the rebellion to reach Spain, where the Council of Castile, devoid of military and financial resources, was forced to seek a negotiated settlement.

Towards the end of 1546, a small and frail bearded priest was to arrive in the Atlantic port of Nombre de Dios. A former official of the Inquisition, he had been responsible for the defence of Valencia against the corsairs of the Turkish Admiral Barbarossa, who had ravaged the Balearic islands of Mallorca and Menorca, and in his role as a Crown official had successfully suppressed the threat of an insurrection of the city's Morisco population. The arrival of Don Pedro de la Gasca had been of little significance to the rebel commander of the port, in which his small squadron of caravels had berthed. Nor had the news of his appointment by the Crown as administrator of Peru, with the title of president of the Audiencia of Lima, caused any alarm to the rebel governor of Panama Pedro de Hinojosa. Forwarding a letter from the Emperor, who had been in Germany at the time the news of the rebellion had been received in Spain, Gasca wrote to Gonzalo informing him also of the decision of the Council of the Indies to repeal the New Laws, and offering him and his supporters a full pardon: pledges that were at first met with polite silence, and later with evasion by Gonzalo. Faced with the humiliation of his virtual isolation, and unable to contact any of the encomenderos of Peru without the co-operation of Hinojosa's fleet, Gasca over the weeks began an unrelenting correspondence with the rebel leaders of the Isthmus, couched in language varying from appeals to their loyalty, to threats and simple bribery. It was a campaign the middle-aged priest waged from his writing desk in the quarters he had been given in the port, and which would within time bring about the defection of Hinojosa, whom Gasca promised to award one of the richest encomiendas in Peru. The defection secured for Gasca not only the Isthmus, but the surrender of the Pacific fleet, of some twenty-two vessels. It also enabled him for the first time to communicate with the rebel encomenderos. In the months to come, with the same quiet determination he had used in securing the allegiance of Panama's rebels, he levied an army of invasion, from not only the Isthmus but the Caribbean islands. Its ultimate success, however, he knew depended on his ability to appeal to the feudal loyalty of Peru's encomenderos as much as to their purses, promising them future awards of Indians and guaranteeing them their lands. What followed was an endless and secret correspondence, smuggled by his caravels into Peru. Carbajal, who had executed a number of encomenderos for being found in possession of Gasca's correspondence, himself wrote to Gasca:

With what genius does a chaplain, of the intelligence some say you to possess, involve himself in an enterprise not even the king with all his forces is able to suppress, nor is capable of, if not by your worthless decrees and letters filled with lies? What you may consider is that the inducements which made the traitors surrender to you the fleet, selling their lord for money, as did Judas, was only so that they could themselves become lords, and you, their chaplain . . . and let us hope that your sins will in time bring you safely into my hands . . .[26]

The effect of Gasca's correspondence soon became evident in risings at Puerto Viejo on the equatorial coast, at Trujillo and Chachapoyas, in the central Andes. In May 1547, Diego de Centeno, who had been in hiding in the Cuntisuyo, also raised the royal standard, and with the support of loyalists from Charcas captured Cuzco. Almost at the same time the city of Arequipa declared for the Crown, imprisoning its rebel governor Lucas Martínez Vegazo, who was brought to Cuzco in chains. Aware by now of what was amounting to a mass desertion, and of the landing at Túmbez of Gasca's armada of 18 vessels, numbering 820 volunteers and Isthmian soldiers, Gonzalo evacuated Lima. Carbajal was ordered to join him at Arequipa with his squadrons of horse and infantry, which had been securing silver from the Charcas and the new silver mines discovered at Potosí. With his combined force now reduced to under 500 men, Gonzalo began his retreat towards the Bolivian altiplano, and with the intention of crossing the southern Andes to the settlement at Santiago, in Chile. It was a decision Carbajal vehemently opposed, believing that only victory on the field would save the rebellion. Gonzalo's retreat was to lead to the desertion of a further number of encomenderos. Among the deserters was Mansio, who on his return to the loyalist-held Cuzco was appointed one of its regidores and charged with the city's defence.[27] Informed of the retreat of the rebel army, Centeno, who had been reinforced by a large contingent of men from the Charcas and the Collasuyo, positioned his troops, of some 460 horse and 540 infantry, near the southern shore of Lake Titicaca, cutting off Gonzalo's retreat south.

At first light of the morning of 20 October 1547, the two armies faced one another on the plains of Huarina. Amid the bleak and windswept landscape of the Andean plateau, the loyalist infantry slowly advanced towards the rebel positions. At a distance of some hundred paces Carbajal's arquebusiers opened fire, refiring for a second and third time with the spare muskets he had ordered them to load beforehand. Positioning his outnumbered pikemen in the formation of squares, time and again he resisted the overwhelming superiority of Centeno's cavalry, and by advancing his arquebusiers he was finally able to break the loyalist positions, horses and men fleeing for their lives.[28] The engagement left 350 of Centeno's men dead and was considered the bloodiest of all the wars of the Conquest. The chronicler Diego Fernández claimed that Carbajal, accompanied by two of his Negro slaves, toured the battlefield, clubbing to death the loyalist wounded. The news of the defeat of Centeno, who had been suffering from

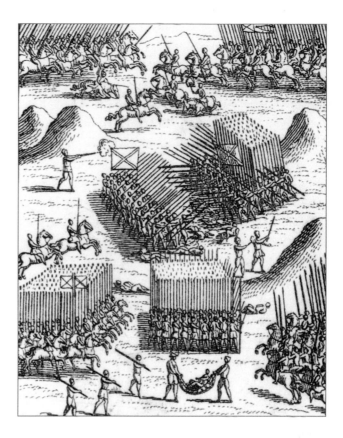

Battle of Huarina. (Herrera: BL.
783. g. 1–4)

pleurisy and had watched the battle from his litter, and who had managed to make his
escape with a small company of horse, was to reach Cuzco with the arrival of the
armoured figure of its Bishop Juan Solano, whose brother had been killed by Carbajal.
Though Mansio had been able to send his young wife and their year-old daughter to the
safety of his encomienda in the Cuntisuyo, he was nevertheless taken prisoner by
Gonzalo's captain Juan de la Torre, who shortly afterwards entered the city with a
squadron of arquebusiers, as the loyalist prisoner Hernando de Cespedes recorded:
'. . . Mansio Serra suffered much ill-treatment and torture for his stance, and for not
wishing to go with Gonzalo to the battle at Huarina; and this is known to me for I had
been taken prisoner at the battle and brought to Cuzco by Gonzalo Pizarro when he had
come there carrying the royal standard of the captain Diego de Centeno'.[29]

Only some weeks after the battle did Gonzalo make his entry into Cuzco, where he
received the rapturous acclamation of the very settlers who had prepared his gallows in
expectation of his defeat, and from whose wooden poles hung the corpses of the city's
Mayor and one of its regidores. Somehow Mansio managed to escape and flee the city,
evading his certain execution at the hands of Gonzalo. For days the rebel soldiers
pillaged the mansions of Cuzco's defectors in an orgy of retribution, raping with

abandon the city's women, Spaniard and Indian. Cespedes recorded that Gonzalo sold some of the loyalist prisoners as slaves.[30] The obese Carbajal ordered that the wives and daughters of Arequipa's loyalists be brought to Cuzco, most of whom had already been raped by their captors. One woman, María Calderón, the wife of the astrologer and loyalist captain Jerónimo de Villegas who was lodged in Mansio's residence, was visited by Carbajal. He ordered his Negro slaves to strangle her for having criticized him publicly, and who then hanged her by the neck from the window of her bedroom – a corner window of the Casa de Sierpes, facing the square of the Nazarenas.[31]

By the end of December 1547, Gasca's army of reconquest had reached the city of Jauja, reinforced by many former rebel encomenderos. 'I was in the valley of Jauja with the president Gasca among his troops he took with him for the castigation of Gonzalo Pizarro and his followers,' recalled Pedro Súarez de Illanes, 'and there I saw and met Mansio Serra, who was well armed, with horses, and in good order, as a fine soldier and hidalgo . . .'.[32] After waiting for the winter rains to pass, Gasca's army reached the Apurímac River and the vicinity of Cuzco in the early part of April 1548. At the valley of Jaquijahuana, a few miles north of Cuzco, the two armies of some 2,000 Spaniards took up their battle positions. One by one, however, the rebel cavalry, and then its infantry, began a mass desertion. Within the hour both Gonzalo and Carbajal were prisoners.

Most chroniclers record that Gonzalo Pizarro met his death with resolve and dignity. His sentence was proclaimed before the entire army by the judge Andrés de Cianca:

> . . . it be declared that the said Gonzalo Pizarro has committed the crime of laesae majestatis against the crown . . . and for which we condemn him as traitor and his descendants in the male line for two generations and in the female line for one generation . . . that he be taken from his imprisonment on a mule with his feet and hands manacled and that he be brought before this royal assembly of His Majesty . . . and that his crimes be proclaimed . . . and that he be brought to this place of execution and that his head be struck off . . . and that after his death it be taken to the city of Lima . . . and that under it be inscribed in large lettering: This is the head of the traitor Gonzalo Pizarro who was brought to justice in the valley of Jaquijahuana where he gave battle against the royal standard in defence of his treason and tyranny . . . and we further order that his house in Cuzco be razed to the ground and that its foundations be scattered with salt . . .'[33]

Francisco de Carbajal, who some chroniclers claim was then eighty years old, shared his caudillo's fate. His former adversary Centeno, who had ordered he be unharmed by the throng of soldiers who clamoured to attack him, was said to have been visibly irritated by the fact that Carbajal did not appear to recognize him, and asked him whether in fact he did recall him. 'My god, sir!', Carbajal is recorded to have exclaimed, 'having only ever seen your buttocks in retreat, I can say I do not.'[34] Stripped of armour he was dragged naked in a basket by several mules to the scaffold, where, before being hung, he was asked by his confessor to say the Our Father and the Hail Mary.[35] Defiant to the end, and to the amusement of the onlookers who crowded his gallows, he repeated just the words: 'Our father, hail Mary.'

Each and every one of the encomenderos and conquistadors of Peru had at one time or another supported Gonzalo's rebellion, including Centeno. Some of them, like the father of the chronicler Garcilaso de la Vega, who had deserted Gonzalo at the field of Jaquijahuana by galloping across to the enemy lines, were pardoned. Others were less fortunate, and little mercy was shown the rank and file of the rebel prisoners who were sentenced to be brought to Cuzco on the backs of llamas and

Diego de Centeno. (Herrera: BL, 783. g. 1–4)

publicly flogged, before being taken to the Pacific ports for deportation as slaves in the royal galleys. All the principal rebel captains taken prisoner were hung and quartered, their heads ordered to be placed on poles in each of the settlements of the colony. A certain Estremaduran called Serra, who may possibly have been a relative of Mansio, was condemned to be flogged and to have his tongue cut out, a sentence Gasca himself

Fountain on the patio, Mansio's mansion, Cuzco. (Nicholas du Chastel)

recorded to the Council of the Indies: '. . . so disgraceful was his rebellion that a day before the battle of Jaquijahuana, being one of the enemy scouts, he had been spotted by our men and urged to join them and serve the king but shouted that they could kiss his backside, and that had they meant the king of France he might well have joined them, even though he had a fine king in Gonzalo Pizarro . . .'.[36]

Mansio's role in the rebellion is virtually unrecorded. The silence of his witnesses to his probanza and their perjured declaration, of having no knowledge of his complicity, among them the former President of the Audiencia of Lima, Melchor Bravo de Saravia, were indicative of the involvement of almost all the principal magnates of Peru in the insurrection. Even though his initial loyalty and imprisonment would have been made known to Gasca, his later involvement must have been serious enough to have warranted the

Convent church of San Francisco, La Paz. (Alexander Stirling)

sentence the judge Andrés de Cianca subsequently passed on him at Cuzco, ordering him to 'pay a thousand gold pesos towards the crown's soldiers and to be banished from Cuzco for a term of two years'.[37] It was a sentence that prompted the Friar Alonso de Medina, one of the most tenacious preachers of Cuzco, to write a theatrical protestation to Gasca denouncing the treachery of each of the colony's cities and encomenderos: 'Tell me Cuzco, why is it that you do not speak? Being as you are a traitor to the Crown? See here, a certain Mansio Serra, traitor in death in your service to Gonzalo Pizarro, and who, when he was dead, neither wished to serve the king; traitor in life, without ever repenting, and allowed to keep his Indians, his mansion and a life of repose . . . see here, Maldonado, the rich, traitor in your youth, and traitor in your old age . . .'[38] Though in his probanza Mansio claims that Gasca subsequently entrusted him with the capture of the few rebel captains still at large in the Cuntisuyo and the Charcas, his service on behalf of the Crown was more than likely a means of reducing his sentence of exile.

To commemorate his victory, which had left only sixteen dead, Gasca ordered the foundation at Chuquiabo, a valley south of Lake Titicaca, of the city of Nuestra Señora de la Paz, Our Lady of Peace, later known as La Paz, the administrative capital of Bolivia, and where the rebel and loyalist dead from the Battle of Huarina were buried many years later. His decision, however, to allow most of the former rebel encomenderos,

Battle of Chuquinga. (Herrera: BL,
783. g. 1–4)

including Mansio, to retain their Indians and lands prompted an outcry of protest from
the volunteers he had brought with him from the Isthmus, who clamoured for what
they saw to be a just reward for their service. Though he had been able to reward some
of his captains with a number of encomiendas, there were not enough within the colony
to appease his followers, fermenting a dissent that soon manifested itself in open
rebellion. Taking with him the blood-stained banners of the rebel army which had
marked his victory, on his arrival in Spain he was rewarded with the bishopric of
Palencia, from where some ten years later, after the abdication of the Emperor, he would
journey from his diocese to greet his sovereign during his final journey to his retreat in
the Estremaduran monastery of Yuste.[39]

Within three years Gasca's legacy would once more throw Peru into civil war with an
abortive rebellion at Sucre of the encomendero Sebastián de Castilla. Eight months later
a further insurrection was led in Cuzco by the encomendero Francisco Hernández Girón,
who attempted to kill the city's governor in protest at the introduction of a law
prohibiting Indian servitude. This revolt, supported by the hundreds of landless veterans
of Gasca's army, lasted for almost a year and once more witnessed the defeat of a loyalist
army at Chuquinga, near Nazca, north of Arequipa. Mansio's role as a captain of horse
and scout for the loyalist army is recorded in considerable detail by witnesses to his

Philip II, an engraving of a Titian painting. (Royal Museum of Fine Arts, Brussels, Belgium)

probanza. Girón, who credited his victory not only to the prowess of his men, among them a regiment of Negro slaves, but to witchcraft, was a month later defeated at Pucará, north of Lake Titicaca, by an army led by Lima's judges, and in which Mansio also served. Captured and taken to Lima where he was hanged, his decapitated head was placed in an iron cage beside the two cages that contained the skulls of Gonzalo and Carbajal. This marked the end of almost seventeen years of rebellion which had left more Spanish dead than during the entire conquest of the Inca empire.

The rebellions of Peru were recorded by four contemporary chroniclers,[40] other than an account based on Pedro de la Gasca's memoirs, written in about 1565 by Juan Calvete de Estrella who had never been to Peru, and that of Garcilaso de la Vega, written in the early part of the seventeenth century. The first account was published by Agustín de Zárate, a treasury official from Valladolid, who had lived in Lima from the outset of the insurrection. Many of the events concerning the Conquest, which he also wrote about, he had researched while staying with the Conquistador Nicolás de Ribera. His affiliation with the rebel cause enabled him to obtain permission from Gonzalo to return to Spain, where he was imprisoned on suspicion of complicity in the rebellion. During his incarceration at Valladolid he wrote his account of the rebellion and of the Conquest, *Historia del Descubrimiento y Conquista del Perú*. After his release in 1554, Zárate obtained a minor post at court which enabled him to accompany the regent, the future King Philip II, to England for his marriage at Winchester cathedral to Queen Mary Tudor. It was during the voyage of the royal galleon from La Coruña to Southampton that Philip read his manuscript and authorized its publication. A year afterwards Zárate's history was published in the Netherlands, and twenty-six years later it was translated into English under the title *The Strange and Delectable History of the Discovery and Conquest of the Provinces of Peru*.

Unlike Zárate, the chronicler Pedro Gutiérrez de Santa Clara, who had arrived in Peru at the outbreak of Gonzalo's rebellion, witnessed Gasca's final victory at Jaquijahuana and accompanied him to Panama on his return to Spain. Of either Spanish or Mexican mestizo parentage, he had served as a conscript in the loyalist army, and in the short time he had lived in Cuzco had befriended the Inca Paullu. A talented linguist, Gutiérrez de Santa Clara included a vocabulary of quéchua in his account *Historia de las Guerras Civiles del Perú*, one of the most descriptive and colourful of all the chronicles of the rebellions. Almost nothing is known of his life, other than he is recorded to have been living in Mexico in 1603, over half a century after leaving Peru. His manuscript, originally entitled *Quinquenarios*, is preserved in the provincial library of Toledo and was published in 1904.

Diego Fernández, known more commonly as el Palentino because of his birthplace in the Castilian city of Palencia, was an official chronicler. A clerk to the Audiencia of Lima, he had arrived in Peru shortly after Gasca's victory. Some years later he was commissioned to write a history of Girón's insurrection. Fernández subsequently wrote an account of Gonzalo's rebellion, leaving possibly the most vivid portrait of Carbajal which he obtained from eyewitnesses, and whose influence on the events of the time he establishes more than any other chronicler. His manuscript, which also contained a brief outline of Inca history, was published in Seville in 1571.

Pedro de Cieza de León is regarded as not only the foremost historian of the rebellions and of the Conquest, but of Inca civilization. Born in Estremadura, though by adoption a native of Seville, where his family held trading interests with the Isthmus and Caribbean islands, he had emigrated to the New World inspired by the treasures and Inca artefacts he had seen as a young boy lining the quays of Seville which Pizarro had sent back from Cajamarca and had been publicly displayed before being melted down. In 1536 Cieza de León was made an encomendero of Urute, in Colombia, and from where, eleven years later, he joined Gasca's army. From Tumibamba to Túmbez, and through the central Andes, he followed Gasca's troops on their march south to Cuzco, visiting the various Inca sites he later recorded in an almost journalistic style, leaving a descriptive sketch of each region and of its people and customs. At Cuzco, as in the settlements of the Collasuyo and Charcas he later visited with Gasca's permission, he was given access to the quipucamayoc and amauta elders, from whom he was able to gather much of the information that formed part of his chronicle of the Inca people. After only four years in the colony he returned to Seville, where in 1553 he published the first part of his history, dying a year later. Only within the last hundred years have Cieza de León's other manuscripts been discovered, revealing a prolific account, ranging from the mythology of the Incas to the Conquest, and later civil wars and rebellions of the Spaniards: a work which the official historian of the Council of the Indies, Antonio de Herrera, in the early seventeenth century plagiarized without reservation.[41] Fourteen years after Cieza de León's death his patron Pedro de la Gasca was buried in the church of La Magdalena at Valladolid, on the walls of whose façade the rebel banners he had taken with him on his journey home can still be seen, sculptured and surmounting the coat of arms his grateful Emperor had awarded him.

THE COYA OF CUZCO

. . . ichach munani, ichach manamuni,
. . . perhaps I do, perhaps I don't.
The Coya's reply to her enforced marriage vows

Garcilaso de la Vega
Comentarios Reales de los Incas

The few records to survive of the Coya Quispiquipi Huaylla, who after her baptism was known to the Spaniards as Doña Beatriz, show her to have been one of the most remarkable if not tragic figures of the conquered Inca dynasty. Nothing is known of her appearance. At the time of Gonzalo Pizarro's execution she was twenty-seven years old. As a young girl she had suffered the loss of her father the Emperor Huayna Cápac, and within a few years had witnessed the killings of both her mother and her brother Huáscar at the hands of Atahualpa's warrior chiefs. Aged twelve, together with her only surviving full-blooded sister, the Coya Marca Chimbo, a year older than her, she had been kept a prisoner in Cuzco to await the triumphal entry into the city of her half-brother Atahualpa, for whose personal harem she had been selected. Nor is anything known of the role of her guardian the cacique Cariapasa, Lord of the Lupaca, into whose care she had been entrusted by her father, only that he returned to Cuzco after the arrival of the Spaniards and urged his bondaged tribesmen, encamped near the city, to return to their lands. What is recorded, however, is that like her sister she was awarded in concubinage by her half-brother the Inca Manco, only to be abandoned by her Spanish lover some five years later after her presumed rape by Almagro's soldiers when they took possession of Cuzco. Nothing is known of her in the immediate years after Mansio left her, nor whether she had been able to keep her son with her. Nor will it ever be known if she had ever loved his father.

The Coya's later marriage to Pedro de Bustinza, a penniless treasury official, who had come to Peru in the retinue of Hernando Pizarro on his return from Spain, did little to alleviate the poverty in which she had been forced to live. This situation did not improve until the licentiate Vaca de Castro awarded her the encomienda of Urcos, south-east of Cuzco, part of the lands that had been granted by Pizarro to his brother Hernando. The only mention made of her during this period is by the chronicler Garcilaso de la Vega who records the death of her husband Bustinza, who Gonzalo Pizarro had appointed Mayor of Cuzco after his victory at Huarina. Betrayed by one of his wife's cousins, Bustinza was captured by loyalists while raising Indian auxiliaries from his wife's lands and taken to Gasca's encampment at Jauja, where he was hanged. Twenty-seven years old and a widow with three sons, the Coya's future was to depend on the outcome of the forthcoming battle at Jaquijahuana, the result of which she knew was to determine the choice of Spaniard both she and her encomienda would be awarded by the victor. It was said that for several days before Gonzalo and Carbajal led the rebel army out of Cuzco the carcasses of dead foxes had been found in the city's streets, killed by plague, an omen regarded by the Indians as foretelling his defeat. Her nephew the chronicler Garcilaso de la Vega recorded:

> The wife of Pedro de Bustinza, who was a daughter of Huayna Cápac, and whose Indians of her encomienda belonged to her and not to her husband, the governors [Gasca] gave in marriage to a fine soldier of good character called Diego Hernández, who it was said – more from malice than truth – in his youth had been a tailor. And when this was known to the princess she refused to marry him, saying that it was not right that a daughter of Huayna Cápac should be married to a tailor; and though the Bishop of Cuzco begged her to reconsider and the captain [Diego de] Centeno and other personages tried to persuade her, none were able to do so. It was then they called upon Don Cristóbal Paullu, her brother, who on visiting her, took her aside to a corner of a room, who told her that it was not in their interest that she refuse the marriage, for it would only bring hardship to the royal family and the Spaniards would regard them as their enemies and never more offer them their friendship. She then agreed to accept her brother's command, though not in very good faith, and thus she went before the bishop and the altar. And being asked by an interpreter if she would accept to be the wife of the soldier, she replied in her language: '*ichach munani, íchach manamuni,*' which means, 'perhaps I do, perhaps I don't.' And so was concluded the betrothal, which was celebrated in the house of Diego de los Ríos, encomendero of Cuzco . . .[1]

The dowry she brought her husband, an elderly soldier of fortune and native of Talavera, who was probably twice her age, was substantial for an Indian. Other than her mansion at Cuzco, which had previously belonged to the Conquistador Vasco de Guevara and was situated behind that of Garcilaso de la Vega's father, her encomienda of Urcos possessed an annual tribute of some 400 male Indians and their families.[2] She was also still regarded by her people with great reverence. The Indian Mazma recalled: 'I have seen the Indians of all the regions and nations show her their obedience and respect as daughter of the lord and king.'[3] At the time she took possession of her lands at Urcos the plight of the colony's bondaged tribesmen had remained unchanged since the early years of the Conquest, though their numbers had been drastically reduced by recurring outbreaks of smallpox and the harshness of their servitude, principally in the mining of silver. The encomendero Antonio de Ribera recorded:

> It has been some fifteen years since the Marqués Don Francisco Pizarro ordered the counting of Indians of the encomiendas of the conquistadors, and which numbered one million and five hundred and fifty thousand Indians. And when Pedro de la Gasca was to make a similar enquiry in order to access the number of Indians to allocate and placate the complaints of the caciques who said they had not enough Indians to produce their tribute, it was discovered that in all the land there were no more than two hundred and forty three thousand Indians, as recorded by the testimonies that were made to the inspectors, and I being one of them . . .[4]

In an Andean population by then consisting of probably no more than 2 million Indians and some 8,000 colonists, 346 of whom were encomenderos at the time Pedro de la Gasca left the colony for Spain, the former Inca territories had since their conquest suffered the loss of almost a third of their population.[5] Their Inca lords, though not bondaged, but dispossessed of their lands and wealth, had over the years been forced to make a living as virtual servants to the settlers with only a few exceptions, chiefly the immediate members of the royal family, among them the Inca Paullu who was to die a year after Gasca's victory at Jaquijahuana. Proud of his allegiance to his people's conquerors, he was buried in all the finery of a Castilian hidalgo in the small chapel he had built adjoining his palace, leaving as his heir to his encomienda his twelve-year-old son Don Carlos Inca. The leadership of the royal house at Cuzco was assumed by Doña Beatriz, following also the death of her sister, whose husband the Conquistador Francisco de Villacastín had been exiled for life by Gasca for his part in Gonzalo Pizarro's rebellion. 'In Cuzco where she resided,' the chronicler Diego Fernández recorded, 'there was no lord, male or female, greater than she.'[6]

The small court over which the Coya presided at her mansion in Cuzco would have been Indian in appearance and custom – for neither she, nor any of her close relatives, ever learned to speak Castilian. The Indian chronicler Poma de Ayala, in a series of pen-and-ink drawings produced at the end of the sixteenth century, portrayed the royal coyas and ñustas dressed in full-length embroidered mantle capes, adorned at the neck by gold pendants: costumes also depicted in late seventeenth- and early eighteenth-century colonial paintings. Like other encomenderos, by then restricted by the Crown to residing in the cities from which their encomiendas were held, she would have been obliged from time to time to make a tour of her lands and tributary Indians, travelling in a litter and accompanied on horseback by her husband Diego Hernández and her sons and yanacona servants. The administration of her encomienda would have been in the hands of Spanish stewards – landless colonists who in general were renowned for their cruelty and blatant dishonesty as foremen, and who in later years were replaced by mestizos, equally despised by the Indians of the encomiendas. The stewards were responsible for gathering the tribute and supervising the agricultural produce of the caciques which twice yearly – on the feast of San Juan (24 June) and at Christmas – would be brought to the city of the encomienda's jurisdiction for sale in its markets: coca, maize and potatoes, clothing and livestock of llamas, alpacas and vicuñas, together with whatever gold or silver had been mined in the tributary lands. In the province of Quispicanchis, some 35 miles south-east of Cuzco, she maintained her principal hacienda at Urcos, the capital of her encomienda. In the neighbouring mountain valley of Andahuaylillas, bordering the River Vilcanota, she was probably responsible for the building of its primitive church. Later, towards the end of the sixteenth century, this was replaced by the Jesuits, but because of its mural paintings is regarded as one of the finest examples of early colonial church architecture.

The Coya's marriage to an almost unknown conscript of Gasca's army was however indicative of the reluctance of the more prominent conquistadors or Spaniards of hidalgo rank to marry the Indian mothers of their children. It was a racism bred in the psychology of men, irrespective of their own humble origins, whose sense of racial purity, *limpieza de sangre*, dominated their attitude to the lineages they wished to establish as grandees of a new order, and who like their countrymen in Spain were at pains to distance themselves from any stigma of mixed blood. The early years of the Conquest, when the veterans of Cajamarca had lived openly with their Indian mistresses, had given way to a semblance of moral conformity imposed on the colony by successive missionaries and by the Crown itself, who publicly criticized the failure of the by then middle-aged conquistadors to marry and set an example to both colonists and Indians alike: something to which they had previously turned a blind eye during Pizarro's governorship. The conquistadors' general refusal to wed their Indian concubines led to a gold rush of women fortune hunters from Spain and from the Isthmus, more than willing to trade their youth and white skin for the fortunes of the gout-ridden and battle-scarred soldiers, most of whom were disfigured by syphilis and the facial warts from which the elder Almagro, among others, was recorded to have suffered. The influx of women, from the noblest families of the Peninsular to the humblest prostitutes, would lay the foundations for the future creole aristocracy of the colony. It would also deprive the mestizo children of the conquistadors of any legal right to their elderly fathers' fortunes, and who would be seen by their young Spanish stepmothers as a threat to their own children. It was a cycle from which few of the conquistadors would be immune, as in the case of Lucas Martínez Vegazo who in his old age married a creole young enough to be his granddaughter, and who would eventually inherit his encomienda.

The Coya's eldest son Juan had been born in 1534 at Cuzco and had been raised by her, together with her two other sons from her later marriage. Though recognized by his father Mansio, he would never be legitimized by him. It was a fate he shared with his cousin and childhood companion Garcilaso de la Vega, both of whom by blood were Inca princes and in turn hidalgos of Spain – a racial and social ambiguity which would encompass them all their lives. 'The children of Spaniards and Indians are called mestizos,' Garcilaso wrote in his old age, 'which is to say we are of mixed race, and a term invented by the early Spaniards who had children by Indians; and as it was a name given us by our fathers I was proud to call myself as such . . . though now in the Indies it is regarded as a term of inferiority . . .'.[7] The chronicler Pedro de Cieza de León recorded that he knew of encomenderos who had fathered some fifteen children by Indian women.[8] As mestizos the Coya's children were deprived of the legal rights of even the humblest colonist, based on the premise that their divided loyalty would represent a potential political threat in the future, and reflected in a decree issued at Valladolid in 1549 by the Emperor which prohibited mestizos from holding public office, and also denying them the right of inheriting their father's encomiendas or carrying arms. Their exclusion from the wealth of the colony would also be apparent in its social hierarchy and racism – a prejudice Garcilaso suffered at the hands of his father's Spanish wife, who reduced his Inca mother to the role of almost a servant before she eventually married an obscure immigrant called Pedroche.[9]

There is, however, little evidence to suggest in the various testimonials of the conquistadors that they regarded their mestizo children with anything other than affection, as is evident in the will of Alonso de Mesa, all of whose children were mestizos. Though maintaining their Spanish identity, the surviving veterans of Cajamarca after years of cohabitating with their Indian women were themselves by then as Indian as their mestizo children, speaking with fluency both quéchua and aymara, the principal languages of their tributary vassals, and participating in many of the native customs. Judging by the various petitions made to the Crown by the mestizos and their Inca relatives it would be the conquistadors, rather than the colony's missionaries, who would testify on their behalf. On three occasions Mansio testified in petitions to King Philip II. 'I know and well understand,' he declared in one of the petitions on behalf of Doña Beatriz's niece María, one of the Inca Manco's daughters, 'that the royal person of the King Don Felipe, our lord, is a Christian king and prince . . . and the merits of the said Manco Inca at the time of the conquest are known to this witness when we made much of this realm's discovery . . . and being, as I am, informed of the poverty of his daughter Doña María Coya who has not sufficient income to sustain her . . . I ask you grant her your benevolence, as it is something she deserves and in which Your Majesty will be well served . . .'.[10] On behalf of Atahualpa's two sons, Francisco and Diego, he declared that should the King award them an encomienda with which to support themselves, 'it would be a just and saintly thing'.[11]

Other than her three sons the Coya's immediate family consisted of two daughters of her half-brother Manco, the ñustas Usezino and Ancacica whom she had sheltered and brought up as her own children after his flight from Cuzco.[12] The Conquistador Francisco de Illescas, a frequent visitor to her mansion, recalled that apart from the two young princesses various other relatives of hers were also lodged there.[13] Among her numerous relatives also residing at Cuzco was her cousin Don Diego Cayo Yupanqui, who had been responsible for betraying her husband Bustinza to Gasca's men, and who as a reward had received the encomienda of Sóndor.[14] Also living in the city were the ñustas Cuxirimay Ocllo (Doña Angelina) and Chimpu Ocllo (Doña Isabel). Doña Angelina, a niece of Atahualpa, had at one time been Pizarro's concubine and was the mother of his sons Francisco and Juan. It appears, however, that because of her past affiliation with Atahualpa she was regarded with hostility by Doña Beatriz and other members of her panaca. It was a rivalry evident in the writings of Garcilaso de la Vega whose mother belonged to the Coya's panaca, and who was responsible for maligning the origins of Atahualpa's mother by claiming quite falsely that she was a subject princess from Quito. A counter-assertion can be found in the chronicle of Doña Angelina's husband Juan de Betanzos, who omitted Huáscar from his list of Inca monarchs, and who referred to his mother the Empress Rahua Ocllo as a concubine. It was an allegation also made by the Inca Titu Cusi Yupanqui, an illegitimate son of the Inca Manco, in his attempt many years later to impress the Spaniards as to his right to the Inca throne. Betanzos, however, on the strength of his wife being the mother of two of Pizarro's sons, obtained for her a rich encomienda in the Yucay valley, which he later appropriated for himself.[15]

Nothing for certain is known of Betanzos' background, other than his apparent birth at Valladolid and service to Francisco de Carbajal at the time of Gonzalo's rebellion, and his ability as a translator. His history *Suma y Narración de los Incas* is one of the earliest accounts of the Inca people and of their culture, most of the information for which he obtained from his wife's relatives and by acting as interpreter to the enquiry the licentiate Vaca de Castro held at Cuzco. The first part of his manuscript was discovered in the library of the Escorial and was published in 1880. A second section, which had been in the library of the Duques de Medinaceli, was discovered in Mallorca and first published in 1987. A dictionary of quéchua he wrote as a foreword to his history has never been found.

It would, though, be through the writing of the Coya's nephew Garcilaso that much of the history of the Inca people would be made known to seventeenth-century Europe. For most of her early adult life his mother Doña Isabel had been the concubine of the Estremaduran hidalgo Sebastían Garcilaso de la Vega, who had arrived in Peru at the time of the siege of Cuzco. After serving under Gonzalo Pizarro in the conquest of the Collasuyo he had been awarded an encomienda at Tapacarí in the valley of Cochabamba, and though he had initially been opposed to Gonzalo's rebellion he had later served under him until his desertion at Jaquijahuana. Pardoned by Gasca, he subsequently became corregidor of Cuzco and married a Spaniard. His mestizo son Garcilaso was born in Cuzco in 1539 and baptized with the family name of Gómez Suárez de Figueroa, though he would later adopt his name. His education, together with that of his cousin Juan Serra de Leguizamón, who was five years older than him, was entrusted to Juan de Cuéllar, a canon of Cuzco, who in 1552 established a small school in the city. Among their fellow students were the sons of the conquistadors Pedro del Barco and Pedro de Candía and Pizarro's son Francisco. So proud was the canon of his

Arms of Garcilaso de la Vega, engraving, from *Comentarios Reales de los Incas*, Lisboa, 1609. (Private Collection)

charges, Garcilaso recalled years later, that he had wished he could have sent each of them to the University of Salamanca.

A year after his father's death in 1559, by then aged nineteen, Garcilaso left Cuzco for Spain and was never to return. After serving against the Morisco uprising in Andalusia in 1570, in the army of Don Juan of Austria, who a year later destroyed the Turkish fleet at Lepanto, he settled in the township of Montilla, and then at Córdoba. Far removed from his homeland, the former pupil of canon Cuéllar's small school at Cuzco wrote one of the greatest narrative histories of the Americas, *Comentarios Reales de los Incas*, a work that influenced the conception of Inca civilization for centuries afterwards. Though at times historically unreliable in anything that would veer from his projection of an heroic and almost utopian Incaic society – denying for example the existence of human sacrifice – his history nevertheless presents an epic account of a people, their religion and customs, portrayed in a literary style unequalled by any of Peru's chroniclers with the exception of Pedro de Cieza de León. Much of what Garcilaso wrote was based on the stories and legends he had heard as a child from his mother's relatives, and from what he had himself observed during his adolescence. As he records in his history many of the veterans of Cajamarca were known to him, including Mansio, and from whom he would have been given first-hand accounts of the Conquest. He also relied on the existing published histories and an unpublished manuscript in Latin by the Jesuit mestizo Blas Valera.

After writing a literary work of translation from Italian, entitled *Los Tres Diálagos de Amor*, in 1605, and a genealogical essay of his father's family, Garcilaso wrote a history of the conquest of Florida by Mansio's former cavalry commander, Hernando de Soto. Four years later he published the first part of his history of Peru, seven years before his own death at Córdoba at the age of seventy-seven. Bequeathing the little he possessed for a chapel dedicated to the Holy Souls of Purgatory in the city's cathedral mosque where he would be buried, he left in his will to his Negro slave Marina de Córdoba an annuity of 50 ducats and a mandate for her freedom.[16] Ignorant of the universal fame the history of his mother's people would bring him, little would Garcilaso have imagined that some three-and-a-half centuries after his death his remains would be brought back to the city of his birth by his sovereign's descendant King Juan Carlos of Spain to be buried in state at Cuzco's church of el Triunfo. His mother Doña Isabel, defrauded by the Spanish husband she had later married, was to die a virtual pauper, leaving a debt of 'one single peso',[17] as she recorded in her will.

In October 1555 when Emperor Charles V announced his abdication in the great hall of the palace at Brussels, bestowing the crown of Spain and of the Indies on his son Philip II, the Coya Doña Beatriz was thirty-four years old. One of the last decrees the Emperor had signed before travelling to his self-imposed exile in Estremadura had been the appointment of a viceroy for his Peruvian territories. At the time of the Marqués de Cañete's arrival at Lima, in 1556, bringing with him one of the largest retinues of officials and attendants ever seen, the only nominal resistance that existed to Spain's sovereignty of her colony was in the Andean region of Vilcabamba – virtually an independent Inca kingdom. Since the Inca Manco's death, his 23-year-old son Sayri Túpac had ruled the remnants of his army of warriors in his fortified mountain enclave, and had repeatedly refused to negotiate a peace agreement with the Spaniards. The presence of his warriors in the vicinity of Cuzco had led to a number of attacks on travellers on the roads from the city to Lima. The Conquistador Juan de Pancorbo recorded:

> . . . at one time I left the city with a number of men in order to ambush Sayri Túpac's warriors who had waylaid many people in the road of the Apurímac, for his Indians had killed a number of Negroes, burning houses and committing other acts of violence on the road; and together with our troop I went in search of them to a mountain station where we learned that Sayri Túpac had some eight hundred warriors, all well armed, and that some two hundred or three hundred of them had taken part in the raids . . . and as I did not possess a commission to go further in search of them I returned to the station, and by order of the justices of the city I later kept guard of the road with the men I was with for several days . . .[18]

One of Cañete's first acts was to write to the Coya Doña Beatriz asking for her help in persuading her nephew Sayri Túpac to receive his envoys. The delegation that subsequently left Cuzco for Vilcabamba, and which also included the Coya's husband Diego Hernández, the chronicler Betanzos and two Dominican friars, was led by her 23-year-old son Juan Serra de Leguizamón, as two of Sayri Túpac's warriors record:

> . . . as I was at the time with Sayri Túpac Inca in the Andes [Vilcabamba] and at war, I saw the friar Melchor [de los Reyes] and another friar companion of his, and also Juan de Betanzos, and that they went to where the Inca was, but he did not wish Betanzos or any other person to enter where he was, and so the friars went ahead alone, and Betanzos returned [to Cuzco] – Chasca, Indian.[19]

> As a warrior in the service of the Inca Sayri Túpac, in his company I saw Juan Serra enter, as he was his first cousin the Inca received him well, and also out of respect to his mother Doña Beatriz Yupanqui, his aunt. And also entered there the friar Melchor. And I heard Juan Serra say to Sayri Túpac that if he left the viceroy the Marqués de Cañete would give him many Indians and houses for his people and many clothes and other goods, so that he would be content; and all this Juan Serra told him many times and in my presence, and I also heard him say the same to his warrior chiefs. I further witnessed Juan Serra take part in the treaty and discussions with Sayri Túpac, and the Inca sent him twice to the Lord Marqués about his leaving, and Juan Serra came two times to see the Inca, bringing with him payment and presents – Paucar Yupanqui, Inca.[20]

The Marqués de Cañete and the Inca Sayri Túpac in Lima. (Felipe Guaman Poma de Ayala, *Nueva Corónica y Buen Gobierno*)

Though the chronicler Juan de Betanzos in his history claimed the credit for the negotiations with the Inca, in fact he had been turned away by his captains as Juan Serra de Leguizamón's probanza shows. In October 1557, leaving behind his younger full-blooded brother Túpac Amaru and his half-brother Titu Cusi Yupanqui in guard of his mountain realm, the Inca finally began his progress from Vilcabamba accompanied by his daughter and young sister-wife Cusi Huarcay (Doña María) and several hundred of his warriors. The caravan of litters that would take him and his family to the valley of Andahuaylas was escorted by his cousin on horseback and by the Coya Doña Beatriz's husband Diego Hernández. Ordering his cousin Juan to ride ahead to Lima to inform the

Viceroy of his arrival, in January 1558 Sayri Túpac entered the capital of the viceroyalty, and at whose gates he was met by the cabildo of the city. Cañete received him with equal honour, seating him by his side in the audience chamber of his palace.

Garcilaso de la Vega recorded that on the night of a banquet given by the Archbishop of Lima, in which the Inca was presented with the documents awarding him a pardon and the grant of his encomiendas of Indians, he had observed in quéchua that he had traded what had once been the empire of Tahuantinsuyo for the equivalent of a thread of the cloth that covered the dining table. The encomiendas awarded him and his descendants in perpetuity included much of the Yucay valley, which had once formed part of the lands of his grandfather the Emperor Huayna Cápac's panaca of Tumibamba. His transformation into a Castilian encomendero would be completed on his later arrival in the ancient capital of his ancestors with his baptism and Christian marriage to his sister, for which a special dispensation from Rome would eventually be secured by King Philip II. Carried in a litter in accordance with Inca custom, he made a tour of the little that by then remained of the monuments of the city in the company of his cousin, to whom the Conquistador Juan de Pancorbo recalled 'he showed great love'.[21] Thousands of his subjects from across the former Inca empire made pilgrimages to the city to render him homage during his stay at his aunt Doña Beatriz's mansion. Among the relatives who came to pay him homage was the nineteen-year-old Garcilaso de la Vega. Before his departure to his encomienda in the Yucay he gave his cousin Juan sole legal right to administer his lands and wealth, and also dictated a will, witnessed by Mansio Serra de Leguizamón and by Doña Beatriz's husband Diego Hernández, in which he left him 1,000 pesos of gold in gratitude 'for the work he has done for me and for his service to me'.[22] The heir to his considerable fortune he named as his only child and daughter who had been baptized with him, and who had been christened Beatriz in honour of his aunt. The lengthy legal authorization he gave his cousin to administer his possessions demonstrates his total dependence on him, and may explain much of Juan's motive in persuading him to leave Vilcabamba:

> Be it known that I, Inca Sayri Túpac Manco Cápac Yupanqui, Inca and encomendero of this great city of Cuzco, of these kingdoms and provinces of Peru . . . authorize you Juan Serra de Leguizamón, my cousin and citizen of this said city, and entrust you to act on my behalf in all matters . . . also in regard to all my lands and possessions and income of maravedí pesos of gold and of the tribute of my Indians . . . and that you be charged with all the administration of my goods, lands and Indians . . . and whatever tributes of coca . . . .this first day of October, 1558 . . .[23]

Some time after the Inca's departure from Cuzco the Coya Doña Beatriz was once more faced with the harrowing experience of witnessing the mummy of her father displayed for private viewing in the mansion of the city's Governor Juan Polo de

Ondegardo. It was an event he proudly recorded several years later with the testimony Viceroy Toledo included in a letter to the Council of the Indies:

> . . . being at the time in charge of the government of these provinces, some twelve or thirteen years ago, with much diligence and through various sources, I was able to discover the said bodies . . . some of them so well embalmed and so well maintained as at the time of their deaths; and four of them, which were those of Huayna Cápac and Amaru Topa Inca and Pachacuti Inca, and that of the mother of Huayna Cápac, who was called Mama Ocllo, and the others, I discovered in bronze cages that had been secretly buried; and also among them I discovered the ashes of Túpac Inca Yupanqui in a small earthen jar, wrapped in rich cloth and with his insignia; for it was this mummy, I had heard, Juan Pizarro burnt, believing that treasure had been buried with it . . .[24]

Though the licentiate Vaca de Castro at one time had the mummies in his possession, nothing is known of what became of them until Ondegardo's announcement of their discovery. It seems more than likely that their location had been revealed to him by the Inca Sayri Túpac on the advice of the Dominican Melchor de los Reyes, who had instructed his conversion to Christianity. Whatever the truth of the matter, they remained in near perfect condition in Ondegardo's mansion until their removal to Lima on the instructions of Cañete, and where they were eventually buried in the grounds of the city's hospital of San Andrés. With silent resignation the Coya accepted the sacrilege.[25] Her only

Eighteenth-century Cuzco portrait representing Doña Bernardina Serra de Leguizamón, the conquistador's granddaughter, engraving by Champin, from Castelnau. (National Arts Library, V&A Museum)

Arms of Doña Bernardina Serra de Leguizamón: eight saltires of Serra as border of arms awarded her grandmother, the Coya Doña Beatriz Yupanqui, engraving by Champin, from Castelnau. (National Arts Library, V&A Museum)

consolation was the reward Cañete gave her for her collaboration, of the encomienda of Juliaca,[26] on the northern shores of Lake Titicaca, the lands of which had formerly belonged to her guardian the cacique Cariapasa, and which in the eighteenth century would be possessed by the marqueses de Valparaíso.

The role the Coya's son Juan had played in the negotiations with the Inca were also rewarded by Cañete, but only with the grant of a virtually insignificant encomienda at Písac in the Yucay, valued at less than 400 pesos of silver annually. It was a pitiful recognition of his services, and is clear evidence of the prevalent discrimination against his mestizo origin. All of the witnesses to Juan's probanza he at that time presented to the Audiencia of Lima, and which was sent to King Philip II, testify to his poverty and dependence on his parents, among them the Conquistador Francisco de Villafuerte, who recalled that Juan had spent a period in jail at Cuzco for failing to pay a debt of 70 pesos of silver.[27] Unlike his childhood companion Pedro del Barco, who led an abortive rebellion of mestizos in Cuzco in 1560, and for which he was exiled to Chile, he appears to have led a virtually reclusive life. At his encomienda at Písac,[28] below the Inca mountain ruins that had once been the summer retreat of his grandfather Huayna Cápac, he built his hacienda in one of the most beautiful Andean valleys. For some thirteen years he remained Písac's encomendero, living there with his wife Doña María Ramírez,[29] whom he had married at Lima at the time he had accompanied his cousin the Inca to the viceregal capital. Nothing is known of his bride's family, nor whether she was Spanish or mestiza. Two children were born to the marriage: Don Juan-Pablo and Doña Bernardina. The small colonial township of Písac, built by Jesuit missionaries and by his son, and whose colourful Sunday market and Inca ruins are today one of the most popular tourist attractions near Cuzco, is all that remains of his legacy. Until his death at the age of thirty-seven,[30] he continued to petition the Crown to award him the encomiendas of Juan de Saavedra, of Quispicanchis,[30] and that of the licentiate de la Gama, each valued at 7,000 pesos of gold in annual income.[31] He received neither.

In 1569 his mother the Coya died.[32] Mourned by her people and by her Spanish husband and her three sons, the last surviving daughter of the Emperor Huayna Cápac and of the Coya Rahua Ocllo was laid to rest at one of Cuzco's churches, its site now unknown and forgotten.

9

THE HOUSE OF THE SERPENTS

Nothing is more certain than death,
and nothing more uncertain than the time of it . . .

The Emperor Charles V's Will

Overlooking the plaza de las Nazarenas in Cuzco stands the convent of that name, known also as the *casa de las sierpes*, the house of the serpents, or the house of Leguizamón. Though converted in the late seventeenth century into the convent church of the Order of Nazarus, much of its façade, patios and structure remain as they would have appeared at the time Mansio Serra de Leguizamón and his family lived there. Above its portico and doorway are sculptured what remain of his family arms, a border of eight saltires awarded his ancestors in commemoration of the victory of Baeza against the Moorish armies on St Andrew's day in 1227, supported by two giant serpents –

symbolic of the mansion's earlier site as the Inca house of learning, Yacha huasi, and of its surrounding area known as Amaru cata, the slope of the serpent. The Jesuit chronicler Bernabé Cobo recorded that several huaca stones formed part of its masonry and were venerated by the Incas of the city as magical and sacred shrines.[1] Built some ten to twenty years after the Conquest, the site had formed part of the original allotments Pizarro had awarded his men after the city's capture, and was one of the few buildings to have partly survived the earthquake that demolished most of Cuzco in 1650. Its yellowing Inca stone masonry and colonial patio are all that remain of the memory of its former occupants, the sounds of their voices and their morrión helmeted and velvet-clad images lost in the distance of time amid the silence of its convent walls.

Mansio's mansion, Cuzco, detail of wall showing snake imagery. (Nicholas du Chastel)

Mansio's mansion converted into the convent of Las Nazarenas, Cuzco. (Nicholas du Chastel)

In 1571 when the Conquistador had led the procession of family mourners from his mansion to one of Cuzco's monastery churches for the burial of his eldest son Juan he was fifty-nine years old. His young wife Doña Lucía had been dead ten years, and who in the fifteen years of their marriage had borne him two daughters and five sons. The eldest of their children was Doña María, born at Cuzco in the closing years of Gonzalo Pizarro's rebellion, and who at the age of eleven had been placed in the city's Franciscan convent of Santa Clara, located in the same square as her parents' mansion, then known as Santa Clara la vieja. It was the first such institution founded in Peru in 1550, and had been established at Cuzco seven years later in the houses that had belonged to the Conquistador Alonso Díaz, principally for the daughters of impoverished veterans of the Conquest. Under its first abbess, Doña Francisca Ortíz, it numbered twenty-four nuns of Spanish parentage, twelve mestizas and forty creole girl students who were educated until they reached marriageable age. Among the founding nuns were the daughters and granddaughters of the conquistadors Bernabé Picón and Francisco de Villafuerte.[2] In defiance of her parents Doña María chose to enter the convent's novitiate. It was an action that led to a lengthy dispute between her father and the nuns, to whom he was eventually forced to donate a dowry of jewels and vestments, valued at 2,000 pesos of gold, together with 700 cattle for the convent's farms.[3] His refusal to give any further donations on behalf of his daughter may explain the wording of much of the Franciscan chronicler Diego de Mendoza's account of the young novice:

Street adjoining Mansio's mansion, Cuzco. (Nicholas du Chastel)

. . . among the glories of this life was Sister María de Leguizamón, one of the twenty-four founding nuns of this convent, daughter of the valorous conquistador Mansio Serra de Leguizamón and of his wife Doña Lucía, citizens of Cuzco, who were well known in this realm for their nobility and wealth, and who at the age of eleven left the home of her parents, and fleeing from there, and from the vanities of the world, entered the convent of Santa Clara . . . and from where not all the influence of her parents would make her leave; neither by enticements nor promises; until they disinherited her, denying her their refuge and her maintenance . . . yet at so tender an age she commended herself to God . . . and the more her parents denied her vocation the more she accepted her spiritual sisters as her family . . . bringing her from the confusion and captivity of Babylon to the doors of Sion . . .[4]

Taking the name of Sister María of the Visitation, Doña María was to become one of the most prominent figures in Cuzco, devoting much of her life to the care of Indians in the native hospital of the city, and eventually was elected abbess of Santa Clara. Friar Mendoza in his history refers to her many demonstrations of sanctity and mortifications. At her death, at the age of sixty, he recalls that a choir of angels was heard singing Vespers in the chapel of the convent, and that some days later she appeared to one of the nuns. Four years after her death, when the convent was transferred to its present site, the friar writes that her coffin was opened and that her body was found to be incorrupted, adding that in order to place her remains in a smaller coffin to be taken for burial in their new church the nuns broke her legs, and that 'blood flowed freely from the wounds . . .'.[5]

Hardly any records survive of Mansio's other children. His son Jerónimo also entered the religious life as a Dominican in the monastery of Santo Domingo at Cuzco, built on the foundations of the Inca Temple of Coricancha, and where his mother Doña Lucía had been buried.[6] The licentiate Cepeda wrote in a letter to King Philip II from Sucre, dated 14 February 1585, enclosing a missive from the Jesuit Alonso de Barzana: 'In order to comply with my office in approving the native speech of the Indians among the

The Archangel St Gabriel, late eighteenth century, Potosí School. (Private Collection)

clergy who reside within this bishopric of Charcas, I can testify that the Reverend Father Jerónimo de Leguizamón, curate of the parish of San Pedro de Potosí, speaks with great propriety the quéchua language.'[7] Only three of Mansio's legitimate children married. His eldest son Mansio, heir to his encomienda of Alca, married Doña Francisca de Caveruelas. Whatever the reason, it was a marriage of which Mansio disapproved, and because of which he disinherited his son, and spent years in litigation fighting the demands of his granddaughters, the eventual heirs to his encomienda.[8] His sons Pablo and Miguel never married. His son Francisco married Doña Elena Girón de Heredia, the daughter of a hidalgo from Seville, and who on his return to Peru is listed as being accompanied by Francisco de Castro, one of his mother's relatives, and two servants.[9] The name of his youngest daughter Doña Petronila's husband remains unknown. Another of his daughters was Doña Paula, whose mother was Indian, and who also formed part of his household. Each of his children and grandchildren ended their lives in anonymity with the exception of the Coya Doña Beatriz's grandson, Don Juan-Pablo de Leguizamón, who was appointed by the Crown corregidor of Yucay, and who was known to the chronicler Bernabé Cobo. In 1617 he is recorded as having written to the

Viceroy with regard to a quantity of Inca treasure he had discovered at his encomienda at Písac.[10] Nothing more is known of their lives.

Though plagued by his gambling debts, and virtually dependent on money lenders, at the time of his eldest son's funeral Mansio Serra de Leguizamón was nevertheless still a figure of considerable importance, though he presented a somewhat forlorn figure. '. . . in later years,' Garcilaso de la Vega recorded, 'the cabildo of Cuzco, seeing how ruined this son of theirs had become because of his gambling, in order to cure him of his addiction elected him alcalde of the city for the term of a year: a service he performed with all care and diligence, for there was much of a gentleman about him, and for the whole of that year he never once touched a card'.[11] Contrary to what Garcilaso wrote from the distance of his Spanish exile, a will made by Mansio several years later shows him to have continued his passion for gaming: '. . . I owe Juan Gómez 800 pesos of silver,' the will, dated 1576, records, '. . . Agustín Alzazan 100 pesos . . . Agustín López Gómez 150 pesos . . . 1,000 pesos Antonio Pereyra, alcalde, won from me at gaming . . . the licentiate Alonso Perez 4,000 pesos . . . 3,400 pesos I owe the said Diego de los Ríos from gaming, and which he won from me . . .'.[12] His debts forced him to sell one of the first mining concessions at Potosí,[13] which he had possibly acquired during the closing years of Gonzalo Pizarro's rebellion. His varying fortunes, however, are demonstrated by a later will that shows him to possess imported tapestries and a variety of silver ornaments which decorated his mansion, together with various sums of gold and silver. According to the testimony of his witnesses to his probanza Mansio maintained his household in apparent comfort, if not luxury, at a time when it was not uncommon for a colonial grandee to accommodate not only his immediate family but a large number of dependants, Negro slaves and Indian retainers.

The most revealing, if not contradictory, insight into Mansio's character, and almost at variance with the energy and time he spent petitioning the Crown to compensate him for the loss of his original award of encomiendas, is the attitude he demonstrated in his later years towards his tributary Indians, and the restitution he would make them in both his wills. Though a number of conquistadors in their old age were to make similar restitutions for their share of booty and treasure they had obtained at Cajamarca and at Cuzco, there is little evidence to deny their

Patio of Mansio's mansion, Cuzco. (Nicholas du Chastel)

sincerity, even if such sentiments were influenced by their impending deaths and the advice of their confessors. Many made no such gestures. Neither did any of the later colonists, responsible for a far greater exploitation and ill treatment of the Indians of their encomiendas than the by then elderly conquistadors, a number of whom, like the trumpeter Pedro de Alconchel of Vilcaconga, were virtually penniless. Nor was any such sentiment shared by the Crown officials of the colony: as in the case of the eight-year-old son of the Judge Melchor Bravo de Saravia who was awarded an encomienda.[14] In his first will Mansio ordered his executors to return to his Indian vassals much of the produce and livestock of his encomienda:[15]

> I declare that the produce and inheritance of Vizan [Alca] . . . belongs to the Indians of my encomienda because it was they who planted it, and they who built its hacienda, and because of which it is theirs and which they are to keep and own, as it was once their own . . . I declare that all the horse mares, goats, Castilian sheep, belong to the Indians of my encomienda . . . and this I return to them so that it be distributed among them . . . I declare that I have received [over the years] in tribute from my Indians of my encomienda some 50,000 pesos of gold, and it is what I owe them, and I beg that they pardon me, for I no longer have any money to repay them . . .[16]

Considering that the produce and livestock of his encomienda – virtually its entire wealth – should by right have been inherited by his children, his action betrays an extraordinary sense of morality shared by few of his countrymen, however late in his life. His encomienda of Aymara tribesmen at Alca in the Cuntisuyo, bordering the Cotahuasi River, was some 140 miles south-west of Cuzco, and north-west of the city of Arequipa. Like all other encomiendas it was held by him for the duration of his life and that of his successor and heir. In a report of inspection carried out in 1572, its population, livestock and annual produce were recorded as comprising: '. . . 938 male tributary Indians; 770 children; 130 elderly Indians; 2,640 women; 8 caciques; 1,860 pesos of mined silver; 1,744 pesos of mined gold; 130 head of cattle, each valued at 2 pesos of silver; woven cloth valued at 175 pesos of silver; maize valued at 187 pesos of silver; wheat valued at 143 pesos of silver; 400 poultry birds, each valued at 50 pesos of silver . . .'.[17]

The encomienda was liable for the payment of a salary for two missionaries (802 pesos of silver), a legal tax (703 pesos of silver), and a payment to the caciques for the labour of their people (200 pesos of silver). Apart from his income of livestock, Mansio received annually some 2,401 pesos of silver. From a smaller encomienda at Vito,[18] of Manarí Indians, near the eastern tropical region of the Antisuyo, he received a further 55 pesos of silver annually. It was an income that included, as Mansio mentions in his last will, plantations of alfalfa, timber and a goat farm in the neighbouring valleys of Cuzco.[19]

By 1571 Mansio had spent thirty-eight years of his life in Peru: a land still virtually unexplored, varying in climate and terrain, from its mountain enclave of Cuzco to its eastern forests of the Antisuyo, and as far south as the Bolivian altiplano and the pampas of Argentina, whose city of Mendoza had been colonized by settlers from Chile, bringing with them the vines that would later found the great vineyards in the foothills of the Andes. In the sub-tropical valleys vast crops of coca were produced, together with fruit and tobacco – known in Spain as the Holy plant because of its reputed medicinal properties. In the great plains and mountain-terraced farmlands maize and potatoes. From the rivers, lakes and Pacific coast, all types of fish were also brought into the markets at Cuzco and other settlements. Though llama meat, guinea pig and maize were the staple diet of the early settlers, within twenty years of the Conquest almost every European crop, livestock and working animal had been imported into Peru. It was a wealth that would transform the encomiendas into farm land and their Spanish masters into landed and mostly absentee aristocrats.

From the earliest days of the Conquest Negro slaves from the Isthmus had formed part of the colony's labour force, mainly in the sub-tropical valleys of the Andes and coastal regions of Lima, Guayaquil and Cartagena. Their ownership was widespread, and many were acquired solely for domestic service, as in the case of the purchase made by Mansio in 1560, of a slave called Francisco for 1,000 pesos of silver.[20] Their ownership was not confined to encomenderos, but was also common among merchants and the religious Orders. A number of freed Negroes are recorded to have later found employment as blacksmiths, tailors and carpenters in Lima and at Cuzco. No accurate record exists of their number, though at the time of Girón's rebellion a company of some 400 were raised to fight in his ranks.[21] The social structure of Peru, like that of the other colonies of the Indies, had been inherited from Spain, and which only varied in the pre-eminence given its conquistadors and encomenderos. In every walk of life the language and culture of its settlers were central to the maintenance of its conquest, influencing many of its surviving Inca lords and caciques to imitate their conquerors in dress and customs. Few Indians learned to speak Castilian, and as such became dependent on their interpreters in matters of law, which only led to their exploitation. Education was virtually restricted to creoles and mestizos and was the responsibility of the religious Orders, as in the case of the Dominican foundation of the University of San Marcos at Lima in 1551.

The Dominicans, who had presided over the colony's religious life since the earliest days of the Conquest, saw their influence further enhanced by the establishment of the Inquisition. At the first *auto-da-fé* at Lima in the winter of 1573 among the Holy Office's victims was the incongruous sounding Frenchman Mateo Salade.[22] Eight years later the English corsairs John Oxenham and Thomas Gerard and the Irishman John Butler were paraded as heretic penitents in the same square.[23] Three future saints of the Catholic Church made their ministry at Lima: the Spaniard Toribio de Mogrovejo, a former professor of law at the University of Salamanca, was appointed Archbishop of Lima in 1580; Martín de Porres, the son of a hidalgo and a freed negress, born at Lima in 1579;

St Ursula, late eighteenth century, Potosí
School. (Private Collection)

and the Creole Isabel de Flores, who would be known as Santa Rosa de Lima and who
had also been born in the viceregal capital, in 1586.

The development of the colony also saw the onus of its wealth become more than ever
dependent on its mining industry: its silver mines discovered in the Bolivian region of the
Charcas,[24] and which had attracted many of the new immigrants to its mining settlement
and city of Potosí. In the chronicles of the Indies no other city symbolized the untold
wealth of the New World, and which even the great sixteenth-century Jesuit explorer
Matteo Ricci illustrated in his map of the world commissioned by the emperors of China.

Potosí's fame derived from a mountain lying in the foothills of the Andes known as the
Cerro Rico, the rich mountain, because of the abundance of its silver. It was discovered in
1545 at the time of Gonzalo Pizarro's rebellion by a yanacona named Hualpa, the son of
a cacique from the Cuzco region, who would end his days in bondage to a succession of
Spanish overseers. By the time of the Viceroy Toledo's visit in 1572 to the city founded at
the foot of the mountain, its inhabitants were to number some 120,000 Spaniards,
Indians and mestizos – by far the largest population of any city in the Americas and most
of the capitals of Europe. Toledo was to award Potosí the title of 'Imperial' and Charles V's
coat of arms, to which his son Philip II later added the motto: 'For the Powerful Emperor,
for the wise King, this lofty mountain of silver will conquer the world.'

Early settlement at Potosí. (Private Collection)

Men and women from every region of Spain and the Indies crossed the cordillera in search of Potosí's windswept and desolate location. Some eighty churches were built in the city, among them San Lorenzo, one of the finest examples of Spanish mestizo architecture in the Americas. Cervantes, who many years later failed to secure an appointment as corregidor of the city of La Paz, described the great mining city as 'a sanctuary for bandits, a safeguard for assassins, a cloak and mask for card sharpers, the aspiration of courtesans, the common disappointment of many, and the special remedy of a few'.[25] By the end of the century it possessed 36 gambling houses, where some 800 professional gamblers and prostitutes plied their trade. The chronicler Bartolomé Martínez y Vela, who recorded Potosí's celebrations to mark the feast of Corpus Christi, described how its Spanish miners would lavish their new found wealth on 'fountains sprouting the finest European wines, the men with chains of gold around their necks, and their dark skinned mestizo women wearing slippers tied with strings of silk and pearls, their hair adorned with rubies and precious stones'. And as a final demonstration of their allegiance to their Christian faith, 'they would cover the streets with bars of solid silver, from one end to another'.

Goods of every type were to be found in Potosí's markets: 'embroidery of silk, gold and silver from France, tapestries and mirrors from Flanders, religious paintings from

The Virgin of Copacabana, gold medallion, late seventeenth century, Potosí School. (Private Collection)

Rome, crystal and glass from Venice, vanilla and cocoa from the Caribbean islands and pearls from Panama'.[26] Portuguese traders also plied illicit merchandise across the selvas and cordillera of the Andes from their port at Río de Janeiro, the beaches of which they named in honour of Potosí's Virgin of Copacabana, the reliquary of which was situated on the southern shores of Lake Titicaca, her gilded Indian features almost hidden by the jewelled offerings of her penitents, who in their thousands would thank or beg her for their fortunes. Describing another of Potosí's religious festivals the chronicler Martínez y Vela wrote that the city's nobility, numbering thirty counts of Castile, 'were to form themselves into bands of men and women, wearing their costumes, with jewels and plumes and waving flags, and just to wrench these flags from one another they knifed and killed each other, leaving more than a hundred dead, men and women'. The Dominican Domingo de Santo Tomás referred to the Cerro Rico in his interview with the Council of the Indies as 'a mouth of hell consuming thousands of innocent Indians'.[27]

The Viceroy Toledo assigned 95,000 Indians to Cerro Rico's mines to labour as mitimae, working for one year, from sunset to sunrise. For every ten Indians only seven were to survive in what was to become a rabbit warren of human suffering, consoled solely by their addiction to coca, and whose labour left its young miners with the broken and haggard features of old men. Their addiction to coca also established an industry for the narcotic's transportation and sale from the Andean sub-tropical valleys of the Yungas, near the city of La Paz which acted as a staging post for the mines, and from the rich harvests of the Cuzco region. By torchlight and working with pick axes, day and night, at any one time some 4,500 Indians mined the silver which was then taken by mule pack to the city's Casa de la Moneda for minting. In a room of stone flooring and cedar wood, mules pulled the giant wheels that stretched through cylinders the stream of metal into bars and coins, one-fifth of which was put aside for the Crown and transported to the Pacific harbour of Arica. The treasure was then taken by small barques to Lima's port of Callao, from where it was transported on caravels that would sail the fifteen days to Panama. Once more it was carried by hundreds of mules across the Isthmus to the Atlantic port of Nombre de Dios, from where the galleons sailed to

Cerro Rico de Potosí. (Alexander Stirling)

Havana to await the treasure fleets from Mexico, before finally crossing the Atlantic to the Andalusian port of San Lúcar de Barrameda.

By the end of the eighteenth century the great mountain was exhausted of its silver: its city and convents, where nuns had once prayed for the souls of their governors, left barren and deserted, its churches and palaces carved with lotus flowers, devils and mermaids, emblems of the moon and of the sun, of winged angels and sad-eyed Indian madonnas, the sole legacy of its former glory.

In 1571 – almost two centuries before the demise of Potosí – Don Francisco de Toledo, third Viceroy of Peru, arrived at Lima. The Emperor Charles V had by then been dead thirteen years; Cervantes was twenty-four years old; and the young Cretan painter Domenico Theotocopoulos, known as *el Greco*, the Greek, had as yet to reach Spain from Italy; neither had the great monastery palace of the Escorial been completed, being already eight years under construction. A younger son of the Conde de Oropesa, and probably named after an ancestor who had died on the walls of Constantinople defending its last Christian emperor,[28] Toledo had been one of the very few courtiers present at the deathbed of Charles V at the monastery of Yuste.[29] Aged fifty-four and a confirmed bachelor, he proved to be one of the foremost colonial administrators of the Indies, and in turn possibly the most ruthless in his treatment of the remnants of the Inca royal family, initiating a genocide that would see their

Casa de la Moneda, Potosí. (Alexander Stirling)

descendants exiled or die from sheer poverty. His purpose was the reform of the colony's bureaucracy which had suffered from the nepotism and scandals of his predecessor viceroys the Marqués de Cañete and the Conde de Nieva, both of whom had died at Lima: the former as a result of being refused an extension to his governorship, and the latter from a head wound after falling from the balcony of his mistress' mansion. The reforms he implemented in the twelve years of his governorship affected not only the bureaucracy of the colony, but the re-organization of its Indian labour. Prone like Philip II to involve himself in the minute detail of government, Toledo established the foundations of a system of administration that survived almost unchanged until Peru and Bolivia's independence in the early nineteenth century. Two other factors that also left a lasting influence on the colony were his establishment of the Inquisition at Lima and the arrival of the Jesuit Order, which was to dominate the future intellectual life of Peru and which would be responsible for much of the scarce humanity shown the Andean people in their evangelization.

Fourteen months after his arrival at Lima Toledo left his capital on a tour of inspection that would last for almost five years. After a sojourn at Huamanga, the present day city of Ayacucho, he travelled south to Cuzco where he was met on the outskirts of the city by a delegation of its officials, among them the city's six surviving conquistadors: Mansio Serra de Leguizamón, Diego de Trujíllo, Alonso de Mesa, Pedro Alonso Carrasco, Hernando de Solano and Juan de Pancorbo, who made him a gift of a roan stallion, its leather saddle trimmed in gold. The reception given him was as lavish as the city had accorded Gonzalo Pizarro almost a quarter of a century previously after his victory at Huarina. Lodged in the mansion of Juan de

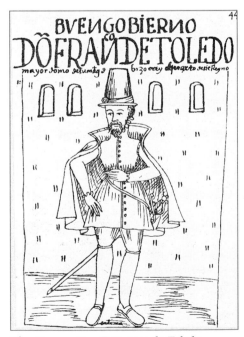

The Viceroy Don Francisco de Toledo. (Felipe Guaman Poma de Ayala, *Nueva Corónica y Buen Gobierno*)

Pancorbo, and then in that of the encomendero Diego de Silva, Toledo presided over the processions of Spaniards and Inca nobles that passed his balcony to honour him. For several days he was fêted with cane and bull fights arranged by the encomenderos, in which several of the elderly conquistadors took part.[30]

The festivities and honours shown Toledo did little to detract from his planned reforms of the city's cabildo and its ruling hierarchy of encomenderos. Within the week he ordered its regidores to elect a landless soldier as one of its alcaldes. Though each of the cabildo's members had agreed among themselves to vote against the election, with the exception of Hernando de Santa Cruz and Mansio Serra de Leguizamón, they eventually succumbed to Toledo's command once he ordered his personal guard to enter their chamber and threaten them with exile to Chile.[31] Mansio, who at the time was procurator-general of the city, refused to be intimidated by Toledo, and sent him possibly one of the most impertinent and patronizing letters he would ever receive:

> The Most Excellent lord Mansio Serra de Leguizamón, in the name of this great city of Cuzco and of its cabildo, and as its Procurator General, I find it necessary to point out that the cabildo of this city, having judicially elected alcaldes by a majority of votes Rodrigo de Esquivel and Martín Dolmos, encomenderos of this city and persons of quality . . . Your Excellency, nevertheless, without the consent of the cabildo and without possessing a single vote personally, awarded one of the offices to Juan López de Izutarregui . . . something Your Excellency should rectify, so that the election and mandates by the cabildo be ratified, as they have been these last forty years . . .[32]

For a further two pages Mansio lectured him on the civil rights of the city, and of its feudal privileges to elect its own officials. Toledo curtly ordered that his candidate be appointed at once – an order that was adhered to without exception.

Toledo's action was repeated throughout the colony, and brought to an end the political monopoly and judicial power the encomenderos had held in the cities and regions of their land holdings. Like the priest-governor Pedro de la Gasca, Toledo earned both the antagonism as well as the begrudging respect of the colony's grandees, conscious of their inability to manipulate a government they had always held as an extension of their own privileged status. From ordering the acquisition of a new premises for Cuzco's jail, to the widening of its central square, his reforms were greeted with approval by the city's settlers. Toledo also demanded funds from the city's cabildo for the building of Cuzco's cathedral which he ordered should take six years to complete, but which in effect took eighty-two years, and is regarded by the architectural historian Harold Wethey as 'the finest church of the western hemisphere'.[33] His nomination of Juan Polo de Ondegardo, a former Governor of Sucre, as Cuzco's Governor was also characteristic of the appointments he made, of men who were lawyers by profession yet possessing experience as administrators, and of an intellectual calibre almost unknown among their predecessors.

Another jurist who had accompanied him to Cuzco was Juan de Matienzo, who for many years had also resided at Sucre, where he had been a member of its audiencia that had been established in 1559. Three other figures who had an equal influence on Toledo's understanding of the history and culture of his colony were the cartographer and explorer Pedro Sarmiento de Gamboa, the Jesuit José de Acosta, who he would later meet at Sucre, and the Andalusian curate priest of Cuzco Cristóbal de Molina. Acosta, who had been born into a converso family in Medina del Campo, was a theologian and naturalist who arrived in Peru in the wake of the first Jesuit mission in 1572, and where he would spend fourteen years before eventually returning to Spain after visiting Mexico in 1586. Four years later he published *Historia Moral y Natural de las Indias*, regarded as one of the greatest naturalist accounts of the New World. He died at Salamanca in 1600.[34]

Toledo's interest in Inca history was in part influenced by his desire to justify Spain's conquest, by proving that its dynasty was not the natural lords of its empire, and which they had won and governed by force of arms: a premise he saw as a means of countering the condemnation levelled against Spain's right of conquest. In his efforts to gather as much information as possible he commissioned the Conquistador Diego de Trujillo to dictate his memoir of the Conquest, and also Pedro Pizarro who resided at Arequipa. However, it was the history he requested Sarmiento de Gamboa to compile that came to be regarded as possibly the most authoritative account of pre-Colombian Inca history. A native of Galicia, who four years previously had been the cartographer and commander of a naval expedition that had discovered the Solomon Islands of the western Pacific, Sarmiento de Gamboa had formerly lived in Mexico where he had been imprisoned for a brief period by the Inquisition on a charge of necromancy – a charge he faced again later after his arrival in Lima. Ignoring the charges, Toledo, who recognized his ability and scholarship, invited him to accompany him on his tour of inspection. The history he commissioned him to write in Cuzco, and which was sent to King Philip II as part of the report of information he had prepared, was discovered by a German scholar in the library of Göttingen University in 1892. Much of Sarmiento de Gamboa's information was based on a series of enquiries held by Toledo at Cuzco and in the Yucay valley, and the evidence of thirty-seven Inca lords of the city. His manuscript, accompanied by a series of cloth paintings of Inca genealogies he had also executed, was read to the conquistadors Alonso de Mesa, Juan de Pancorbo, Pedro Alonso Carrasco and Mansio Serra de Leguizamón, who submitted a brief outline of their own understanding of the Inca dynasty.[35] Mansio also added his name to a lengthy statement written by Cuzco's Governor Polo de Ondegardo, in which the practice of human sacrifice by the Incas is recorded, but which by its general tone had possibly more to do with the rhetoric of its principal author in his desire to vindicate Toledo's premise.[36]

Sarmiento de Gamboa's varied life later saw him serving in the colony's flotilla of ships in pursuit of Sir Francis Drake after his raid on the port of Callao, and then as Governor of the settlement at the Strait of Magellan.[37] On his return to Spain his ship

Ruins at Tiahuanacu, engraving by Champin, from Castelnau. (National Arts Library, V&A Museum)

was captured by English corsairs and he was taken prisoner to London and granted an audience with Queen Elizabeth, with whom he recorded he conversed in Latin, and who, at the instigation of Sir Walter Raleigh, ordered his release. A great deal of the knowledge Raleigh acquired about Peru he obtained from Sarmiento de Gamboa, and which influenced his subsequent search for the legendary kingdom of *el Dorado* and his exploration of Guyana, the name of which was a misspelling of the Emperor Huayna Cápac's name. Other than a record of his appointment to a command of an escort of the Indies treasure fleet, nothing more is known of Sarmiento de Gamboa's life, nor of the year or place of his death.

Toledo's tour of inspection also led to the re-establishment of the Inca tributary service of mita labour, mainly at the mercury mines at Huancavelica, whose miners were plagued by its poisonous fumes, and at Potosí. From Cuzco to the southern settlements of northern Argentina male Indians between the ages of 18 and 50 were obliged to spend 4 months of every year working in their mita service, and from which not even the Inca nobility was immune, numbering then 1,274 male adults.[38] Another of Toledo's mandates concerned the rebel enclave at Vilcabamba, whose warriors, though few in number, had since the death of the Inca Sayri Túpac maintained a defiant independence under the successive rule of his brothers Titu Cusi and Túpac Amaru. The failure of his negotiations led Toledo to order a military campaign against Vilcabamba.

By April 1572, the largest army seen at Cuzco since the defeat of Gonzalo Pizarro was mustered on the outskirts of the city. Its command was given to Martín Hurtado de Arbieto and Juan Alvárez Maldonado. Toledo also appointed as captains his nephew Jerónimo de Figueroa and the captain of his personal guard Martín de Lóyola, a great-nephew of St Ignatious, founder of the Jesuit Order. Each of Cuzco's encomenderos, in lieu of their feudal obligation to the Crown, were obliged to accompany the expedition with a contingent of their tributary Indians. Several thousand Cañari and Chachapoya Indians were also assembled under their caciques as auxiliaries. Toledo also ordered the conquistadors Alonso de Mesa, Hernando de Solano and Mansio Serra de Leguizamón, who had entered Vilcabamba some forty years previously, to accompany the expedition as advisors. A total of 250 Spaniards in full armour, among them the Coya Doña Beatriz's widowed husband Diego Hernández and her son Pedro de Bustinza, rode out of the city amid a fanfare of trumpets and beating drums.

The soldier Miguel López recalled their first engagement against the Inca Túpac Amaru's warriors: '. . . being as we were at the bridge of Chuquichaca we heard news that warriors were on their way to attack the royal encampment, at which time Mansio Serra drew his arms and began to walk towards the enemy, encouraging our troops and telling them that it was all that was needed to conquer that land, and that they should march and walk with him as he was doing, and he went ahead on foot to where it was said the Indians were coming . . .'.[39] Thirty-eight years after the events at Vilcabamba one of the Spanish conscripts Baltasar de Ocampo wrote a description of the campaign and of the capture of the Inca, and of his subsequent execution at Cuzco, related to him by a Mercedarian friar of the city:

Our men then occupied the bridge [of Chuquichaca], which was a measure of no small importance to our force. For the enemy did not remember to burn it and destroy the said bridge . . . leaving some of our men to guard it, and to forward supplies to the front, the rest of the force continued the pursuit . . . the road was narrow in the ascent with forest on the right, and on the left a ravine of great depth. Our troop could not advance in formation of squadrons, but only two abreast . . . Advancing in further pursuit of the enemy we took many prisoners, both chieftains and common people. When we forced them to tell us the route the Inca had taken, they told us he had gone towards the valley [of Simaponeto]; and that he was making for the country of the Manarís, a warlike tribe and his allies, where canoes had been prepared to enable his escape . . . Lóyola overtook the fugitives, capturing the Inca and taking many other prisoners. Only two Spaniards were killed. The Inca and other Indians were brought back to the valley . . . here Indians would be settled and a city of Spaniards founded. It was called San Francisco de la Victoria de Vilcabamba . . . leaving a garrison of 50 soldiers we marched to Cuzco with the Inca Túpac Amaru and his chieftains who were prisoners. On reaching the archway of Carmenca, which is the entrance to the city of Cuzco, the general [Martín Hurtado de Arbieto] marshalled all his troops. The commander Juan Alvárez Maldonado, as adjutant, chained Túpac Amaru and his captains together. The Inca was dressed in a mantle and doublet of crimson velvet. His shoes were made of wool of the country, of several colours. The crown or headdress called mascapaicha was on his head with a fringe over his forehead, this being the royal insignia of the Inca . . . so they proceeded in triumph for their victory directly to the palace where the Viceroy Don Francisco de Toledo then lived . . . in line of order the commander marched there in triumph and presented his prisoners to the Viceroy. After His Excellency had savoured his conquest, he ordered that the Inca and his chieftains be taken to the fortress which is in the parish of San Cristóbal, of Colcampata . . . at the end of two or three days, after being taught and catechized, Túpac Amaru was baptized. This was done by friars of Our Lady of Merced . . . the Inca was taken from the fortress through the public streets of the city with a guard of 400 Cañaris armed with lances . . . he was accompanied by the priests Alonso de Barzana, of the Company of Jesus, and by Father Molina [the chronicler priest of Cuzco], one on either side of him . . . the open spaces, roofs, and windows in the parishes of Carmenca and San Cristóbal were so crowded with spectators that if an orange had been thrown down it could not have reached the ground anywhere, so closely were the people packed. As the executioner, who was a Cañari Indian, brought out his knife with which he was to behead the Inca, an extraordinary occurrence took place. The whole crowd of natives raised such a cry of grief that it seemed as if the day of judgement had come, and all those of Spanish race did not fail to show their feelings by shedding tears of grief and pain. When the Inca beheld the scene, he only raised his right hand on high and let it fall. With a lordly mind he alone remained calm, and all the noise was followed by a silence so profound that no living soul moved, either among those who were in the square or among those at a distance . . . the Bishop of Popayán, the provincial of the Order of Merced, the prior of the Order of San Agustín, the prior of Santo Domingo, the provincial of San Francisco . . . the rector of the Company of Jesus . . . all went to the viceroy. They went down on their knees and besought him to show mercy and spare the life of the Inca. They urged he should be sent to Spain to be judged by the king in person. But no prayers could prevail with the viceroy. Juan de Soto, chief officer of the court, was sent on horseback with a pole to clear the way, galloping furiously and riding down all kinds of people. He ordered the Inca's head to be cut off at once in the name of the viceroy . . . the executioner then came forward and, taking the hair in his left hand, he severed the head with a knife at one blow, and held it high for all to see. As the head was severed the bells of the cathedral began to ring, and were followed by those of all the monasteries and parish churches in the city . . . when the head was cut off it was put on a pole and set up on the same scaffold in the great square . . . there it became each day more beautiful . . . and the Indians came by night to worship the head of their Inca . . .[40]

Mansio's letter to King Philip II.
(Patronato 125, AGI, Seville)

The Inca Túpac Amaru was twenty-eight years old. As he had walked to meet his death through the streets of Cuzco a Spaniard recalled that his sister the Coya Doña María, who was witnessing the spectacle from the window of a house, cried out to him: 'Where are they taking you, my brother, prince and sole king of Tahuantinsuyo?'[41] The Mercedarian friar who described much of what had taken place at Cuzco to the soldier Ocampo also mentioned that several nights after the execution Mansio Serra de Leguizamón's grandson Juan-Pablo, having woken at dawn, gazed out from his bedroom window and witnessed the thousands of Indians kneeling as they worshipped the blooded features of his cousin.[42] It was a macabre and humiliating end to a dynasty that had attempted to maintain the remnants of its sovereignty, and what would prove to be an ignominious role of the elderly conquistador once more tainted with the blood of his mestizo son's family.

For a further eighteen years Mansio remained living in Cuzco, outliving all the veterans of Cajamarca, and even Toledo himself, who returned to Spain nine years after Vilcabamba and who died in the care of his relatives in his family's fiefdom in Estremadura. All that is recorded of Mansio's final years is the evidence he gave on behalf of the testimonials of the Inca Sayri Túpac's widow, in which he pleaded with the King to grant her a pension, and that of the priest Cristóbal de Albornoz who had dedicated much of his ministry to eradicating the cult of Taki Onqoy, a mystical Indian ghost dance held at the huaca shrines, not dissimilar to the trance-like ghost dance of the North American Indians, which also bewailed the destruction of their people at the hands of their conquerors.[43] His signature also appears on a document a year before his death in support of the Jesuits in their ongoing dispute with the other religious Orders at Cuzco.[44] In that same year Mansio's younger son Francisco presented to King Philip II at the palace monastery of the Escorial the last of the petitions he wrote for compensation for the loss of his encomiendas, pleading his past service and reduced circumstances, and couched in the formal language of the age:

Most Powerful Lord: As vassals of Your Highness, we have every right to give infinite thanks to God Our Lord for having granted us in these times so Catholic a King, and so zealous in our welfare and justice, and because of which we may take the liberty of declaring our needs . . . I, as one of the least vassals of Your Highness, being favoured by such reason, take the opportunity of expressing myself to you; something I have in so many years never been able to do, and which I can no longer do in person, yet which my son Francisco Serra de Leguizamón is able to perform on my behalf, and to kiss the royal feet of Your Highness: to inform you of the zeal that I showed in the discovery of the Indies and of Peru, in the company of the governors Pizarro and Almagro. And in the discovery, conquest, pacification and foundation of so prosperous a New World, and for which God in his infinite goodness granted me particular privilege to serve Your Royal Crown with great advantage over many of those who came with me; and if I were to relate the particular dangers in which I placed myself, the success of which was to benefit Your Highness, it would cause incredulity and appear more than a miracle; but as all this is now commonly held, and which none can deny, I now presume, if I may, being impeded to do so personally, to inform you that I am now in great poverty because the viceroys have not wished to reward my services, not because I do not feel grateful of having rendered such service to so Catholic Monarchs, but human life, children and one's family oblige me to beseech Your Highness for redress . . . and for this motive, because of my old age, my son presents himself to Your Highness in my name. I beg Your Highness that you reward him considering my service to you for the Christian king you are, and because it is what my need requires; for here I have with me many sons and daughters God has given me who are dependent on my service to Your Highness . . .[45]

Mansio's petition remained unanswered. It was the price he had paid for his rebellion. Ghosts and memories were all that now remained to him: of his youth in Castile, and of his crossing of the Atlantic; of Veragua and Cajamarca; the killings, and the tortures he had himself endured; images of war and of love, orphaned faces and voices, lost for ever in the silence of old age. For several months he had been on the verge of death and recovered sufficiently to dictate his last will and testament he addressed to his sovereign. In the darkness of his bedchamber, the walls hung with the armour and arms he had worn as a young man, the elderly hidalgo who would be remembered for having gambled the gold face of the Inca sun, and in whose veins ran the blood of the Cid of Vivar, breathed his last.[46] Dressed in the threadbare black habit of a friar of the Order of San Agustín, his body was taken for burial in a procession led by the religious Orders of the city and by its cabildo to the convent of San Agustín, where it was placed in the tomb that had been erected for him in the chapel of Santa Lucía, surmounted by his coat of arms. He was seventy-eight years old: the last of the conquistadors of Peru.

APPENDIX 1

MANSIO SERRA DE LEGUIZAMÓN'S WILL, CUZCO, 1589

Recorded at Cuzco and addressed to King Philip II, dated 18 September 1589. Archivo General de Indias, Seville, Patronato 107. The transcription and translation are by the author.[1]

. . . I, the Captain Mansio Serra de Leguizamón, resident of this great city of Cuzco, capital of these kingdoms of Peru, and the first who entered it in the time of its conquest: being as I am, infirm and bedridden yet of sound mind, judgment and memory, and fearful of death as is natural, and which comes when one least expects it, authorize and let it be known that I make this my last will and testament of my own free volition, listing its legacies and codicils in the following order:

Firstly, for the peace of my soul and before beginning my testament I declare that for many years now I have desired to address the Catholic Majesty of Don Felipe, our lord, knowing how Catholic and Most Christian he is, and zealous for the service of God, Our Lord, seeing that I took part in the name of the Crown in the discovery, conquest and settlement of these kingdoms when we deprived those who were the lords Incas, who had ruled them as their own. And it should be known to His Most Catholic Majesty that we found these realms in such order that there was not a thief, nor a vicious man, nor an adulteress, nor were there fallen women admitted among them, nor were they an immoral people, being content and honest in their labour. And that their lands, forests, mines, pastures, dwellings and all kinds of produce were regulated and distributed among them in such a manner that each person possessed his own property without any other seizing or occupying it. And that nor were law suits known in respect of such things, and that neither their wars, of which there were many, interfered with the commerce and agriculture of their people. All things, from the greatest to the smallest, had their place and order. And that the Incas were feared, obeyed and respected by their subjects as being very capable and skilled in their rule, as were their governors. And as we were to dispossess them of their authority in order to subjugate them in the service of God, Our Lord, and take from them their lands and place them under the protection of Your Crown, it was necessary to deprive them entirely of any command over their goods and lands which we seized by force of arms. And as God, Our Lord, had permitted this, it was possible to subjugate this kingdom of so great a multitude of peoples and riches, even though we Spaniards were so few in number, and to make their lords our servants and subjects, as is known.

I wish Your Catholic Majesty to understand the motive that moves me to make this statement is the peace of my conscience and because of the guilt I share. For we have destroyed by our evil behaviour such a government as was enjoyed by these natives. They were so free from the committal of crimes and exorbitance, both men and women, that the Indian who possessed one hundred thousand pesos worth of gold or silver in his house left it open by merely placing a small stick across the door, as a sign he was out. And according to their custom no one could enter nor take anything that was there. And when they saw we put locks and keys on our doors they imagined it was from fear of them that they might not kill us, but not because they believed anyone would steal the property of another. So that when they discovered we had thieves among us, and men who sought to force their wives and daughters to commit sin with them, they despised us. But now they have come to such a pass in offence of God, owing to the bad example we have set them in all things, that these natives from doing no evil have changed into people who now do no good, or very little; something which must touch Your Majesty's conscience as it does mine, as one of the first conquistadors and discoverers, and something that requires to be remedied. For now those who were once obeyed as kings and lords of these realms, as Incas with power and riches, have fallen to such poverty and necessity that they are the poorest of this kingdom and forced to perform the lowest and most menial of tasks, as porters of our goods and servants of our houses and as sweepers of our streets. And in accordance with the Viceroy Don Francisco de Toledo's order, exempting them from such service if they acquired a trade, some of them are now shoe makers and work in similar such lowly occupations. And because many such things are permitted it is necessary for Your Majesty to be made aware of this for the sake of his conscience, and of the conscience of those who are guilty of such offences. I inform Your Majesty that there is no more I can do to alleviate these injustices other than by my words, in which I beg God to pardon me, for I am moved to say this, seeing that I am the last to die of the conquistadors and discoverers, as is well known, and that there is no one left but myself, in this kingdom or out of it. And now I have unburdened my conscience of this, I declare and order my will and testament in the following order:

Firstly, I wish to offer my soul to God, Our Lord, who gave it life and who replenished it through His Passion and with His Most Precious Blood, and order that my body be placed in the earth from where it was formed . . .

I order my body be buried in the convent of San Agustín of this city, in the chapel of the Brotherhood of San Nicolás and Santa Lucía, and that my executors conform to this and donate to the convent a sum apart from the one thousand pesos of gold I have already donated for the offering of Masses for my soul, and which I order they adhere and comply with . . .

I order my body be buried in the habit of San Agustín and that it be clothed in an old habit of one of the friars, and that a new habit be paid for and given him . . .

I order on the day of my burial all the priests of the city offer a Mass for my soul, and that the cabildo of the Holy Church accompany my body, together with all the Brotherhoods of which I am a member, with four religious from each of the monasteries; and that they all offer Masses for my soul, and that their expenses be paid . . .

I order a further two hundred Masses be offered for my soul, a hundred in San Nicolás de Tolentino and the other hundred as a requiem, and that the expenses of these be also paid . . .

I order that when my body be interred a stone monument be placed with my coat of arms and with a large cross, and that a lighted taper be hung over it in perpetuity, and that it will also be the burial place of my heirs . . .

I order fifty Masses be offered for the conversion of the natives of this realm . . .

I order twenty Masses be said for the souls of those for whom I have been responsible, and for those who are unknown to me . . .

I order the said Masses be said in the convent of San Agustín, and that fifty of the Masses be said in the convent of Santo Domingo, and that all the expenses be paid . . .

I order thirty pieces of eight be given to the poor of the hospital of the natives of this city . . .

I order the caciques, Indians and community of Alca, my encomienda, be neither asked for nor pay any tribute during the feast of San Juan to that of Christmas at the end of the year, and I relieve them of this obligation . . .

I declare that at the time of Cajamarca and of the distribution of treasures among the conquistadors that I, as one of them, was awarded two thousand pesos of gold, and that in the distribution in Cuzco, some eight thousand pesos, more or less. And that I was given the figure of the sun which was of gold and kept by the Incas in the house of the Sun, which is now the convent of Santo Domingo and where they practised their idolatry, which I believe was worth some two thousand pesos; all of which being some twelve thousand pesos of gold. And I wish my executors to record this sum for the peace of my conscience and to pay this exact sum from my estate . . .

I declare the doctor Alegría treated in my house for almost a year, even though for short periods of time, and I order his heirs be paid whatever my executors deem fit . . .

I order if any debts of mine by deed be made known they be paid, and that if anyone will swear I owe him even ten pesos he be also paid . . .

I declare the lawyer Galín de Robles owes me one thousand pieces of eight I lent him. I order that this sum be recovered from him . . .

I order that what is owed me by the corregidor of Cuntisuyo, in which province my encomienda is situated, be collected from him, for I believe he is still in debt to me for my having overpaid him for the doctrina at Alca and Potosí, and what he already owed me in the past . . .

I declare that at the time my daughter Doña María de Leguizamón entered the convent of Santa Clara of this city, my wife and I bequeathed her with many jewels and finery, and later some seven hundred cattle, all of the greatest value and worth some two thousand pesos of gold; this I record so that the said convent will make no further demands on my estate . . .

I declare that Gómez de Mazuelas, my father-in-law, made a gift to his grandchildren, my children, of twelve cows and a bull, and that I myself gave them cows and bulls for the purpose of breeding, and that I paid for their maintenance; and that of these cattle, part were gifted to the convent of Santa Clara because of the said Doña María, my daughter, and part to the monastery of Santo Domingo, where my son Jerónimo de Leguizamón was a friar. And that a part was also given to Mansio Serra de Leguizamón, my eldest son, together with other cattle I gave him. I record this so it be understood that their estate has received more than enough, and that the said Mansio received from me some two thousand pesos until his death, and that I provided for him and for his wife and children from the time of his marriage, which is some twenty years, so that his heirs be denied any further claim to my estate; for they have already received more than they were entitled . . .

I declare my landed estates comprise of my house of abode and the other houses surrounding it, to the value of some eight thousand pesos of gold, more or less; some lands and fields of alfalfa in the valley of Tubembaque; in the township of Alca in my encomienda several houses, plantations and lands; and in the valley of this city and in that of Huanacauri a small estate for the breeding of goats and the manufacture of timber wood . . .

I declare I own five bars of gold, three large and two of medium size, marked and stamped, that I believe are worth some three thousand pesos and which I order be taken and deposited in the convent of San Agustín, where they are to be kept safe until they be divided among my heirs . . .

I declare I own in silver a large decorated urn and a smaller one, a serving dish and two bottles, also thirteen small plates and two jars, three spoons, a chamber pot, three salt cellars, a candelabra, a figure of the Saviour, all in silver, which I also entrust to the care of the Reverend Friar Juan Pacheco, Prior of the convent of San Agustín . . .

I declare I am still owed the tribute of my Indians of Alca, which is their payment for the Feast of San Juan of this year . . .

I declare I own a tapestry, trunks, chairs, tables, beds, linen, a jewel case, a Negress, a horse, a coat of mail, a sword, a helmet of steel, and much other furniture and furnishings . . .

I declare that a year after my death the slave Filipa, in the service of my daughter Doña Petronila de Leguizamón, shall be granted her freedom in perpetuity, and this I order by deed . . .

I order Juan Fernández, mulatto, who has served me for many years, be given two hundred pieces of eight . . .

I declare that for the time she has served me Francisca Montañesca be given from my estate one hundred and fifty pieces of eight . . .

I declare Doña Paula de Leguizamón is my natural daughter, who I recognize as such and who lives in my house, and order she be given two thousand pieces of eight from my estate for her welfare . . .

I declare that in the time of my youth I had a natural son Don Juan Serra de Leguizamón, now deceased, whose mother was Doña Beatriz Manco Cápac, youngest daughter of Huayna Cápac, once Emperor of these realms, and that I provided for his marriage and household, and that the Viceroy of those times the Marqués de Cañete awarded him the encomienda of the valley of Písac, for being my son and for having brought his cousin Diego Sayri Inca from the mountain of Vilcabamba. And that the Indians of the said encomienda now enjoy the lordship of Juan Serra de Leguizamón, my grandson, his son, and help in the maintenance of Doña Bernardina de Leguizamón, his sister and legitimate daughter of my son, who are my grandchildren. I beg them to pardon me, as I beg Your Catholic Majesty because of my past service to reward them in their lifetime, and this I ask humbly of so Catholic a king and lord . . .

I declare my legitimate children from my marriage to Doña Lucía de Mazuelas, now deceased, to be Francisco Serra de Leguizamón, Doña Petronila de Leguizamón, Pablo Serra de Leguizamón, and Miguel de Leguizamón, all unmarried. And the said Doña María de Leguizamón, who is a nun, and Jerónimo de Leguizamón, Dominican friar, and Mansio Serra de Leguizamón, my eldest son, who has been dead now many years and married against my orders and wishes; leaving three legitimate children, the eldest of whom, Doña Lucía, who succeeds her father in accordance with the laws of our lord the king as my heir to the encomienda of Alca. And that regardless of my present state of poverty she has brought a law suit against me, and knowing as I do she will never look after my other children I have no recourse but to plead my past service to the Crown for their benefit.

This I now plead in this hour of my death, as one of the discoverers and conquistadors of these realms whose service was of great value in those early days when we were lost in the hands of the natives, and much later at the time of their rebellions, as is well known; and who through his diligence and actions contributed to the pacification of this kingdom, and for which in that first year of the conquest I was granted by the Marqués Don Francisco Pizarro the encomienda of Alca; and that the province of Catanga and Callanga, being the richest in the realm and which he also granted me, he later found necessary to take from me and award to Paullu Inca, as successor of the Incas and lords of this realm, for siding against his brothers and family in the pacification of this kingdom. And that neither I, nor my children, have ever benefited from its surrender which I made for the good of the realm. And because of which I have been left poor with only the town of Alca of my province of Cuntisuyo, with which I have maintained my children, and from which income I helped pay towards the wars between the Spaniards, even though my province was on three occasions taken from me for my loyalty to Your Majesty, and of which the traitors enjoyed the tributes. So I have been forced to place one daughter in a convent, and the other, yet unmarried, in my house; for neither can I leave them or my other legitimate children enough to feed them for a year.

Thus, I humbly beg His Royal Catholic Majesty the King Don Felipe, our lord, to take into his consideration my legitimate children, who I name as my universal heirs. And exclude from my estate my son Francisco, who on two occasions I have sent to Spain with expenses of ten thousand pesos in gold, and Mansio, my eldest son. And this I approve and ratify in the hope Your Majesty will consider these children of so loyal a vassal, who for the benefit of the Crown surrendered his provinces and who was never to benefit from the rewards of his efforts; this I beg Your Majesty for the peace of his conscience.

I name as my executors the Reverend Friar the Prior of San Agustín, Don Bernardino de Lozada and Pablo Serra de Leguizamón, my legitimate son, who I give full power to sell or keep whatever goods for the compliance of this my will. And I declare it be my wish that the house of my abode be not sold by my executors and that my said children live there for the rest of their lives, and without anyone depriving them of that right. And by this will I make null and void a previous will I authorized before Antonio Sánchez, public notary, and whatever other testaments and agreements, either verbal or written; and that only this be recognized, written on nine pages, including this one, the first two in one hand, and the other six, and this page, in another, and I wish they be recognized as my last will and testament . . . And this I authorize before the Public Notary and witnesses in this city of Cuzco, in this my dwelling where I lie bedridden, this Eighteenth day of September, in the year of Our Lord, Fifteen Hundred and Eighty Nine . . .

APPENDIX 2

PROBANZA DE MÉRITOS, LIMA, 1562

The Conquistador Mansio Serra de Leguizamón's testimonial of his past service, addressed to King Philip II, dated 1562. Archivo General de Indias, Seville, Patronato 126. The transcription is by Josefa García Tovar and the translation is by the author. The numbers in brackets refer to item statements. An explanatory list of the witnesses who confirmed the statement given here is provided at the end of the appendix.[1]

Probanza of Mansio. (Patronato 126, AGI, Seville)

Notary: In the city of the Kings, of these realms and provinces of Peru, this Twenty Eighth day of January, of the year Fifteen Hundred and Sixty Two, before the Lord President and judges of the Audiencia and Royal Chancery who reside in the afore-mentioned city, and before me, Francisco López, notary of His Majesty and of the court of the Royal Audiencia, Mansio Serra de Leguizamón, encomendero of Cuzco, presented himself, and whose sworn testimony I record.

Conquistador: Most Powerful Lord, I, Mansio Serra de Leguizamón, encomendero of Cuzco, declare that I have been in these realms of Peru thirty-one years, in which time I have served Your Majesty in all that has been commanded of me, at my own expense and purpose; of which I wish to inform Your Royal Person so that my past services be known to him, and which I ask and beg be sent to him, in conformity with these documents and royal seal: and in so doing petition Your Royal Person to grant me in this realm the favour of ten thousand pesos in [annual] rent of Indians, and that my heirs be shown favour in positions of honour; and such evidence I commend to the testimony of my witnesses, and for which they be questioned regarding the following: (2) In the conquest of Veragua in the province of Nicaragua I served in the company of the captains Juan de Pánes and Juan Téllez, and which province we placed under His Majesty's dominion, and where I experienced great risk to my life and the loss of many pesos of gold.

Nicolás de Ribera: I first met Mansio Serra in the province of Veragua when he had gone there in its conquest with the captains he mentions. And a second time I went there in the company of the Adelantado Don Diego de Almagro who had been provisioned to go there by the licentiate Gaspar de Espinosa, Governor of Tierra Firme [Panama], in order to bring men from the said province; and he was among those he brought with him to this realm, and this is known to me for I accompanied Don Diego de Almagro; and as for what he says of the province of Veragua, so devastated by rain and with such bad aspect, it would have been impossible for him, and for those who were with him in its conquest, not to have suffered great danger and hardship.

Conquistador: (3–4) I came to these realms of Peru in the company of the Adelantado Don Diego de Almagro, bringing with me my arms, horses and servants, in search of Don Francisco Pizarro, who had departed previously. And so as not to show disservice to His Majesty, the ship in which I came, belonging to Juan Díaz, a citizen of Panama, sailed ahead of the armada. And I took part in the imprisonment of Atahualpa among the company of Don Francisco Pizarro, His Majesty's Governor, and did all that was commanded of me, and I helped place this land at peace; and by so doing rendered His Majesty singular service, and because of which Atahualpa gave us a great sum of gold which was sent to His Majesty.

Lucas Martínez Vegazo: I recall having seen Mansio Serra at Cajamarca after the imprisonment of Atahualpa, and as a great deal of time has passed since those events I do not remember whether he took part in his imprisonment, or whether he arrived with the Adelantado Don Diego de Almagro who came with men and reinforcements a little after Atahualpa was taken prisoner; though I saw him serve there as a fine soldier, and do all that was commanded of him. And it is true that a great sum of gold and silver was sent to His Majesty, which Atahualpa had given after his capture, and which the Spaniards gathered, and of which His Majesty's Royal Fifth was sent him with Hernando Pizarro, which was of great service and benefit to His Majesty, and those who took part in this enterprise served him greatly, and which I witnessed with my own eyes.

Pedro de Alconchel: What I know of this is that I was at Cajamarca with the Marqués the Governor Don Francisco Pizarro when a few days after Atahualpa, who was the sovereign lord of these realms, had been made prisoner, the Adelantado Don Diego de Almagro arrived there with a number of men, and I saw that among them was Mansio Serra; and that from that time onwards I witnessed him serve in all that was commanded of him in the conquest of this kingdom.

Juan Pantiel de Salinas: Being as I was at Cajamarca with the Governor Don Francisco Pizarro I met Mansio Serra there, who served in the war as a fine soldier, and who had come there with the Adelantado Diego de Almagro.

Nicolás de Ribera: I witnessed Mansio Serra come to this realm in the armada of the Adelantado Don Diego de Almagro; and he may well have sailed ahead in the ship in which he mentions, but I have no recollection of this, other than the Adelantado Don Diego de Almagro landed on the coast of Peru in the Bay of San Mateo, which is some 150 leagues, more or less, in distance from Cajamarca; and it was there I saw Mansio Serra in the company of the Adelantado and the rest of his men, and who on their march conquered and pacified the natives, experiencing great hardship and lack of provisions, until they reached Cajamarca where the Governor Don Francisco Pizarro held Atahualpa prisoner; and who by the arrival of the Adelantado and his men was greatly pleased, for they arrived there at a time of great need of assistance because of Atahualpa's imprisonment and the threat from the multitudes of his warriors. It is also true that Atahualpa gave a great amount of gold and silver for his ransom which was sent to His Majesty and which was divided among the soldiers.

Bernabé Picón: At the end of the year Fifteen Hundred and Thirty Two I came from the provinces of Nicaragua with other soldiers to this realm of Peru and landed on the coast and Bay of San Mateo, and some two days' march from there was encamped the Adelantado Don Diego de Almagro, and where I met and saw Mansio Serra who had come with the Adelantado from Panama; and from there we went with the Adelantado as far as Tangarará, which is where the city of San Miguel was founded, and which is now called Piura.

Luis Sánchez: What I know is that in the year Fifteen Hundred and Thirty Two the Adelantado Don Diego de Almagro sailed from Tierra Firme to this realm of Peru in search of, and in aid of the Governor Don Francisco Pizarro who had gone ahead, and that among the men who sailed with the Adelantado was Mansio Serra who landed at the Bay of San Mateo; and from there to Cajamarca, which is some 150 leagues, more or less, the Adelantado, Mansio Serra and the rest of the men who were with them, pacified all the villages and provinces they passed until they reached Cajamarca, where the Governor Don Francisco Pizarro had a short while before made Atahualpa, the sovereign of these realms, his prisoner; and all those who marched with the Adelantado experienced great hardship, in the fighting, hunger and deprivations, for the land was at war, and in the crossing of the mountains and many rivers, and in certain areas clearing the roads along which we marched; and the Governor was much pleased with the arrival of so important a reinforcement, and at such good time; for he was greatly stretched in men and greatly hindered by having Atahualpa as his prisoner and surrounded by so many of his warriors; and this is known to me, for I served with the Adelantado and took part in what I record, and in which Mansio Serra served in all that was ordered of him as the fine soldier he was. It is also publicly held that the imprisonment of Atahualpa and the reinforcements the Adelantado brought to Cajamarca were the most important services rendered Your Majesty; for before our arrival the Governor Don Francisco Pizarro was on the point of losing all, for those who were with him were few, and the Indian warriors in great number; and it is true that Atahualpa gave for his ransom great treasure in gold and silver which was sent to His Majesty with Hernando Pizarro, and much more remained behind for it was not possible then to take it all; and I saw Mansio Serra serve Your Majesty until we reached Cajamarca and from there onwards, doing all that was commanded of him as a good soldier.

Conquistador: (5) I accompanied the governors Don Francisco Pizarro and Don Diego de Almagro on their march to Cuzco, of which they had received news, and on the way to which we met with many difficulties and risk because of the state of the roads; reaching the valley of Jauja we encountered a great number of warriors who had burnt its bridges, and with whom we had many engagements in fighting, making use of our arms and horses to disperse them.

Nicolás de Ribera: I witnessed the Governor and the Adelantado leave Cajamarca with all the rest of the people, among them Mansio Serra, in their discovery and conquest until they reached the valley of Jauja where there were a great many Indian warriors, and with whom they fought and battled until they defeated them and drove them from the valley, in which great hardship and risk were met.

Juan Pantiel de Salinas: This is known to me for I left Cajamarca in the company of the Governor and of the Adelantado for the seizure of Cuzco; and one of those who went with them was Mansio Serra, who served in all that was ordered of him during our march through the various provinces before reaching the valley of Jauja, where we engaged and fought the natives.

Pedro de Alconchel: I witnessed Mansio Serra leave Cajamarca with the Governor and the Adelantado in search of the city of Cuzco, and along the road we made discoveries and conquests of the provinces through which we marched until we reached the valley of Jauja where we found a great multitude of Indian warriors; and we did battle with them until with great difficulty we drove them from the said valley, and in all of which served Mansio Serra, as witnessed by me.

Bernabé Picón: The Marqués Don Francisco Pizarro, as Governor of these realms by order of His Majesty, and the Adelantado Don Diego de Almagro, who at that time was his captain-general, left Cajamarca and entered the interior of the land as far as the valley and province of Jauja, where Atahualpa's chiefs and his warriors attacked and fought us at the entrance of the valley; and this witness saw Mansio Serra accompany the said Governor and Adelantado, serving them in all that was commanded of him, as was ordered of us all.

Lucas Martínez Vegazo: It is known to me that Mansio Serra accompanied the governors and men of Cajamarca to Jauja, and that in the same valley of Jauja Mayta Yupanqui, Atahualpa's chief, in command of a great multitude of warriors, attacked us Spaniards and we fought the Indians until we broke and dispersed their squadrons, pursuing them and killing them for some 12 leagues, and among the Spaniards was Mansio Serra, who greatly served Your Majesty, and this I know, for it is what I saw.

Luis Sánchez: I witnessed the Governor Don Francisco Pizarro and the Adelantado Don Diego de Almagro, together with all the people, and Mansio Serra among them, leave Cajamarca for the seizure of Cuzco, discovering and conquering and fortifying all the valleys and provinces of the Indians on their march to the valley of Jauja, which is more than 100 leagues, and where we found many warriors and chiefs of Atahualpa; and with whom a great engagement and battle took place with much difficulty and risk, until they were defeated; and this I know to be true for I served there, and was witnessed by me.

Conquistador: (6) In the advance to Cuzco the Captain Hernando de Soto went ahead with seventy hand-picked soldiers, I among them, for much of the land was still at war; and we reached the province of Vilcastambo, against whose Indians we fought, some thirty thousand in number,* and I took prisoner many of their scouts after a great deal of fighting and risk.

Pedro de Alconchel: After we defeated the warriors in the valley of Jauja the Governor the Marqués Francisco Pizarro ordered the Captain Hernando de Soto, who was his general,

---

* Though each witness appears grossly to exaggerate the number of Indian warriors, having never before seen such multitudes, it would nevertheless have been impossible for them to give an accurate assessment.

to take with him sixty soldiers, and to go ahead and scout the road for the seizure of the city of Cuzco; for certain Indian spies had informed us that Quisquis, Atahualpa's captain-general, was going to reinforce the city with many Indian warriors; and I witnessed the Captain Hernando de Soto go on ahead, and as Mansio Serra was young and very diligent he took him with him; and it is commonly held that in the province of Vilcas, in its township they took part in a battle until they defeated the people there, and then went on ahead.

Lucas Martínez Vegazo: It is true that after having defeated the Indians of the valley of Jauja and having regrouped, the Marqués Don Francisco Pizarro sent the Captain Hernando de Soto with fifty horsemen and some foot soldiers in pursuit of the Indian warriors on the road to Cuzco; in which march we fought the natives and met great danger, for the Spaniards having gone lightly armed and without their porters, and among those who went ahead in the vanguard was I believe Mansio Serra; yet so much time has passed I cannot remember well whether he was there or not.

Juan Pantiel de Salinas: I witnessed in the valley of Jauja the Governor Don Francisco Pizarro order the Captain Hernando de Soto to leave on the road to Cuzco and confront the people that were there and to discover and conquer the land and report on it, and I saw that among the sixty or more men he took with him was Mansio Serra; and on reaching Vilcas they were met by a great number of Indian warriors with whom we did battle and fight against with difficulty and great hardship, and I saw that Mansio Serra served there as a fine soldier, doing all that was commanded and asked of him.

Bernabé Picón: What I know of this is that while the Marqués Don Francisco Pizarro was at Jauja I saw him summon the Captain Hernando de Soto, and if I recall correctly, summon also the soldiers mentioned, for I was one of them, so that we could report on the road ahead to Cuzco; and he sent us forward, including Mansio Serra, and when we reached Vilcas we were faced by a great number of warriors with whom we fought three engagements on the day we reached there, and I saw Mansio Serra capture certain of their scouts, as he says.

Nicolás de Ribera: I witnessed the Captain Hernando de Soto leave the valley of Jauja with certain men given him in order to scout the land ahead for the seizure of Cuzco, and what is said of this is commonly held; though I did not see this, because from Jauja I returned to the bay [of San Mateo] by order of the Governor Don Francisco Pizarro to take possession of it in His Majesty's name, and of all that had been discovered; for he had news that Don Pedro de Alvarado was coming from Honduras with armed men to enter this realm.

Luis Sánchez: It is true that a few days after we had defeated the natives of the valley of Jauja the Governor Don Francisco Pizarro sent up to a hundred and twenty men, footmen and cavalry, to march with him for the seizure of Cuzco, and ordered that the rest of the people remain in the valley of Jauja with the treasurer Riquelme, in guard of the treasure of His Majesty, which was some million [pesos of gold] more or less, and also in guard of the treasure of the individuals who were to leave with the Governor; and the hundred and twenty men, among them this witness and Mansio Serra, left with the Governor, and on the road the Governor ordered the Captain Hernando de Soto to go ahead, taking with him sixty or seventy foot men and horsemen; and they went in advance inspecting the land, for the Indians we had defeated in the valley had retreated to the city of Cuzco and on their march had destroyed bridges and recruited more men; and the captain went ahead with the men, taking with him Mansio Serra, until we reached the province and township of Vilcas where we had a lengthy engagement with the native warriors, in which we fought very hard and at great risk until we defeated them; and then we went in pursuit of them until the crest of Vilcaconga, fording and swimming across a river with much difficulty, for the natives had burnt its bridges, and it was winter and the rivers were in flood.

Conquistador: (7–11) From the province of Vilcas, after having cleared our way, the Captain Soto and the aforementioned men, and I among them, went on towards the city of Cuzco until we reached the crest of Vilcaconga, 8 leagues distance from Cuzco; and where we once more engaged the natives and did battle with them, and which was with great difficulty; and in the battle many of our men were killed and wounded, as were many horses, and those that remained were wounded. And that among all the men the captain had taken with him, I alone was chosen to return along the route we had taken to show the governors where to ford the river [Apurímac] and bring them to where we were; and in great danger I returned through the lines of the Indians who surrounded us, and I was able to inform Don Diego de Almagro of what had taken place and show him and those who were with him the way to where the captain was besieged, and urge them to go there at all speed. And having informed Don Diego and those who were with him, within hours they relieved Captain Soto and his men after marching a full day, and at great risk because of the multitude of Indians. On the orders of Don Diego I remained by the river in guard of it, and so as to show the Governor Don Francisco Pizarro and the reinforcements where to ford and the route to take; and this I showed him, and with all speed we marched to relieve Don Diego and His Majesty's servitors, and where I had helped bury our dead and cure our wounded of the royal encampment, and also bury the horses so the Indians would not discover our losses.

Juan Pantiel de Salinas: After defeating and pacifying the warriors in the province of Vilcas the captain and his men went forward towards the crest of Vilcaconga, which is 8 leagues from the city of Cuzco, and where the Chief Quisquis was in guard of the crest with other warrior chiefs who were of Atahualpa's army; and in defence of the crest they gave battle and placed us at great risk of our lives, and they killed some of us Spaniards and wounded others and horses, and during which fighting I saw Mansio Serra serve as a good soldier and honourable man. After our battle on the crest of Vilcaconga we were in great danger and only protected by the night. And at night we buried our dead and the horses that very night. As the captain's adjutant at his command I selected Mansio Serra, being as he was a person of diligence and enthusiasm, to go back and show Don Diego de Almagro and his men where to ford the river, and that same night they reached us. It was a service Mansio Serra performed of great merit and importance.

Pedro de Alconchel: It is true and publicly held that the Captain Hernando de Soto and those who were with him in the vanguard on reaching Vilcaconga encountered Quisquis and a great number of warriors, with whom they fought into the night, and five Spaniards were killed and eighteen horses and seventeen Spaniards were wounded other than those who had been killed. And being by the tambos of the River Apurímac, this witness, together with the Governor and the Adelantado, were informed by Indian scouts the warriors Quisquis had with him at Vilcaconga and the Marqués ordered the Adelantado Don Diego de Almagro to take with him some thirty horsemen in search of Captain Soto, until he found him and rescued him; and this witness went with him, walking at great speed along the road until we heard the news of how they were surrounded on the mountain crest, and that five Spaniards had been killed, and that seventeen or eighteen were wounded; and the Adelantado reached them that same day of the battle when it was already dark, and then in groups, the rest of the men arrived who had walked the whole of that night, and the Adelantado chose Mansio Serra, for being not only young but conscientious and quick footed, to return and inform the Marqués Don Francisco Pizarro of what had taken place, and to show him the way across the river, the bridge of which had been burnt; and I saw him leave on that mission, which was one of great risk and danger, and he then returned with the Marqués to the crest where we were all gathered; and of this and of the rest, it was a great service he performed that day, and of so much importance. And if that same night the Adelantado Don Diego de Almagro and this witness and other horsemen had not come to their aid, some thirty men, more or less, not one of them would have escaped because a great number of warriors surrounded them.

Lucas Martínez Vegazo: After the events at Vilcas the Spaniards who were with Captain Soto went with him to the crest of Vilcaconga at great peril and difficulty, and at which crest the natives killed five Spaniards and wounded some others, and also horses, and among those who were there, and who I remember fighting there with the rest of the Spaniards was Mansio Serra. I cannot recall whether it was Mansio Serra who was sent by the Captain Soto, but I believe it was he, being as he was the strongest runner among us. And as I was with Captain Hernando de Soto's men I was not able to know what happened at the river and ford, which was 7 leagues, more or less, from where we were besieged. After the killing of the five Spaniards and with less than a shot left of our crossbows, and being positioned high up the crest and encircled by the natives, the rescue arrived in the middle of the night, in groups of ten and twenty, each one making their way to the crest until dawn; and I know of this because it is what I witnessed with

my own eyes, and in which I took part, and with great difficulty and danger to our lives.
Bernabé Picón: After the Captain Hernando de Soto and those who were with him had fought in the township of Vilcas, seeing that the Indians had retreated towards Cuzco, he left in pursuit of them following them on the road which brought him to the crest of Vilcaconga, which crest and mountain Atahualpa's chiefs had fortified with a great number of warriors, and where we had a great and perilous battle with the natives, in which five Spaniards were killed and many others wounded, as were our horses; and we all served and experienced great risk and peril, so much so that if the Adelantado Don Diego de Almagro had not come with the help of some thirty horsemen that night, at the hour of two or three, we would have suffered much danger because many of us Spaniards were wounded, five killed, and the rest greatly exhausted, and the Indian warriors were all about us in great numbers, and had we not been reinforced we would have all perished. And I witnessed Captain Hernando de Soto, seeing that there was no bridge across the Apurímac, and which we his men had forded across, order Mansio Serra to show the governors where to ford the river, and which he carried out as ordered of him.

Luis Sánchez: It is true that when the Captain Hernando de Soto and his men reached the crest of Vilcaconga, which is some 8 leagues from Cuzco, they found there in its defence Quisquis, Atahualpa's captain-general, with many other warrior chiefs and a great number of warriors, and against whom a great battle was fought, and seven Spaniards died, and almost the rest were wounded, and some of them very badly; and in the same manner died and were wounded horses; and the battle took place at dusk, and as night was falling the natives were ignorant of the damage they had caused us, nor did they realize the great harm they had done the captain and us men, nor did they know the stranglehold they held over us, for had they known they would have overwhelmed us; and for that reason the captain and the men fortified ourselves high above the crest until almost two o'clock, more or less, until the Adelantado Don Diego de Almagro with the rest of the horsemen came to our aid, and we all grouped ourselves together at the top of the crest until dawn; and the natives, conscious of our rescue, did not turn away until the arrival of Don Francisco Pizarro with the rest of the men. What we experienced at the crest of Vilcaconga was more perilous than anything else I witnessed in all the Conquest, and I witnessed all the men render His Majesty there singular service.

Conquistador: (12) The governors and those who went with them, I among them, marched in good order towards the city of Cuzco, and close to the city, some half a league, more or less, some hundred thousand Indians came out to confront us in three squadrons, and we battled with them until we dispersed them and placed them under His Majesty's sovereignty; and a number of Spaniards were wounded and horses were killed, and we had to delay our march for another day, and in the morning in battle order we entered the city of Cuzco and its square and took possession of its strongholds.

Pedro de Alconchel: After the Governor and the rest of the men arrived at the crest of Vilcaconga the men formed themselves into their ranks and marched towards the city of Cuzco, and near the city, some half a league, we were met by Quisquis with a great number of his warriors in their squadrons, and we fought with them from the time of vespers until nightfall; and on the morning of another day the Marqués and all the men arrayed in their ranks entered the city, and in all this I witnessed Mansio Serra doing all that was commanded of him as the good soldier he was.

Lucas Martínez Vegazo: It is the truth, and what I witnessed take place and the multitude of Indians was great, though I do not know their exact number.

Juan Pantiel de Salinas: The governors began their advance on the city with all the men, and among them Mansio Serra, and on their march to seize the city of Cuzco, half a league away, Quisquis, captain-general of the Indian warriors, with a great number of men, which as far as I could tell were some eighty thousand in number, came out in its defence; and with whom we fought all day until almost nightfall when they retreated, leaving many Spaniards and horses wounded; and another day in the morning we entered the city and took possession of it in the name of His Majesty.

Bernabé Picón: At our entry to Cuzco we were met by a great number of warriors who were in guard of the city, and we fought with them until at nightfall we made them disperse to a hill; another day in the morning the Governor and all the men entered the city of Cuzco and took possession of it, and in which I saw Mansio Serra among the small number of our men, for in all there were no more than one hundred and twenty.

Luis Sánchez: The Governor Don Francisco Pizarro and all the men left the crest in good order on the road to the city of Cuzco, and half a league away we met the same chief who with all his men had abandoned the crest of Vilcaconga, and who he had reinforced; and what this witness believes were some hundred thousand warriors, and who in their squadrons formed themselves in defence of the city, and with whom we once more fought until God was served and they were repelled; and another day by force of arms we entered the city in the morning after great peril and hardship, in which Mansio Serra like all the rest of the men took part at great risk to his person like a good soldier.

Conquistador: (13–14) As the city of Cuzco had been won the Governor Don Francisco Pizarro commanded the Captain Soto to go to the province of Cuntisuyo with fifty horsemen and also some foot men in pursuit of Atahualpa's warriors chiefs, and I was among those who served there for more than two months, punishing them and fighting them, and working in the most rugged of country, suffering great hunger, until we found their chiefs in the midst of their many warriors, and we fought them, defeating them and capturing some of them. The Governor then ordered us to return to Cuzco, for he feared our enemies would attack us; and we returned to where he and the rest of the men were in guard of the city, and which the Indians had surrounded, putting our lives in much danger because of their numbers and the hunger and necessities from which we suffered.

Pedro de Alconchel: After the city was won the Governor Don Francisco Pizarro ordered the Captain Hernando de Soto and some thirty horsemen and twenty foot men to go to the province of Cuntisuyo where Quisquis had retreated to a fortress with all his warriors; on which expedition I went, together with Mansio Serra, and being some days in the province Quisquis fled towards Jauja, where some fifty or seventy Spaniards had remained in guard of this city of the Kings,* for it was there it was first populated; and as he had fled the captain and us men returned to Cuzco; and in that expedition we spent some fifteen days, more or less, experiencing great difficulty because of the bad mountain passes and the roads and rivers we had to cross.

Lucas Martínez Vegazo: It is true the Captain Soto left the city of Cuzco after we Spaniards had won it, taking with him horsemen and foot men in pursuit and in search of the chiefs and warriors of the Inca, and we had many encounters with them and scrapes, crossing passes and rivers of great danger; and I do not recall the time the expedition lasted, other than great risk and difficulty was experienced, and which Mansio Serra could not have failed to also experience like the others, because I was there and saw this with my own eyes. It is true the Captain Soto and the men who were with him returned to Cuzco, and the Marqués Don Francisco Pizarro once more sent him in pursuit of the warriors, and the Adelantado Don Diego de Almagro went with him, and in order to relieve Jauja where the Marqués had left some of the Spaniards in guard of the gold and silver of His Majesty, and which had been gathered after Hernando Pizarro had left for Spain; and we Spaniards experienced great risk to our lives and hardship, and which also Mansio Serra experienced, for I witnessed part of the expedition, and the rest of which is well known.

Luis Sánchez: After the city was won the Governor had news that Quisquis, captain-general of the natives, had taken his position in the province of Cuntisuyo, some 15 leagues from the city of Cuzco, and he sent there his captain Hernando de Soto and soldiers in pursuit, among them this witness and Mansio Serra. In all we were in the province a month serving there, more or less, until the natives retreated to Jauja; and the Captain Soto, seeing that he could not pursue them on horseback because of the density of the terrain and mountains, returned to Cuzco. And after a few days of our return the Governor distributed to the Spaniards who had come there with him and those who had remained at Jauja the gold and silver which had been collected, and later

---

* All the witnesses refer to Jauja as the city of the kings so as to indicate that it was the first capital of the governorship, a name later given to Lima because of its foundation on the Feast of the Epiphany.

he founded the city and distributed the land among eighty encomenderos, and one of whom he named was Mansio Serra, and whom he awarded Indians and lands, and which he retains to this day, and for which he served and fought so well.

Bartolomé Picón: After the Captain Soto and the Adelantado Don Diego de Almagro had gone to drive him out of the Cuntisuyo, Quisquis and his men had marched to Jauja, where this city of the Kings was first founded, and knowing this the Governor commanded Captain Soto and some thirty or forty horsemen, I among them, to ride in relief of the Spaniards who were in the valley of Jauja. And I heard it said how the Governor had populated the city of Cuzco, and how he had made Mansio Serra one of its encomenderos and awarded him a distribution of Indians; and when I returned to the city I found him in possession of his allotment and with his distribution of Indians.

Conquistador: (15) In recognition of the service I rendered Your Majesty and the great expenditure I had incurred, I was among those when the land was divided to be awarded two distributions as a person of rank, and for my service, and for which I was given seals.

Pedro de Alconchel: I saw that the Marqués was always conscious of those who served him well in the war, and because he also was greatly fond of Mansio Serra for being so diligent and so deserving he made him an encomendero of Cuzco and gave him a distribution of Indians.

Juan Pantiel de Salinas: I saw Mansio Serra named as an encomendero and awarded his distribution, and which he did not sell, being a person who had earned it by his merit.

Conquistador: (16–19) I was one of the forty soldiers chosen to remain in the city of Cuzco in its defence in the company of the Captain Beltrán de Castro, which was when the governors had gone to meet with Don Pedro de Alvarado who had come from Guatemala with his soldiers. While on guard of this city it was learnt that the Incas planned to kill us all and recapture Cuzco, bringing with them as their chief Villac-Umu [Inca High Priest of the Sun]. In order to forestall their purpose, I and a number of my companions disguised ourselves as Indians, and taking with us our arms we went on foot to where Villac-Umu was encamped with a great number of warriors. And taking heart I was the first to seize him and we brought him as our prisoner to Cuzco and handed him over to the Captain Beltrán de Castro, and which was a great service we rendered Your Majesty. And as Villac-Umu was our prisoner the Incas wished to pay us a ransom for his freedom, and they gave us a great sum of gold worth more than two hundred thousand pesos, which we gave to the Captain Beltrán de Castro, and we soldiers, who had been responsible for his capture, refused any share of the ransom which was sent to His Majesty and his royal officials.

Nicolás de Ribera: I was at Pachacámac when the Adelantado and then later the Governor returned to Jauja, and I saw that Mansio Serra did not come with them, but had remained in Cuzco in guard of the city with forty encomenderos, as is well known. And being at Chincha the news reached us of what is recorded, and how the land was saved, and this witness and other soldiers then went to populate the village of Sangalla.

Pedro de Alconchel: I know that Mansio Serra was one of the forty Spaniards left in guard of Cuzco under Beltrán de Castro, and this is publicly known. This witness, who at the time was with the Governor Don Francisco Pizarro in this city of the kings, was present when the news of this was brought, and the Marqués received a letter concerning the event in question; and I believe Mansio Serra did what he states because he was brave and diligent in war. And though I was not in the city of Cuzco when these events took place, I know them to be true and publicly held, and those who had remained in guard of the city gave that amount of gold to the Marqués Don Francisco Pizarro who received it on behalf of His Majesty, and which was spent.

Diego Camacho: I know Mansio Serra remained in guard of the city of Cuzco, for I went there for the first time before its siege, and met there Mansio Serra, who was one of its encomenderos, possessing there a house, horses and Indians. And being in the city of Cuzco news reached us of how Villac-Umu, who was the most important person after Manco Inca Yupanqui [recognized by Pizarro as native ruler], was with many warriors in the province of Cuntisuyo; and it was agreed that one night he be captured and brought back prisoner: an act Mansio Serra carried out, together with another citizen called [Francisco de] Villafuerte and nine or ten other soldiers. And I saw him brought back to the city and placed in the custody of the Captain Beltrán de Castro. It was an act of great boldness and which could not have been carried out without much danger and courage, especially as Villac-Umu was camped in such barren terrain and among so many of his warriors, and which was of great service to His Majesty.

Lucas Martínez Vegazo: It is true up to some forty encomenderos, more or less, remained in the city with the Captain Beltrán de Castro, among them Mansio Serra; and he would have been unable to avoid being involved in what is recorded, for no other Spaniards had entered the city other than those who were in guard of it, and many had left on horseback and on foot, and only forty remained at great risk and danger to their lives, there being so few of them in the city, and the land being so barren and full of the Indian people, and this I know for I was one of the forty who remained in the city.

Luis Sánchez: The Governor departed from the city, leaving in guard of it forty encomenderos under his captain Beltrán de Castro, I and Mansio Serra among them, and to found at Jauja, where the treasurer had remained with a number of people, this city of the Kings in the valley there. And in which time the forty encomenderos of Cuzco came into the possession of thirty-six thousand pesos of gold and six thousand marks of silver, and which was to be distributed among them; and being informed that Your Majesty, our Emperor, had need of this, we gathered it all together, registering it by seal in the presence of the Captain Beltrán de Castro and Diego de Narvaez, notary; and what took place is as recorded: for we were in guard of the city day and night with our lives at great risk because there were so few of us, and this city being the capital of this realm, and where all the captains and cousins of Atahualpa were gathered in great number with all their vassals; and where Mansio Serra and this witness performed great service to God, Our Lord, and to His Majesty.

Conquistador: (20–1) On their return from Quito and the city of the Kings, captains and soldiers were commissioned to go to the province of Callao, I among them and the brothers of the Governor Don Francisco Pizarro; and we went to the said province with our arms and horses and served there, pacifying and conquering the land after many engagements with the natives who were in considerable numbers, and we Spaniards few, ill fed and with a great many tasks to perform. After which I accompanied Juan Pizarro and Gonzalo Pizarro, His Majesty's captains, to the provinces of Cuntisuyo where the natives had killed their Spanish masters; and we punished them and placed them under the royal dominion, after much fighting and effort.

Diego Camacho: Because of the killings by the Indians in the province of Cuntisuyo of an encomendero by the name of Pedro Martín [de Moguer] and another encomendero called Simón Suárez, I saw the Captain Juan Pizarro and Gonzalo Pizarro, and Mansio Serra among them, leave the city with other soldiers to exert reprisal on that province; and being as I was in the city of Cuzco I heard it said that the reprisal had been carried out at the capture of the mountain fortress of Ancocagua, where more than eight thousand Indian warriors had taken refuge, and that a great deal of fighting took place; I saw them leave for the reprisal and also return from there, for Pedro Martín who the Indians killed was my brother.

Lucas Martínez Vegazo: The Indian frogs killed Pedro de Moguer, their master, and beforehand had killed another Spanish master of theirs called Becerril; and the Captain Juan Pizarro and Gonzalo Pizarro and other men went on the reprisal, and which they carried out, and among them was Mansio Serra who served Your Majesty as a good soldier and as your vassal; and I know this because I myself served in the reprisal, and which I witnessed with my own eyes and saw Mansio Serra fighting amid great danger.

Conquistador: (22–3) I was in Cuzco at the time of the general uprising, and I served much in its defence and did all that was commanded of me; experiencing both lack of food and necessities; and the natives took possession of the city's fortress [of Sacsahuaman], and were some two hundred thousand in number,* and the Spaniards were few, many of whom had been killed and wounded; and the siege and fighting continued for some three to four months until in battle order we went to the fortress

---

* The probable figure was between 100,000 and 200,000, a number of whom would have been porters.

which was defended by some thirty thousand of their finest warriors; but by day it could not be captured and we were to wait for a further year. I and other soldiers dared enter the fortress, in which action I fought and was wounded in the stomach; and even though badly wounded and on the point of death, and though seeing the Captain Juan Pizarro and others killed, I was the first to cry victory.

Diego Camacho: I saw and know that when the natives' uprising broke out and when they laid siege to Cuzco Mansio Serra fought in defence of the city, serving there all the time, which was some fourteen months, with his arms and horses, in the day and at night, taking part in the engagements and battles with the natives, in which we all ran great risk and fought with much difficulty: for we were surrounded by more than three hundred thousand Indian warriors, and they had put us under such duress that they burnt the greater part of the city; and seeing this, and realizing the danger, the Captain Juan Pizarro decided that we had to capture the fortress where a great number of warriors had fortified themselves; and so it was decided, and among those who went up there was this witness and Mansio Serra, and some seventy soldiers in all; and for some days we had the fortress besieged and one night Mansio Serra and a few others volunteered to gain entry through a small opening they had seen, and thus they entered, and all the others after them, and we captured the surrounding area to the fortress at great peril and much fighting, and that night Juan Pizarro was killed. Hernando Pizarro, who had remained in the city, then came up and we held to the siege until the fortress was captured: scaling its walls with ladders, and in all this, as in the earlier siege of the city, Mansio Serra's service was of principal importance.

Bartolomé Díaz: I accompanied the Adelantado Don Diego de Almagro when he came from the provinces of Chile in aid of the city of Cuzco when Manco Inca had the city cut off at the time of his uprising in this realm; and on entering the city I met there Mansio Serra, and for this reason I know he took part in its defence, for the Adelantado and those who went there with him were the first Spaniards to gain entry to the city; and this is public knowledge.

Juan Pantiel de Salinas: I know and it is the truth that at the time of Manco Inca's rising and siege of the city of Cuzco Mansio Serra and the rest of its citizens served in its defence, and I saw him serve on foot and on horseback as a fine soldier and man of honour in all that was necessary, by day and by night; and he was one of those who went with the Captain Juan Pizarro in the assault of the fortress: an act of great risk and importance, and this I know for I took part in this, and the fighting was very intense until the Indians abandoned their siege.

Bernabé Picón: I know and witnessed in the months of March or April, in the year 1536, Manco Inca, the sovereign lord of these realms, besiege the city of Cuzco with a great number of his warriors; and among the few Spaniards who had remained there was Mansio Serra, with his arms and horse, and who served as a good soldier, hidalgo and person of honour, by day and by night, in all that was required of him; and he was one of those who went at great risk to assault the fortress with the Captain Juan Pizarro, which was garrisoned by a great number of Indians who had caused us great injury; and during which the Indians killed the Captain Juan Pizarro and some other Spaniards and many were wounded, among them Mansio Serra; though it is something I can no longer remember even though I was one of those who stormed the fortress; however, I did see that Mansio Serra was one of the eight or nine soldiers who first gained entry one night in a breach of the walls of the fortress; and to which was due the capture of the fortress, and was of prime importance.

Lucas Martínez Vegazo: Manco Inca Yupanqui, Atahualpa's brother, who the Indians of this land had begged the Marqués Don Francisco Pizarro to recognize as lord of these realms, saying he was descended from God, as was his sovereignty; and after rewarding him, and seeing himself obeyed by the natives of the land, he attempted to rise up against the Spaniards and kill them; and this he put into effect by his siege of the city of Cuzco with some two hundred thousand Indian warriors, a number recorded by both Indians and Spaniards; and they put the Spaniards who were in the city under great pressure, for they burnt the houses they captured and put barricades across the streets and fought us from the roof tops, and took control of the city in great order, killing some Spaniards and horses and wounding them; and as the city was on the verge of being lost, and with it the whole of the realm, some men were selected to capture the fortress, and it was won at night for in the day on a number of occasions it was impossible to enter because of the great number of warriors in its defence; and through a gap in its walls, in a remote part of the fortress and away from where the Spaniards were laying siege, some twelve or fifteen Spaniards entered, killing and wounding the natives and shouting 'Spain! Spain!' and 'Victory!' And from the other sides of the fortress the rest of the Spaniards made their entry and also took part in the killing, during which the Captain Juan Pizarro was killed from a deep wound in his head from a stone, and also a certain Gallego was killed and other Spaniards were wounded; and in all this Mansio Serra took part and it is evident he fought well, being a good soldier and fine young man; though I took part in this I do not remember whether or not it was Mansio Serra who was the first to enter the fortress and cry victory.

Luis Sánchez: At the time Manco Inca with all his chiefs rose in rebellion against God, Our Lord, and His Majesty, and attacked the city of Cuzco with great force of warriors, and who was said to have been some three hundred thousand in number, putting the city to the torch and shedding its blood, in which the majority of the city was burnt; and so much peril was experienced by its few defenders that only six Spaniards remained protecting the square of the city beside its strongholds, fighting day and night until the Captain Juan Pizarro put his life at risk before all others and volunteered to attack the fortress which overlooks the city, and which was held by some fifty thousand Indian warriors, and from where they did us great harm because of its position and being on a hill; and the Captain Juan Pizarro, taking with him half of the men, among them Mansio Serra, went there, and I remained with the rest of the people in the stronghold in the city's square. And the Captain Juan Pizarro, Mansio Serra and the rest of the men who went to the fortress took part in a great battle there as they tried to capture the fortress, but which they were not able to do because of the strength of the Indians and the fortress' defences; and after a great deal of fighting Our Lord was served for after three days the fortress was taken and captured, in which Juan Pizarro and some other soldiers were killed, and the rest exhausted by their labour; and soon afterwards Hernando Pizarro went to their relief and helped them in taking possession of the fortress; yet after which a great deal of fighting resumed, for the siege was to last some fourteen months, in which Mansio Serra served with all honour with his arms and horses, doing all that was commanded of him as a fine soldier, hidalgo and person of great valour, putting his life each day in danger and peril.

Conquistador: (24) I was among those who accompanied Hernando Pizarro to Ollantaytambo where Manco Inca had retreated with many of his men in a fortress beside a river, and where we engaged his warriors who killed six Spaniards and wounded many others, and because of which we were forced to return to Cuzco in great danger of our lives.

Diego Camacho: In the company of Mansio Serra this witness and seventy horsemen went to the said province and fortress, which we attacked on the day of our arrival. The Indian warriors, having ventured out of the fortress, a great battle took place until that night, in which many Spaniards were killed and wounded; and abandoning our encampment and tents we were forced to flee to Cuzco that very night, losing everything we had taken with us; for had we remained until morning not one of us would have returned alive because of the great number of warriors and the ruggedness of the land.

Conquistador: (25) I was also among the men who accompanied the Captain Heredia to the Cuntisuyo for its pacification, in which expedition I served some seven or eight months as caudillo* with forty of my soldiers, and who through our labour and in great danger destroyed the fortress encampments of the Indians, placing them under the royal dominion.

Francisco Hernández de los Palacios: I know that Mansio Serra accompanied the Captain Heredia in the pacification of the provinces of Cuntisuyo, serving there, with his arms and horses as a fine soldier and man of honour, in the fighting we faced until the provinces were conquered; in which we all experienced great hardship and danger as the land was of dense forest and the mountain passes were of barren and rough ground,

---

* Caudillo means military leader.

and this is known to me as I was present on the expedition with the said Captain Heredia, and it is what I saw.

Rodrigo López Bernal: What I know is that some Spaniards had been killed in the province of the Cuntisuyo which had risen against His Majesty, and this witness accompanied the Captain Nicolás de Heredia and I saw Mansio Serra serving there as captain and caudillo with his horses and arms, both day and night, in all that was expected of him; and much was risked for there were few of us Spaniards in comparison to the great number of Indians who attacked us and surrounded us in very barren terrain, making it impossible for us to reach the river [Cotahuasi] for the water we needed to drink; and that night in the tambo fortress of Alca, Mansio Serra and the Indians in his service left our encampment in order to break the siege, entering the fortress from the high ground of a slope, passing their sentries and putting them to the sword so that they could not warn their warriors; and in this manner in the middle of the night they climbed to the upper villages where the great multitude of warriors were camped, and catching them asleep they killed many of them, and then gave the Spaniards who had remained below the signal to climb up and follow them. In these and other acts I wish to inform Your Majesty that Mansio Serra was one of those who served with the greatest diligence and valour, and with the lustre of a soldier and hidalgo, at his own cost and mission; which expedition I recall lasted eight or ten months.

Francisco de Illescas: Many of my friends went on the expedition, and when they returned they told me on a number of occasions that Mansio Serra had been one of the most hard working among them, as was always the case with him, being as he was such an agile man and so fine a soldier; and in which conquest, of great risk and hardship, I heard he lost a horse.

Conquistador: (26–7) Together with the Captain Gonzalo Pizarro I went in pursuit of Manco Inca into the Andes [Vilcabamba] where he was encamped; and I was one of the first of the squadron in the subsequent battle in helping to capture the Inca's woman and his warrior chief who was called Cusi Rimache; and I assisted in the pacification of the province where I served for eight months, suffering hardship and hunger and the expenditure of a large sum of pesos of gold: for I went there well armed, with my horses and servants, and served there as a caudillo until all the land was at peace. And in the campaign I captured a bridge that is close to Vilcabamba,* and which is the first fortress the Inca possessed there, and I captured many of their scouts, and served Your Majesty greatly.

---

* Chuquichaca bridge across the Urubamba River.

Bernabé Picón: I know that in the year Fifteen Hundred and Thirty Nine I saw Gonzalo Pizarro go to the province of Vilcabamba where Manco Inca had fortified himself and I witnessed his defeat, and that also Mansio Serra went there serving as a person of honour and a good soldier with his arms and horse.

Francisco de Illescas: I know that Mansio Serra went with the Captain Gonzalo Pizarro in pursuit of Manco Inca who had retreated to the province of the Andes, for I served on that expedition with the captain, though because of illness I had to return. And Mansio Serra, going on ahead, I know served throughout the expedition; and it is commonly known that a great deal of work was carried out and at great risk as the land was rugged and of dense forest, and where the natives ambushed them along the mountain passes of the roads, and in that journey they captured Cusi Rimache, brother of the Inca, and the Inca's woman and a great number of warriors; and I know for certain that Mansio Serra did all that he records, and I saw him well armed and on horseback, in the service of Your Majesty.

Conquistador: (28–31) At the time of the rebellion of Don Diego de Almagro, the younger, and the death of the Marqués Don Francisco Pizarro, I left Cuzco for the coast in order to take a caravel in search of the licentiate Vaca de Castro, accompanied by eight friends, all well armed, mounted and provisioned; and because Almagro the younger had been informed that I had gone in search of the licentiate, he took from me my house in Cuzco and my Indians; and I and my friends were captured by García de Alvarado, his captain, who dispossessed us of our arms, horses and Negro slaves, all of which were worth some eight thousand pesos of gold, and having robbed us and hung one of our companions he brought us to Cuzco as his prisoners.

Luis Sánchez: What I know of this is that after the death of the Marqués Don Francisco Pizarro, Don Diego de Almagro the younger was informed by his captain Gregorio de Soto who had gone to Cuzco that Mansio Serra was in the province of Cuntisuyo in his encomienda, together with some friends of his, and he ordered they be taken prisoner; and hearing of this they fled towards the coast where they were captured by García de Alvarado, Don Diego's captain, who brought them prisoner to Cuzco. And I later saw Don Diego award Mansio Serra's encomienda to Martín de Bilbao, another captain of his, and he also took from him his house.

Diego Camacho: I witnessed Don Diego de Almagro take the Indians of a number of citizens of Cuzco for not following his rebellion and leaving to join Vaca de Castro; and he did as such with Mansio Serra, for he was one who fled and who was later brought back prisoner.

Francisco de Illescas: After Don Diego de Almagro killed the Marqués Don Francisco Pizarro, being as I was in the city of Cuzco at the same time as Don Diego, I heard it said that Mansio Serra and Mazuelas and Montenegro and others had gone to the coast in search of the Governor Vaca de Castro;* after which I saw García de Alvarado, Don Diego's captain, enter the city with prisoners, among them Mansio Serra and other soldiers; and I heard it also said that García de Alvarado had hung one of them, Montenegro, and robbed them of all their goods and arms. And as Mansio Serra was his prisoner, Don Diego de Almagro took from him his Indians and awarded them to Martín de Bilbao, his captain, who acquired their tribute, and who I saw bring him tribute; and during the time Mansio Serra was a prisoner he suffered ill treatment and torture because he had stood against them.

Conquistador: (32) Because of my refusal to follow Gonzalo Pizarro when he came to Cuzco and was declared Procurator-General, accompanied as he was by many armed men, he ordered I be tortured and caused me much injury, and he seized from me my Indians and my house, which he gave to his ally and vassal Guerrero; and he kept me prisoner and threatened to have my head cut off, which he would have done had it not been for his fear of people's reaction.

Hernando de Cespedes: For not following Gonzalo Pizarro's cause in his rebellion, and because of which he was held to be his enemy, he took from Mansio Serra his Indians he had in the city of Cuzco and gave them to a certain Guerrero, his ally; and who this witness saw enjoying their tribute and also inhabiting Mansio Serra's house; and I heard him publicly say that Gonzalo Pizarro had given him Mansio Serra's Indians and house; and Mansio Serra suffered much ill treatment and torture for his stance, and for not wishing to go with Gonzalo to the Battle of Huarina; and this is known to me for I had been taken prisoner at the battle and brought to Cuzco by Gonzalo Pizarro when he had come there carrying the royal standard of the captain Diego de Centeno.

Luis Sánchez: At the time I was in the city of Cuzco and witnessed Alonso de Toro, Lieutenant-Governor of Gonzalo Pizarro, take Mansio Serra prisoner and do him much injury, and it was believed that he would kill him for being his enemy, and that is what I remember.

Francisco de Illescas: I was in Cuzco [at the outbreak of the rebellion] and witnessed Gonzalo Pizarro take Mansio Serra's Indians in the city for refusing to be one of his followers, and he gave them to a certain Guerrero who was a native of his land, who I saw make use of their service and of their tribute, of gold, silver, crops and clothing, sending his factor for their collection; and I also witnessed that when Gonzalo Pizarro came to Cuzco he wanted Mansio Serra and his woman thrown out of his house, and because of people's reaction he did not do so, and allowed Mansio Serra to retain a section of it, the rest he gave to his ally Guerrero, to whom he had given his Indians;

* Gómez de Mazuelas, Francisco de Montenegro.

and other than this I believe they took from him many other things in his house, also his cattle and farms he had in his villages; and this I heard, and also that he lost a great quantity of gold and that he had been unable to join us. And he was unable to leave Cuzco, being in virtual custody until Gonzalo Pizarro himself left the city: for no one fled without being brought back a prisoner and hung; and only after Gonzalo Pizarro and his men had left Cuzco was he able to make his escape from his confinement and flee the city on horseback. After which I saw him [years later] in the encampment of the President [Gasca] in the battle against Gonzalo Pizarro's army, in which he served as a hidalgo and vassal of His Majesty should serve, and taking part in the imprisonment of Gonzalo Pizarro.

Hernando de Cespedes: (44) I know that Mansio Serra has always been opposed to the opinion of the rebels and I do not know, nor have I heard it said he was involved with them against His Majesty's service, only that he served in what was offered him; and I have witnessed him treated with great honour, and as a hidalgo maintaining a house and a family and supporting many soldiers and servants of Your Majesty; and I was especially witness to this when many prisoners were taken to Cuzco after the Battle of Huarina and who Gonzalo Pizarro sold.

Conquistador: (33) I served in His Majesty's army of the President Gasca and did all that was commanded of me as a gentleman and person of honour until the battle [of Jaquijahuana] in which I fought with my arms and horses until Gonzalo Pizarro and his allies were made prisoner.

Diego Camacho: Having joined the royal camp of the President Gasca in the province of Huaylas I saw Mansio Serra later join us and fight under the royal standard at the Battle of Jaquijahuana until Gonzalo Pizarro and his followers were taken prisoner; and I witnessed him serve in the battle, going there in good order with his horses, arms, slaves and servants, like an encomendero and man of great standing.

Rodrigo López Bernal: I saw Mansio Serra fight at the Battle of Jaquijahuana under the royal standard until Gonzalo Pizarro and his captains were taken prisoner and sentenced, for I took part in the battle and the same squadron in which Mansio Serra served as a principal commander, with his arms, horses and servants.

Pedro Súarez de Illanes: I was in the valley of Jauja with the President Gasca among His Majesty's troops he took with him for the castigation of Gonzalo Pizarro and his followers, and there I saw and met Mansio Serra, who was well armed, with horses, and in good order, as a fine soldier and hidalgo; and I witnessed his service until the Battle of Jaquijahuana when Gonzalo Pizarro was taken prisoner.

Conquistador: (34–5) I was to serve His Majesty on the orders of the licentiate Gasca in the capture of a number of Gonzalo Pizarro's partisans who had fled to the provinces of Cuntisuyo and of Charcas, among them the Captain Diego Guillen and the priest

Vizcaino. And seeing how zealous I was in the service of His Majesty the licentiate confided in me various commissions of great importance.

Pedro Súarez de Illanes: After the battle the Captain Guillen and other followers of Gonzalo Pizarro fled to the provinces of Callao and Cuntisuyo, and I heard it publicly said that the President Gasca had commissioned Mansio Serra to find them and capture them, and that this he did.

Francisco de Illescas: This witness saw that Mansio Serra, being a person in the licentiate's confidence, was entrusted to bring from Cuzco to this city of the Kings and from Huamanga certain prisoners who had been followers of Gonzalo Pizarro and who had been sentenced to serve their punishment, and that he left with them.

Conquistador: (36) At the time of Francisco Girón's rebellion, only by the force of my arms was I able to prevent him harming Gil Ramírez Dávalos who at the time was corregidor of Cuzco, and I helped him flee the city and took him to my villages and fed and cared for him, and did all that I could in His Majesty's service.

Francisco de Illescas: Though I was not in Cuzco at the time of Francisco Hernández Girón's uprising, I was told by Piedrahita and others that Mansio Serra prevented any harm being done to Gil Ramírez Dávalos, and that he had sheltered him.

Conquistador: (37–8) When the Mariscal Alonso de Alvarado came from Charcas to assist His Majesty against Francisco Hernández I went to receive him well armed with my men and horses. And being ordered to go to the enemy's camp near Nazca and to the plains of the province of Parinacochas, taking with me some Spaniards, I went there to discover the movements and intentions of the enemy. And I carried out my mission with much diligence, inspecting the enemy encampment and scouting its movements as a good caudillo and captain; and I informed the Mariscal of what exactly was taking place in the rebel encampment; all of which was of great difficulty for the land there is very rocky, and impossible to reach by horse without being detected.

Hernán Gómez: When the Mariscal Alonso de Alvarado brought his army against Francisco Hernández Girón, he sent Mansio Serra, being a person of diligence and in his confidence, to the provinces of Charcas and of Cuntisuyo with a number of soldiers, to scout the land and discover the state of the rebel army and of its movements, and to enquire which way should His Majesty's army march; and something he carried out for several days and which was of great importance; and after this he went to the province of Parinacochas, and there also did scout the land; and when the army of the Mariscal reached the province of Parinacochas I saw that Mansio Serra was there and that he had with him the caciques of all that province, and who he had brought with him, so that their men could serve us as scouts and in carrying information; and it is known to me that he experienced great difficulty in his mission because of the barrenness of the lánd, and much of which he crossed on foot, and that he surveyed the vicinity of the enemy camp at great risk to himself.

Juan de Rivamartín: As one of the commanders of the royal army of the Mariscal I know that Mansio Serra took with him a number of soldiers to the lands of his Indians which are between the provinces of Cuntisuyo and Parinacochas, and near the road the rebel was to take his army; and the mariscal was informed of their movements. And because he was known by the natives of that province and respected by them, he was also sent to organize provisions for the royal encampment; and this he complied in doing with those men he had taken with him to a tambo in Parinacochas, which is today the encomienda of Alonso de Hinojosa, citizen of Cuzco, and which had previously belonged to Don Baltazar de Castilla; and on the orders of the Mariscal I went there to organize the provisions, and one night at midnight, a night of terrible cold, I met Mansio Serra who was returning to inform the Mariscal of what he had learnt; and the land was barren and rocky, most of which could only be crossed on foot.

Francisco Ruiz: I was the quarter master of the Mariscal's army and I witnessed Mansio Serra join us, and I saw him appointed by the Mariscal to undertake a mission to scout the mountain passes, bridges and roads we would march through, and where we would be able to take our artillery; and as he was a man with great experience of that land, and a person who could be trusted, the Mariscal nominated him for that mission; and I saw him leave us, and his mission he accomplished at great danger to himself with diligence and care until he returned to our encampment in the province of Parinacochas after crossing some 80 leagues, and the Mariscal received him warmly and thanked him in the name of His Majesty.

Francisco de Illescas: Coming as I did in the army of the Mariscal Alonso de Alvarado from Charcas against Francisco Hernández Girón, I saw Mansio Serra receive the Mariscal on the outskirts of Cuzco and join the royal standard, with his arms and men; and later in the city of Cuzco, being as he was a person in whom the Mariscal held great confidence, he was sent as a caudillo and captain with a number of soldiers to the provinces of Cuntisuyo and Parinacochas and Caraveli, and other regions, to scout out the land and enquire the whereabouts of Francisco Hernández's encampment, and to give us information about his army; and I saw him leave the city well armed and provisioned for war; and later when I visited his house I saw the letters and dispatches he sent informing us of Francisco Hernández's encampment; and which must have been of great danger to his person, being so close to the enemy, and had they caught him they would have hung him, as they had hung numerous others.

Conquistador: (39) I helped provision the army of His Majesty, and in which I served alongside Alvarado, bringing him many provisions of war, and at great cost to myself in pesos of gold.

Diego Camacho: At the time I saw Mansio Serra in the royal encampment I saw him treated as someone of great authority and as a hidalgo, and he had with him arms, horses and his personal soldiers, in all of which he must have spent a great deal of his wealth.

Francisco de Illescas: I saw Mansio Serra bring with him his tents and servants as a man of quality, and that there he shared his table with many soldiers, giving them what he possessed.

Conquistador: (40–2) I gave favour to many soldiers, supplying them with muskets and powder and horses, and other articles of war for the service of His Majesty, and all at great cost to myself in pesos of gold; and by order of the Mariscal, taking with me some hundred soldiers, I went to cut off certain mountain passes and bridges where the enemy would march, and this I carried out with diligence and alacrity. And in the company of the Mariscal Alonso de Alvarado I entered in the Battle of Chuquinga well armed, with my horses and my servants, and I was one of the vanguard in the battle and urged the soldiers to fight, and I fought there as a gentleman and servitor of Your Majesty until we were defeated, being one of the last to leave the field of battle on foot, and where I lost a great sum of gold, of some ten thousand pesos.

Hernán Gómez: It is true the Mariscal sent Mansio Serra with certain soldiers to cut off the passes of that part of Chuquinga, where the army of the rebels would have to flee through if it were defeated in the valley; a mission he accomplished at great risk, but as the rebels won the battle it was to no avail though a great service, and this I know for I was in the army of the Mariscal. I believe that Mansio Serra returned in time to take part in the battle, because that very night after our defeat, leaving the field in the upper valley and fleeing the enemy, I saw Mansio Serra who was himself fleeing on foot with only a naked sword in his hand, and robbed of all his possessions, and we walked together the whole of that night until day break, when we each went our own way; and I know he lost a great deal of his wealth in the battle, for I had seen him in our encampment well provisioned with his horses, arms and his servants with his dining plate and tents.

Diego Camacho: I know Mansio Serra entered in the Battle of Chuquinga in the company of the Mariscal Alonso de Alvarado; and this I know because I served in the squadron of horse of Sancho Duarte; and we all left the field defeated and robbed of our possessions, and I know that he must have lost a great deal of his wealth for I had seen him in the encampment well provisioned with his arms, horses and slaves which were of great worth.

Juan de Rivamartín: I remember that after the battle Mansio Serra like the rest of our men, was forced to flee; and much later I heard that he had gone to the Cuntisuyo, which is a barren land, and where the rebel [Girón] attempted to entice him to join his cause, promising to reward him; and which I heard said by many persons and is public knowledge.

Ordoño de Valencia: I witnessed Mansio Serra at the Battle of Chuquinga with the Mariscal Alonso de Alvarado, and this I know for I saw him enter in the fighting and I

believe he did all he says as a good servitor of His Majesty and as a gentleman and
hidalgo; and I witnessed that he was one of the last to leave the field, having been
robbed of all his possessions, his horses, mules, slaves and arms and personal baggage,
but which I believe was worth in gold slightly less than he says, but which he lost.

Francisco de Illescas: I saw Mansio Serra return after cutting off the passes and enter the
battle well armed and provisioned; and of what he says I believe for he was a man of
honour and brave, though the battle was won by the enemy who defeated the Mariscal
and his men, and each one escaped as best he could; on reaching the Cuntisuyo some
ten days later, more or less, I learned that Mansio Serra was there, and that he had left
the battlefield on foot. I later saw him on horseback with his men, and I heard it said
that he had borrowed the horse or purchased it; and his loss would have been great
because when he entered the battle he was well armed with horses, slaves and
provisions, all of which he lost, and when I met him again all he possessed were the
clothes he wore. In the province of Cuntisuyo where Mansio Serra had his Indians I saw
that he shared what he could to enable others to go with him in search of the royal
army of the lord judges; and from there, he and I and other soldiers travelled through
the most arid and desolate land in order to evade the enemy, in all some 150 leagues
until we found the royal camp at Huamanga, having taken with us some ounces of
gunpowder and other arms we had made for us in Cuntisuyo.

Conquistador: (43–4) In order to avoid being captured by Francisco Hernández and his
followers I walked for some 200 leagues across the most arid of roads in search of the
lord judges, and who I later joined, bringing with me many Spaniards and provisions for
the royal service and some ten ounces of gunpowder, and I served under His Majesty's
royal standard and did all that was commanded of me. And at the battle at Pucará I
fought in the front rank with my horses and servants, and served and fought well like a
good soldier and gentleman in leading the soldiers until Francisco Hernández and his
followers were captured and brought to justice.

Francisco de Illescas: I saw that once Mansio Serra reached Cuzco with the royal army he
once more armed himself with horses and his retainers, for I myself sold him two horses;
and with the royal army he went in good order up to Pucará and in the night of the
battle there I witnessed him serve in a squadron of horse, and I believe he did that night
do what he says as a vassal of His Majesty and as a man of honour, as he has always
demonstrated; and in the morning in the retreat of the enemy I saw him give them
chase and saw that his horse had lost an eye, gorged by either a lance or by musket
shot.

Pedro Súarez de Illanes: I witnessed Mansio Serra serve in the royal camp, well armed and
with his horses, retainers and tents, feeding his men from his own table, and in all of
which he must have spent a great deal of gold; and I saw him take part in the battle at
Pucará that night against Francisco Hernández and again in the morning; and as the

night was so dark and frightful we all had a great deal of work to do and at great risk, and as I was in the squadron of Juan Román I was not able to see what Mansio Serra did, though I am certain he served as a fine soldier and man of honour.

Melchor Bravo de Saravia: I know that Mansio Serra fought at Pucará on the night of the battle, though Francisco Hernández was not taken prisoner nor killed that night but many days later in the valley of Jauja, from where he was brought to his city [of the Kings] to be tried.

Francisco Ruiz: I saw Mansio Serra at Pucará and I served there that night on foot as a musketeer; as he was among the cavalry and the battle was at night I was not able to see a great deal, though I am sure he served in the manner he says he did, understanding and knowing as I do his goodness and quality, and having seen the things he has done of great manliness.

Pedro de Alconchel: Throughout the whole of the Conquest, as also in the battle, I witnessed Mansio Serra serve as a nobleman and a valiant gentleman, always doing his duty and putting himself in danger and at risk, and at his own cost, for we all served in like manner and he could not but have spent a great deal of his wealth.

Lucas Martínez Vegazo: In the twenty-eight years I have known Mansio Serra in this realm I have seen him serve Your Majesty with honour and at his own expense, and in which he could not fail to have spent a great deal of money; being as he was an encomendero and a lord of Indians he was obliged to offer his aid, and which is the custom in times of war and of peace; and I have not heard it said he ever served against Your Majesty in either a battle or any such encounter that has taken place with the rebels.

Nicolás de Ribera: Having known Mansio Serra some thirty-one years more or less, I always saw him serve at his own expense as a good soldier and hidalgo, and he could not have failed to have spent a great deal of his wealth, and for which he never received any repayment or aid, because at the time of the conquest of this realm it was the custom though now no longer so among encomenderos.

Conquistador: (45–7) I declare I have been in these realms thirty-one years, in which time I have served Your Majesty with all diligence and honour and at my own expense as a gentleman of ancient lineage, having expended in such service and in the past wars and rebellions of these kingdoms more than fifty thousand pesos of gold, and having always complied with Your Majesty's summons in times of peace and of war with my person, arms and wealth, my servants and soldiers, whom I have always maintained, though I am at present poor and in debt. And though the Marqués Don Francisco Pizarro awarded me two encomiendas, one in the Cuntisuyo called Alca, and the other in the Antisuyo, which to placate Don Pablo Inca he took from me and gave him, which was the encomienda of Callanga; and until this day I have only had one of these encomiendas to maintain myself.

Melchor Bravo de Saravia: Ever since I have known him I have always seen Mansio Serra comport himself as a hidalgo, bringing with him his servants and other persons, in times of peace and of war.

Hernán Gómez: In the war and in times of peace I have always seen Mansio Serra treated with great respect and honour as a gentleman and hidalgo and a man of great quality, supporting as he did his family and many soldiers who he often had with him in his house; maintaining also horses, mules, slaves and arms, and always giving aid to whosoever was in need: and because of which he did indeed spend greatly and because of which it is natural that he has debts and now lives in need of sustenance.

Francisco de Illescas: Because of his great expenditure over the years in His Majesty's service, and for which he received neither aid nor recompense, and because of the little value of his Indians, Mansio Serra lives in great need and possesses many debts, for I myself have seen his debtors visit him.

Francisco Ruiz: In the time I have known Mansio Serra I have only ever seen him served from the Cuntisuyo where he possesses his encomienda of Alca, and which I believe is of little worth with the high cost of prices and its great distance from Potosí and his mines there.

Conquistador: (48–9) I am a gentleman and hidalgo of a noble house, and as such I am held, as were my parents and grandparents, and loved and acknowledged as such in the township of Pinto, where I come from.

Francisco de Illescas: The township from which Mansio Serra comes is but a league in distance from my own, and when meeting people from his land I have always heard it said that his parents were hidalgos, and that as such they enjoyed the privileges of hidalgos in the township of Pinto; and as such I have always held him; for if it were not so it would be known to me. I have also known Mansio Serra to have been married to the daughter of Gómez de Mazuelas, encomendero of Cuzco, and that he has either seven or eight children from the marriage; and in order to maintain so many children and his house with such honour, I know that he is unable to pay the whole year for their upkeep.

Hernando de Cespedes: In the years I have known Mansio Serra I have always seen him treated and esteemed as a gentleman and hidalgo, and in such rank he is held, and which is not only portrayed in his manners and behaviour, but which is publicly known; for there are many persons in this realm from his native land, and the lineages of Spain are equally well known in these realms.

Lucas Martínez Vegazo: I have always held Mansio Serra as a hidalgo, and as such he has lived. I saw that he was married to the daughter of Mazuelas in Cuzco, and that a number of children were left him from his marriage, though I do not know how many, and that the income he receives from his Indians is little and not in accordance with his rank, for he is now in need and in debt.

Notary: (50) Is it known to the witness or ever heard by him that the said Mansio Serra was ever involved in any meeting, or party to in battle with any of the rebellions which have taken place in this realm against the service of His Majesty, or ever committed any such disservice?

Witnesses: All denied any knowledge.

Notary: (51) . . . inscribing my signature Francisco López, who had been among the men who had gone immediately afterwards [from Cajamarca] to place Cuzco under the royal jurisdiction, in the company of reserves of the Captain Hernando de Soto and Mansio Serra and Martínez Vegazo as they marched southward from Vilcasbamba to Cuzco, all of which he witnessed . . .

The Witnesses

Pedro de Alconchel: Aged 70. Estremaduran. Illiterate.

Rodrigo López Bernal: Aged 55. Origin unknown. Illiterate.

Diego Camacho: Aged 43. Origin unknown. Able to sign his name.

Hernando de Cespedes: Aged 45. Origin unknown. Literate.

Bartolomé Díaz: Aged 47. Castilian. Able to sign his name.

Hernán Gómez: Aged 35. Origin unknown. Able to sign his name.

Francisco Hernández de los Palacios: Aged 46. Estremaduran. Literate.

Francisco de Illescas: Aged 50. Castilian. Illiterate.

Pedro Suárez de Illanes: Aged 35. Origin unknown. Illiterate.

Martín Mercado de Peñalosa: Judge of Audiencia. Aged 38. Castilian.

Bernabé Picón: Aged 55. Origin unknown. Able to sign his name.

Nicolás de Ribera, el viejo: Aged 70. Andalusian. Literate.

Juan de Rivamartín: Aged 44. Origin unknown. Literate.

Francisco Ruiz: Aged 45. Origin unknown. Literate.

Juan Pantiel de Salinas: Aged 50. Castilian. Able to sign his name.

Luis Sánchez: Aged over 50. Origin unknown. Illiterate.

Melchor Bravo de Saravia: Judge. Aged 50. Castilian.

Hernán González de la Torre: Aged 48. Andalusian. Literate.

Ordoño de Valencia: Aged 30. Origin unknown. Literate.

Lucas Martínez Vegazo: Aged 49. Estremaduran. Able to sign his name.

APPENDIX 3

INCA TESTIMONIES, CUZCO, 1561

In 1561 the Conquistador's son Juan Serra de Leguizamón also presented his Probanza de Méritos to the Audiencia of Lima at Cuzco, addressed to King Philip II. Archivo General de Indias, Seville, Lima 205. The transcription is by Josefa García Tovar and the translation is by the author. The numbers in brackets refer to item statements. Among his witnesses a number of Incas and Indians of Cuzco gave testimony on his behalf in their native quéchua (they are listed at the end of this appendix). The following are extracts from their testimonies relating to Juan's mother the Coya Doña Beatriz and to his cousin the Inca Sayri Túpac.

Juan Serra de Leguizamón: [12 January 1561, Lima] Most powerful Lord, I, Juan Serra de Leguizamón, declare I am the grandson of Huayna Cápac, once lord and king of these realms, and son of Doña Beatriz Yupanqui, his legitimate daughter, and desiring as I do to beg your royal person to favour me in my need. And I ask of Your Highness that in accordance with your royal ordinances the following questions be put to the witnesses I present: (2) If it be known to them that Huayna Cápac Yupanqui was king and lord of these realms of Peru, of its mountains and valleys, from Chile as far as the lands of Pastu, and that among his many children born to him was my mother Doña Beatriz Yupanqui. And that at the time of her birth at Surampalli in his domain of Tumibamba he gave her for her guardian and service the Cacique Cariapasa, Lord of the Lupaca, for being his legitimate daughter of his queen, mother of Huáscar Inca who was later to succeed him as king and lord of Cuzco; and that ever since the death of Huayna Cápac she has been obeyed and honoured as his legitimate daughter by all the Indians and native lords of these realms.

Don Juan Sona: It is publicly held and commonly known that Doña Beatriz Yupanqui was born there and that she is the daughter of Huayna Cápac; and this is known to me, being as I am the principal cacique of the orejones, and as such she is obeyed and respected by myself and all the Indians of this land.

Don Diego Cayo: It is the truth that Huayna Cápac was king and lord of these lands; for when he lived all his laws and commands were obeyed; and it is publicly known that Doña Beatriz was born at Surampalli which is in the province of Tumibamba, and that she is the daughter of Huayna Cápac, for since her birth until the present time she has always been obeyed and respected as daughter of that lord, and this witness has always obeyed her and respected her as such.

Pastac: It is so that Doña Beatriz Yupanqui was born in the lodgings at Surampalli and that she is the daughter of Huayna Cápac: for I witnessed her birth, and because of which great feasting was ordered, being as she was the daughter of so great a lord, the feasting lasting for ten days and ten nights. And from that time to this very day she has been obeyed and honoured because of her birth which I witnessed, having accompanied and served Huayna Cápac in his wars from this city of Cuzco to his seat of Surampalli.

Mazma: I went with Huayna Cápac from this city to his seat of Surampalli at the time of the war, and in which I served the Inca; and there I witnessed the birth of Doña Beatriz Yupanqui, among the other daughters born to him at that season; and after her birth and in the presence of Huayna Cápac I saw him order Cariapasa to serve his daughter Doña Beatriz and to be her guardian, for Cariapasa was a warrior chief of many people.

Juan Serra de Leguizamón: (3) If it is known to them that as Doña Beatriz Yupanqui was the legitimate daughter of Huayna Cápac she inherited the rank of his legitimate wife, her mother, who was also the mother of Huáscar Inca, who was later king. And that in her house she sheltered and raised all the granddaughters of Huayna Cápac, daughters of Manco Inca, the father of Sayri Túpac; and because of which a great many calamities were averted at the time Manco Inca was in rebellion.

Mazma: After the death of the mother of Doña Beatriz this witness saw her inherit the rank of her mother, and I have seen the Indians of all the regions and nations show her their obedience and respect as daughter of the lord and king.

Don Martín Napti Yupanqui: I have witnessed Doña Beatriz raise two daughters of Manco Inca, her brother, the one called Usezino, and the other Ancacica.

Pastac: I witnessed two daughters of Manco Inca raised since they were very young by Doña Beatriz Yupanqui in her house; and it is common knowledge that Manco Inca was her brother.

Juan Serra de Leguizamón: (4) If it be known to them that the Licentiate Vaca de Castro, Governor of these realms, like all the other governors before and after him, attempted in every manner to entice the Inca [Manco] to make peace, and this they were not able to do because of the Inca's death; and that his son Sayri Túpac was his heir, and that he remained [in the Andes] with all the people and warrior chiefs of his father.

Chasca: What I know of this is that the Adelantado Don Diego de Almagro, who was Governor of these realms, sent various persons to speak to Manco Inca, though I do not know to what effect; though at the time I was there, as one of Manco Inca's warriors with the rest of his people he had prepared for war. And at the time of Manco Inca's death he left as his heir Don Diego Sayri Túpac Inca, his son, who succeeded him in his sovereignty and to the same people he had with him in his rebellion.

*Don García Suma Yupanqu*i: It was at the time publicly known that Vaca de Castro attempted with great effort and manner to bring Manco Inca in peace: for many Incas of this city went to the Andes [Vilcabamba] to see him on the orders of Vaca de Castro, the Governor.

Juan Serra de Leguizamón: (5) That after the death of Manco Inca no Spaniard was able to enter the Inca Sayri Túpac's domain in order to ask him to leave there in peace other than Francisco de Pino, guardian of the sons of Don Paullu Inca, and only with a safe conduct and accompanied by Martín the tongue [translator], at the time of the President Gasca; and that he was not able to achieve anything with him.

Chasca: All the time Manco Inca and his son Sayri Túpac were in rebellion in the Andes I accompanied them until the time we left there in peace; but when Francisco de Pino and Don Martín came there Sayri Túpac was at war. And they entered and met with the Inca to ask him to leave there in peace; and the Inca sent me and other chiefs of his to the President [Gasca] to tell him that he would come in peace, but to ask of him where he would live; and this witness and the other chiefs spoke to the President who told us that if he left there within three months he would give him the Indians that had belonged to Huayna Cápac and some houses and estate in Pomacorca [in the valley of Písac] and lands in Mayo, in this valley called Guancaro. And thus I told the Inca of what the President had ordered me to say, and the Inca was then about to leave with all his people but for one principal Christian captain who told him that he was too young, and that he should not leave until he was much older, and for that reason he did not leave.

Guasco: It is true, because I saw Francisco de Pino and Don Martín the tongue at the time they went there on behalf of the President, and that Sayri Túpac did not leave there because a captain of his called Supa impeded him because the Inca was very young at the time Pino was with him, and nothing came of this.

Juan Serra de Leguizamón: (6) The Lord Viceroy [Marqués de Cañete] tried to send many persons to enter the Andes where Sayri Túpac was, so as to persuade him to leave there in peace, and no one wished to go there except for two friars of Santo Domingo and Juan de Betanzos, the translator; but no one was allowed to enter there other than myself.

Chasca: What I know of this is that as I was at the time with Sayri Túpac Inca in the Andes and at war, I saw the Friar Melchor and another friar companion of his, and also

Juan de Betanzos, and that they went to where the Inca was, but he did not wish Betanzos or any other person to enter where he was, and so the friars went ahead alone, and Betanzos returned [to Cuzco].

Guasco: I was in the company of Sayri Túpac at war in the Andes, and I witnessed that a friar called Melchor de los Reyes and Juan de Betanzos go there, but the Inca only let the friar enter.

Juan Serra de Leguizamón: (7–8) If it is known to them that I was involved in the treaties and negotiations with the Lord Viceroy and the Inca, and that I came and went three times to the Viceroy, until after much persuasion on my part I was able to bring the Inca from there in peace, together with his warrior chiefs and lords: and because of which the roads and regions of that part of the Andes are now tranquil and free from war.

Paucar Yupanqui: As a warrior in the service of the Inca Sayri Túpac, in his company I saw Juan Serra enter [Vilcabamba], and as he was his first cousin the Inca received him well, and also out of respect to his mother Doña Beatriz Yupanqui, his aunt. And also entered there the Friar Melchor. And I heard Juan Serra say to Sayri Túpac that if he left [Vilcabamba] the Viceroy the Marqués de Cañete would give him many Indians and houses for his people and many clothes and other goods, so that he would be content; and all this Juan Serra told him many times and in my presence, and I also heard him say the same to his warrior chiefs. I further witnessed Juan Serra take part in the treaty and discussions with Sayri Túpac; and the Inca sent him twice to the Lord Marqués with regard to his leaving [Vilcabamba], and Juan Serra came two times to see the Inca, bringing with him payment and presents.

Guasco: When Juan Serra entered there he was received very well by Sayri Túpac as his cousin and out of respect to his mother Doña Beatriz Yupanqui; for this I witnessed with my own eyes as I was in the company of the Inca, who I heard tell him to say to the Viceroy that if he wished to speak to him of his leaving he would only do so through Juan Serra and that he would not allow anyone else to enter there. It is also true that Juan Serra travelled from there to see the Viceroy one or two times, and I myself witnessed him persuade the Inca to leave, promising him and his captains many things, all of which I saw him do with great effort. It is also true that before then the Inca's warriors had been commanded to attack the roads and rob the travellers of that region, all of which ceased after he left.

Don Martín Napti Yupanqui: On several occasions I heard Sayri Túpac say after he left in the tambo of Vilcas, where I had gone from this city, that it was his cousin who had brought him there in peace; and this is known to me because I raised Sayri Túpac when he was a young child and because I saw Juan Serra go to the city of the Kings, and then return to where the Inca was, bringing with him dispatches and safe conducts for him to leave in peace.

The Witnesses

Chasca: Aged 50. Indian.

Guasco: Aged 50. Indian of Cayambe.

Mazma: Aged 79. Indian of Mayo, in the valley of Jaquijahuana.

Pastac: Aged 80. Indian of Cuzco.

Don Juan Sona: Aged 68. Inca of Cuzco.

Don Diego Cayo Yupanqui: Aged 58. Inca.

Don García Suma Yupanqui: Aged 70. Principal Inca lord of Cuzco.

Don Martín Napti Yupanqui: Aged 73. Inca of Cuzco.

Paucar Yupanqui: Aged 37. Inca.

GENEALOGIES

CHILDREN OF THE EMPEROR HUAYNA CÁPAC

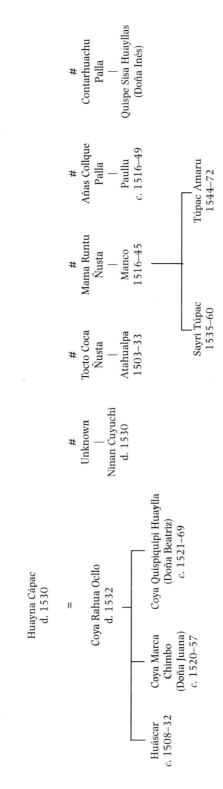

Huayna Cápac
d. 1530

=

Coya Rahua Ocllo
d. 1532

#
Unknown
|
Ninan Cuyuchi
d. 1530

#
Tocto Coca
Ñusta
|
Atahualpa
1503–33

#
Mama Runtu
Ñusta
|
Manco
1516–45

#
Añas Collque
Palla
|
Paullu
c. 1516–49

#
Contarhuachu
Palla
|
Quispe Sisa Huayllas
(Doña Inés)

Huáscar
c. 1508–32

Coya Marca
Chimbo
(Doña Juana)
c. 1520–57

Coya Quispiquipi Huaylla
(Doña Beatriz)
c. 1521–69

Sayri Túpac
1535–60

Túpac Amaru
1544–72

= Marriage
Concubine

DESCENDANTS OF MANSIO SERRA DE LEGUIZAMÓN

Mansio Serra de Leguizamón

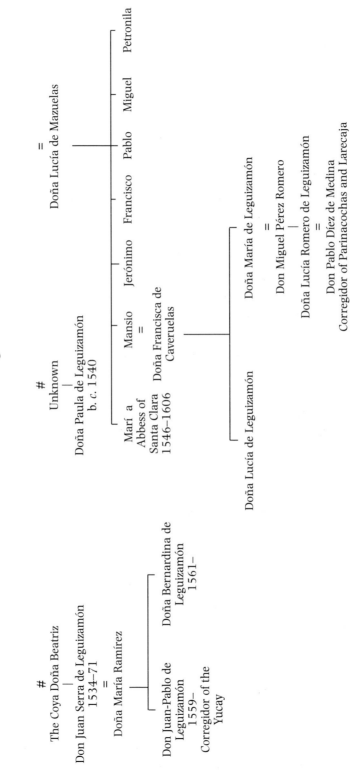

= Marriage
Concubine

GLOSSARY AND PLACE NAMES

adelantado: military title, denoting the command of a frontier region.

Alca: encomienda, in the Cuntisuyo, later founded as a town of that name.

alcalde: mayor.

Altiplano: highland plateau of the Collasuyo.

amauta: Inca bards and elders.

Andes: mountain range; the quéchua name derived from the name Antisuyo.

Antisuyo: eastern region of the Inca empire.

Apurímac: river, on the north-western approach to Cuzco.

Arequipa: city, founded in 1540 because of its proximity to the Pacific Ocean.

Audiencia of Lima: Royal Court of Chancery of the Viceroyalty of Peru; governed by its judiciary and President.

ayllu: Inca or Indian family clan.

Aymara: language of ethnic tribes of the Cuntisuyo and Collasuyo.

cabildo: municipal council of a city.

cacique: word of Caribbean Amerindian origin, denoting a tribal chief, introduced by conquistadors to Peru.

Cajamarca: Inca township, in the central Andes, north of Cuzco.

Callanga – Catanga: encomiendas, in the Yucay valley, Antisuyo.

Cañari: equatorial tribe from the region and city of Tumibamba; auxiliaries of the Spaniards from the earliest days of the Conquest; awarded by Pizarro lands in the Yucay valley and exemption from tributary service.

captain: commander of a squadron of horse or infantry.

captain-general: commander of an army or province.

Chachapoyas: tribe, north Andean region.

chicha: maize wine.

Chile: most southern region of the Inca empire; its settlement of Santiago was founded in 1541 by Pedro de Valdivia.

Chinchasuyo: northern region of the Inca empire.

Chuquinga: Battle of, in Cuntisuyo, 30 March 1554; defeat of royalist army of the Mariscal Alonso de Alvarado by Francisco Hernández Girón.

Coca: narcotic plant sacred to the Inca nobility; from which cocaine is derived; grown in abundance by encomenderos in sub-tropical valleys for the mining markets of Potosí.

Collasuyo: southern region of Inca empire.

conde: count (title).

converso: convert to Christianity, of Jewish ancestry.

Copacabana: religious colonial shrine on a promontory of Lake Titicaca; Aymara name signifies 'stone from where all can be seen', and refers to the view from its former Inca temple; early chapel replaced by a sanctuary dedicated to the Virgin, built between 1610 and 1619. A wooden sculpture of the Madonna, holding a lighted candle, was donated to the sanctuary by the Indian sculptor Tito Yupanqui in 1592 and still adorns its principal altar. The Augustinian chronicler Antonio de la Calancha in the mid-seventeenth century published a history of the sanctuary *Historia del Santuario de Copacabana y del Prado*.

cordillera: mountain range.

corregidor: governor of a city or province.

Council of the Indies: governing body of the Indies.

Coya: title of the sister-queen of the Inca Emperor and of their daughters.

creole: children of Spaniards born in Peru.

Cristiano viejo: old Christian lineage.

curaca: quéchua name for a tribal leader.

Cuzco: capital of the Inca empire of Tahuantinsuyo, established as a Spanish municipality in 1534.

Don – Doña: courtesy title of royalty, nobles and principal governors and military commanders, among them Pizarro and Almagro, some of whom were hidalgos. Though in later years its use would become more common, in sixteenth-century Peru only the wives and daughters of hidalgos and conquistadors were addressed as Doña. Though Mansio's courtly relatives were accorded the title of Don, neither he nor his father, though hidalgos, were ever addressed as such. A few of the Inca princes were however awarded the title, among them the Coya Doña Beatriz Yupanqui and her son Don Juan Serra de Leguizamón, as recorded in Mansio's Will.

encomienda – encomendero: land grant of Indian vassals awarded by the Crown in lieu of feudal service and requisite of the evangelization of their domains.

Guayaquil: equatorial coastal city, founded as Santiago de Guayaquil in 1535.

hidalgo: term of ancient Spanish nobility; *hijo de algo*, son of a man of rank.

huaca: Inca nature shrine.

Huanacauri: huaca mountain shrine, south-west of Cuzco.

Huarina: Battle of, on south-eastern shore of Lake Titicaca, 20 October 1547; defeat of Diego de Centeno's loyalist army by Gonzalo Pizarro.

Iñaquito: Battle of, near Quito, 18 January 1546; defeat of the Viceroy Blasco Núñez Vela's army by Gonzalo Pizarro.

Inca: name of ruling ayllu of Quéchua tribe; title of Emperor.

Indian – Indies: name given by the Spaniards to the natives of the Americas and Caribbean islands because of their belief that the continent formed part of India.

Inti: sun deity.

Isthmus of Panama: known formerly as Castilla del Oro because of its purported abundance of gold, and later as Tierra Firme; port city of Panama on its southern coast was founded as a result of the discovery of the Pacific Ocean by Vasco Ñuñez de Balboa in 1533.

Jaquijahuana: Battle of, in the valley and plain of that name, north of Cuzco, 9 April 1548; defeat of Gonzalo Pizarro's army of encomenderos by the President La Gasca.

Jauja: Inca township, in central Andes; founded by Pizarro as the first Spanish municipality in 1533.

La Paz: city, in the Collasuyo; Nuestra Señora de la Paz, Our Lady of the Peace, founded in 1548 to commemorate the defeat of Gonzalo Pizarro's rebellion; administrative capital of Bolivia.

La Plata: city, in the southern Collasuyo founded in 1538; deriving its name because of its abundance of silver mines; known also by its indigenous name of Chuquisaca and Charcas, the name of its region; renamed Sucre in 1825, in honour of Mariscal Antonio de Sucre; capital of Bolivia.

league: 3½ miles.

León: capital of the early settlement of Nicaragua.

licentiate: lawyer.

Lima: city, capital of the Viceroyalty of Peru; name of lands of the Curaca Taulichusco, where Pizarro in 1535 founded the capital of his governorship, and which he named Los Reyes, the city of the Kings, in honour of the Feast of the Epiphany.

Lupaca: Aymara tribe of the Cuntisuyo and Collasuyo, though principally of the north and western region of Lake Titicaca.

maestre-de-campo: lieutenant to a commander of cavalry or infantry.

mariscal: commander of cavalry or army; empowered to act as a legal authority during a campaign.

marqués: marquis; title awarded Pizarro by the Emperor Charles V, 10 October 1537.

mestizo: of Indian and Spanish parentage.

mitimae: labourers of the subject tribes; transported to various regions of the empire for a period of time – mita – by Incas and then Spaniards.

Morisco: of Moorish parentage.

morrión: curved steel helmet used by conquistadors.

Mudéjar: Moors allowed to live in Christian lands; also a term to describe Moorish influence in architecture.

mulatto: of Negro and Spanish parentage.

Nazca: western region of the Cuntisuyo; pre-Colombian civilization; site of giant earth carvings.

New Castile: Pizarro's governorship of Peru.

New Spain: Mexico.

New Toledo: governorship of the region of the Collasuyo awarded Almagro.

ñusta: niece or daughter of Emperor by a concubine.

orejón: name given by the Spaniards to Inca lords because of the gold and silver ear ornaments they wore.

Pachacámac: quéchua name for the creator; Inca temple shrine, south of Lima.

Pachamama: earth deity.

palla: daughter of a curaca and tribal lord.

panaca: name for the Inca lineages and their custodians; the spiritual and secular heirs of the emperors, numbering eleven in all.

Parinacochas: north-western region of the Cuntisuyo.

Pastu: most northern region of the Inca empire.

Peru – Birú: name the early Spanish explorer of the Pacific coast Pascual de Andagoya mistakenly gave the Inca empire of Tahuantinsuyo.

peso: name of coinage, originally meaning weight. Estimated present day value of gold and silver: Peso de Oro – £25. Peso or mark of silver – £17. Peso of stamped silver (*plata ensayada*) – £25. Unmarked silver – £20. The value in Spain during the early colonial period would have been possibly threefold.

piece of eight: coinage; approximately equivalent to ½ peso of gold.

Písac: encomienda, situated in valley of that name in the Yucay.

Piura: equatorial township.

Potosí: city, in Bolivia, founded in 1545 because of the great wealth of its silver mine, the Cerro Rico.

procurator: legal title of a governorship.

Pucará: Battle of, north of Lake Titicaca, 8 October 1554; defeat of Francisco Hernández Girón by the royalist army of the judges of Lima.

Puerto Viejo: the old port, north of Guayaquil.

Quéchua: language and ruling tribe of the Inca empire.

Quipucamayoc – Quipu: guardians of the quipu, coloured strings used for mathematical, historical and astrological records.

Quito: northern capital of Inca empire; founded in 1534 as San Francisco de Quito; capital of Ecuador.

regidor: alderman.

San Mateo: equatorial bay.

Sapa Inca: emperor.

Sucre: *see* La Plata.

Surampalli: country retreat of the Emperor Huayna Cápac, to the south of the north Andean city of Tumibamba.

suyos: regions.

Tahuantinsuyo: name of the Inca empire of the four suyos – Antisuyo, Chinchasuyo, Collasuyo and Cuntisuyo.

tambo: Inca storehouse or fortress.

Titicaca: lake in the Collasuyo, sacred to the Incas; 12,500 ft above sea level and 3,500 square miles; bordering Peru and Bolivia.

Tucumán: southern province of the Collasuyo in Argentina.

Túmbez: early Spanish settlement on the equatorial coast.

Tumibamba: equatorial Andean capital of the Cañari tribe; birthplace of the Emperor Huayna Cápac who gave it the name of his panaca; founded as the Spanish municipality of Cuenca in 1557.

Veragua: north-westerly province of Nicaragua.

Vilcabamba: Inca fortress settlement, north-west of Cuzco; built by the Inca Manco; known as the Lost City of the Incas; probable site is Espíritu Pampa.

Villac-Umu: title of the shaman and High Priest of the Sun.

Viracocha: cosmic Andean deity.

Vitcos: Inca township, near Vilcabamba, north-west of Cuzco.

Yanacona: nomadic servant caste.

Yucay: valley, north of Cuzco; personal fiefdom of the Emperor Huayna Cápac; renowned for its climate and beauty, known as the Sacred Valley of the Incas.

yupanqui: quéchua title, denoting royalty.

NOTES

The original spelling of the family name – Serra de Leguizamón – has been retained, though the phonetic spelling – Sierra de Leguízamo – was adopted by various notaries, and also by some of the Conquistador's children. His last will and testament, Archivo General de Indias, Seville, Patronato 107, is referred to as SL (Appendix 1). His testimonial, Probanza de Méritos del Capitán Mansio Serra de Leguízamo, Archivo General de Indias, Seville, Patronato 126, is referred to as MSL (Appendix 2). The Indian testimony in his son Juan's testimonial, Probanza de Méritos de Juan Sierra de Leguízamo, Archivo General de Indias, Seville, Lima 205, is referred to as JSL (Appendix 3). His son Francisco's testimonial, Archivo General de Indias, Seville, Patronato 126, is referred to as FSL. The transcription is by Josefa García Tovar and the translation is by the author, as are all other translations.

Prologue

1. Carlos Alonso, *Pedro de Perea, Obispo de Arequipa*, Archivo Agustiniano, Vol. LXI, Madrid, 1977. M.A. Cateriano *Memorias de los SS. Obispos de Arequipa*, Arequipa, 1908.
2. Family: Expediente de Hidalguía de Martín Díez de Medina, Legajo 106, Año 1568, Sala de Hijosdalgo, Real Chancillería de Valladolid. José Rosendo Gutiérrez, 'Mancio Sierra de Leguízamo', in *Revista Peruana*, Lima, 1879. Briones: José Manuel Martínez, *Briones y sus Monumentos*, Asociación de Amigos de Briones, Logroño, 1995.
3. Antonio de la Calancha, *Corónica Moralizada del Orden de San Agustín en el Perú*, ed. Ignacio Prado Pastor, Universidad Nacional de San Marcos, Lima, 1974.

1. Heirs of the Cid

1. Geoffrey Parker, *Philip II*, Chicago and La Salle, Illinois, 1996, p. 202.
2. Gobernantes del Perú, *Cartas y Papeles del Siglo XVI*, ed. Roberto Levillier, Documentos del Archivo de Indias, Madrid, 1924, Vol. VII, p. 118.
3. Richard Fletcher, *The Quest for El Cid*, Oxford University Press, 1989, p. 15.
4. Henry Kamen, *The Spanish Inquisition*, London, Weidenfeld & Nicolson, 1997, p. 23.
5. John Lynch, *Spain Under the Hapsburgs*, Oxford University Press, 1981, Vol. 1, p. 109.
6. Edicto de Expulsión, 31 March 1492. Conversos: in 1449 the Royal Secretary Fernán Díaz de Toledo, in a report to the Bishop of Cuenca, recorded that all the leading noble lineages of

Castile, including the Henríquez, from whom both Queen Isabella and King Ferdinand were descended, could trace their descent to conversos. Limpieza de sangre was still a requirement for entrance to the corps of officer cadets up to 1859. Kamen, *The Spanish Inquisition*, p. 254.

7. Ibid., p. 131.
8. Lynch, *Spain Under the Habsburgs*, Vol. 1, p. 13.
9. The Crown seized control of the grandmasterships of the Orders in 1495. Ibid., Vol. 1, p. 5.
10. All twenty of Mansio's witnesses testify to his hidalgo lineage; MSL. The baptismal records at Pinto of the period have been lost. The date is surmised from the age he gives in his evidence as a witness to various testimonials, though adding the words 'more or less', as was the custom at the time. The name of Mansio is the diminutive for Manso, a legendary lord of Vizcaya.
11. Raúl Rivera Serna, 'El Primer testamento de Mancio Serra de Leguízamo', in *Mar del Sur*, Lima, p. 27.
12. Xela Ximénez was one of the township's representatives to King Alfonso XI, when in 1332 he conferred Pinto's lordship to the neighbouring town of Madrid. Sergio Ascencio Hernández, *Los Señores Feudales y otras Antigüedades de la Villa de Pinto*, Ayuntamiento de Pinto, 1996, p. 129.
13. Richard Ford, *Handbook for Spain*, London, Centaur Press, 1966, Vol. III, pp. 1367, 1371, 1374.
14. Lope García de Salazar, *Las Bienandanças e Fortunas Capítulo: Del linaje de Leguiçamón e de su Fundamento, e Donde Sucedieron*, ed. Maximilano Camarón, Madrid, 1884. Lineage: Expediente de Don Tristán de Leguizamón y Esquivel, Caballero de Santiago, 4418, Bilbao, Año 1530, Archivo Histórico Nacional, Madrid. Alberto García Carraffa, *El Solar Vasco Navarro*, Vols 1–6, 1933–5. Estanislao de Labayru, *Historia de Vizcaya*, Bilbao, 1899–1903. Andrés de Mañaricua, *Santa María de Begoña*, Bilbao, Banco de Vizcaya, 1950.
15. Lope García de Salazar, *Las Bienandaças*.
16. Ramón Menéndez Pidal, *La España del Cid*, Madrid, Espasa-Calpe, 1956, Vols 1 and 2. Fletcher, *The Quest for El Cid*.
17. *Poema de Mio Cid*, ed. Ian Michael, Madrid, Clásicos Castalia, 1984.
18. In *Poema de Almeria* (1147–9) MS, line 225. Governor of Toledo, 1109–14. Referred to as the Cid's nephew in a letter to Doña Jimena, the Cid's wife, Carta de Arras, July 1074. Colin Smith, 'Personages of the Poem de Mio Cid', *Modern Language Review*, 66, 1971, 580–98.
19. Lope García de Salazar, *Las Bienandanças, e Fortunas, Capítulo: De las Muertes que Fisieron Tristán de Leguiçamón e Martín de Zaballa*.
20. Mañaricua, *Santa María de Begoña*, Apéndice IV.
21. Luis Roldán Jordán, *Iglesia Parroquial de Santo Domingo de Silos, Apuntes Históricos y Arqueológicos de la Villa de Pinto*, Ayuntamiento de Pinto, Vol. 3, pp. 53–66. Hernández, *Los Señores Feudales*.
22. Ibid., pp. 112, 113.
23. Alonso de Mesa's testimony, JSL, FSL.
24. Pablo Alvárez Rubiana, *Pedrarias Dávila*, Madrid, 1944.
25. Catherine Delamarre y Bertrand Sallard, *Las Mujeres en Tiempos de los Conquistadores*, Barcelona, 1994, p. 344.
26. No record of the year of his departure exists in the Archive of the Indies.
27. Tomás Ayón, *Historia de Nicaragua*, Madrid, 1956, Vol. 1, p. 2. José Gamez, *Historia de*

Nicaragua, Managua, Colección Somoza, 1975. Slavery: Hugh Thomas, *The Slave Trade*, London, Picador, 1997; Frederick Bowser, *The African Slave in Colonial Peru*, Stanford University Press, 1974.

28. William McNeill, *Plagues and Peoples*, Oxford, Blackwell, 1977.

29. Name derived from an allegorical poem, written in about 1520 by a physician from Verona Girolamo Fracastoro, describing the odyssey of an explorer in search of King Solomon's mines who discovers a tribe in the Indies stricken by a disease given them by a shepherd called Sypilius. Delamarre y Sallard, *Las Mujeres*, pp. 92–4.

30. Alfredo Castillero Calvo, 'Origines Históricos de Veragua', in *Revista de Indias*, Madrid, Vol. 107.

31. MSL, 2.

32. Ibid., 2.

33. Luque could well have been acting on behalf of the wealthy merchant and official Gaspar de Espinosa. John Hemming, *The Conquest of the Incas*, London, Papermac, 1993, p. 24. The formation of a company between Pizarro, Almagro and Luque is also recorded by Nicolás de Ribera, el viejo, in his Probanza de Méritos, *Revista del Archivo Nacional*, Lima, 1937–8.

34. William Prescott, *History of the Conquest of Peru*, London, G. Allen & Unwin, 1913, Appendix, p. 479.

35. Ibid., Appendix, pp. 481–5.

36. Gobernantes del Perú, Vol. II, p. 138.

37. Pedro Pizarro, *Relación del Descubrimiento y Conquista de los Reinos del Perú*, ed. Guillermo Lohmann Villera, Pontifica Universidad Católica del Perú, Lima, 1978, p. 151.

38. *Nobiliario Hispano-Americano del Siglo XVI*, ed. Santiago Montoto, Madrid, 1927, Vol. II, pp. 326–9.

39. Gonzalo Fernández de Oviedo, *Historia General y Natural de las Indias*, ed. Juan Pérez de Tudela, Madrid, Biblioteca de Autores Españoles, 1959, Tomo CXXI, p. 33.

40. Ibid., p. 61.

41. Pedro Pizarro, *Relación*, p. 168.

42. James Lockhart, *The Men of Cajamarca*, Austin, University of Texas, 1972, p. 159.

43. MSL, 2.

44. Pedro de Cieza de León, *Descubrimiento y Conquista del Perú*, ed. Carmelo Sáenz de Santa María, Madrid, Historia 16, 1986, p. 115. Francisco Cansino, one of the witnesses in Nicolás de Ribera's Probanza, testified that there were 200 men 'more or less', *Revista del Archivo Nacional*, 1937–8.

2. *The Realm of the Hummingbird*

1. Sir Clements Markham, *The Incas of Peru*, Lima, Librerias ABC, 1971, p. 57.

2. Population: Rubén Vargas Ugarte, *Historia de la Iglesia en el Perú*, Lima, Santa María, 1953, Vol. 1.

3. Gobernates del Perú, Vol. VII, p. 124.

4. Agustín de Zárate, *Historia del Descubrimiento y Conquista del la Provincia del Perú*, Biblioteca de Autores Españoles, Madrid, 1853, Tomo Segundo, Libro 2, Capítulo 5.

5. Waldemar Espinoza Soriano, 'Los Orejones del Cuzco', *Proceso*, Huancayo, 1977, pp. 104, 106, 107.

6. Bearded white men. Pedro de Cieza de León, *La Crónica del Perú*, ed. Manuel Ballesteros, Madrid, Historia 16, 1984, p. 367.

7. Felipe Guaman Poma de Ayala, *Nueva Corónica y Buen Gobierno*, ed. Franklin Pease, Caracas, Bibioteca Ayacucho, 1980, Vol. 2, p. 291.

8. Gobernantes del Perú, Vol. VII, p. 124.

9. Blas Valera, *Relación de las Costumbres Antiguas de los Naturales del Perú*, in *Antigüedades del Perú*, ed. Henrique Urbano y Ana Sánchez, Madrid, Historia 16, 1990.

10. His statement in his will that thieves were unknown in the Inca realm was quite unwarrantedly ridiculed by the Peruvian scholar Raúl Porras, irrespective of the fact that the Friar Martín de Murúa, whose chronicle Dr Porras edited, is also quite explicit in supporting such a claim because of the severe penalties imposed on theft. Raúl Porras Barrenechea, *Los Cronistas del Perú*, ed. Franklin Pease, Lima, 1986, pp. 575–80. Friar Martín de Murúa, *Los Origenes de los Incas*, ed. Raúl Porras Barrenechea, Lima, 1946, pp. 98, 113.

11. Espinoza, *Los Orejones*, p. 95.

12. Garcí Díez de San Miguel, *Visita Hecha a la Provincia de Chucuito en el Año 1567*, ed. Waldemar Espinoza Soriano, Lima, Casa de la Cultura del Perú, 1964, pp. 106, 107, 204, 298.

13. John Hyslop, *Inka Road System*, Orlando, Florida, 1984, XIII.

14. Gobernantes del Perú, Vol. VII, p. 118.

15. Cristóbal de Molina, el Chileno, *Conquista y Población del Perú*, Biblioteca Peruana, Lima, Tomo III, p. 325.

16. 'Discurso de la Sucesión y Gobierno de los Incas', reproduced in Julío Luna (ed.), *El Cuzco y el Gobierno de los Incas*, Lima, Miranda, 1962, pp. 31–5, 40–1.

17. Polo de Ondegardo, *El Mundo de los Incas*, ed. Laura González y Alicia Alonso, Madrid, Historia 16, 1990, p. 97.

18. Garcilaso de la Vega, *Comentarios Reales de Los Incas*, ed. Carlos Araníbar, Lima, Fondo de Cultura Económica, 1991, Vol. 1, p. 335.

19. The Italianate Afuera Hospital of San Juan Bautista. Don Juan Tavera, Cardinal Archbishop of Toledo, minister and diplomat, former head of the Inquisition.

20. Pedro de Cieza de León, *El Señorio de los Incas*, ed. Manuel Ballesteros, Madrid, Historia 16, pp. 97–8.

21. 'Informaciones Acerca del Señorío de los Incas Hechas por Mandado de Don Francisco de Toledo, Virey del Perú, 1570–2', in Fernando Montesinos, *Memorias Antiguas Historiales y Politicas del Perú*, Colección de Libros Españoles Raros, ed. Jiménez de la Espada, Madrid, 1882, p. 254.

22. José de Acosta, *Historia Natural y Moral de las Indias*, ed. José Alcina Franch, Madrid, Historia 16, 1987, p. 424.

23. María Rostworowski de Díez Canseco, *Historia de Tahuantinsuyo*, Lima, Instituto de Estudios Peruanos, 1992, p. 150.

24. The Coya Rahua Ocllo was a daughter of the Inca Túpac Yupanqui and belonged to his panaca of Túpac Yupanqui, as did Huáscar and her daughter Doña Beatriz.

25. Poma de Ayala, *Nueva Corónica*, p. 103.

26. Commonly known as Huáscar because of his birthplace at Huascarquíshuar, near Muina. Juan de Betanzos, *Narrative of the Incas*, Palma de Mallorca MS, ed. Roland Hamilton and Dana Buchanan, Texas, University of Austin, 1996, p. 176. Name of Hummingbird: B.C. Brundage, *Lords of Cuzco*, Norman, Oklahoma University, 1967, pp. 3, 351. Children of

Huayna Cápac: Ella Dunbar Temple, 'La Descendencia de Huayna Cápac', in *Revista Histórica*, Lima, Vols 11 (1937), 12 (1939), 13 (1940), 17 (1948).

27. Doña Beatriz Yupanqui. Her Inca name was Quispiquipi Huaylla. Her territorial title name of Huaylla referred to the lands given her by her father in the valley of Huaylla in the Yucay, and which would later form part of her lover Mansio's encomienda of Callanga. Noble David Cook, *Tasa de la Visita General de Francisco de Toledo*, Lima, Universidad Nacional Mayor de San Marcos, 1975, p. 202. She was also known as Doña Beatriz Manco Cápac, the patronymic of her royal lineage: SL; José de la Puente Brunke, *Encomiendas y Encomenderos en el Perú*, Seville, Diputación Provincial, 1992, pp. 359, 379. She is often confused with her half-sister Doña Inés, the Ñusta Quispe Sisa Huayllas, whose mother Contarhuacho was the daughter of the cacique of Ananhuaylas.
28. JSL, 2.
29. Max Uhle, *Las Ruinas de Tomebamba*, Academia Nacional de Historia, Quito, 1923, p. 11.
30. Cieza de León, *La Crónica del Perú*, pp. 206, 207.
31. The Ñusta Tocto Coca was Huayna Cápac's cousin and belonged to the panaca of Pachacuti, named after their grandfather.
32. Date of death. Garcilaso de la Vega gives the year 1523; Sarmiento de Gamboa Christmas Day 1524; López de Jerez 1525; and Cieza de León 1527. Concepción Bravo suggests the date may have been as late as 1530 – a supposition based on a lateral interpretation of historical and archaeological evidence, and on the theory Quéchua witnesses calculated their years on a different cycle to the Christian calendar, which in all probability is correct. Concepción Bravo Guerreira, 'La Muerte de Huayna Cápac', in *Revista de Indias*, Madrid, 1977, p. 722.
33. Acosta, *Historia Natural*, p. 325.
34. Cieza de León, *Señorio de los Incas*, p. 195.
35. He was reputed to have been five years younger than Atahualpa who Francisco López de Jerez claimed was thirty years old at Cajamarca in 1533. Francisco de Xerez, *Verdadera Relacíon de la Conquista del Perú*, ed. Concepción Bravo Guerreira, Madrid, Historia 16, 1988, p. 123.
36. Panaca lands. María Rostworowski de Díez Canseco, 'Nuevos Datos Sobre Tenencia de Tierras en el Incairo', in *Revista del Museo Nacional*, Lima, 1962, p. 134.
37. Garcí Díez de San Miguel, *Visita*, pp. 106, 204.
38. Betanzos, *Narrative of the Incas*, p. 244.

3. *The Killing of the Great Turkey Cock*

1. Garcilaso de la Vega, pp. 592, 593.
2. Negro markings. James Lockhart, *Spanish Peru, 1532–1560*, Madison, University of Wisconsin Press, 1968, p. 206.
3. Lockhart, *The Men of Cajamarca*, pp. 122, 157, 168, 175, 190.
4. Diego de Trujillo, 'Relación del Descubrimiento del Reyno del Perú', in Francisco de Xerez, *Verdadera Relación*, p. 195.
5. Hernando de Aldana, an Estremaduran, able to speak the rudiments of quéchua.
6. Ibid., pp. 200–3.
7. Cristóbal de Mena, *Conquista del Perú, llamada la Nueva Castilla*, Biblioteca Peruana, Vol. 1, Lima, 1968, pp. 150, 151. Mansio stated that no Spaniard ever met Huáscar, which was probably the case as such a meeting would have been known to his mistress Doña Beatriz,

Huáscar's full-blooded sister. Gobernantes del Perú, Vol. VII, p. 124.

8. Evidence of Francisco Cansino, 'Probanza de Nicolás de Ribera', in *Revista del Archivo Nacional*, 1937–8.

9. MSL, 3–4.

10. Ibid., 3–4.

11. First conqueror. Mansio declared in his probanza, 'se hallo en la prisión de Atahualpa', by which he could have only meant he took part in the guarding of the Inca, but which can equally be interpreted to mean he took part in his capture. MSL, 3–4. Dr Porras in his biographical sketch of Mansio quite reasonably believed he had made the latter claim, and which influenced his depiction of him as a picaresque rogue. Porras, *Los Cronistas*, pp. 575–80. It appears even more bizarre that Mansio could have made such a claim in front of the notary of the Audiencia of Lima, identified as the chronicler Francisco López de Jerez, who had been present at the Inca's capture. MSL, 51.

12. Doña Inés was the mother of Pizarro's illegitimate children Francisca and Gonzalo. María Rostworowski de Díez Canseco, *Doña Francisca Pizarro*, Lima, Instituto de Estudios Peruanos, 1989.

13. Miguel de Estete, *Noticia del Perú*, Lima, Biblioteca Peruana, Vol. 1, p. 378.

14. Pedro Pizarro, *Relación*, pp. 67, 68.

15. Treasure chamber. Hemming, *Conquest of the Incas*, p. 49.

16. *Información Hecha en Cuzco, a Petición de Francisco y Diego Hillaquita sobre ser Nietos de Guaynacapa e Hijos de Don Francisco Atahualpa*, MS, AGI, Patronato 187, R.21.

17. Thierry Saignes, 'Caciques, Tribute and Migration in the Southern Andes', University of London, Institute of Latin American Studies, Occasional Papers, No. 15, 35.

18. The three foot soldiers: Pedro de Moguer, Juan de Zárate and Martín Bueno. Moguer was the half-brother of the witness Diego Camacho, MSL, 20–1.

19. Rafael Loredo, *Los Repartos*, Lima, Miranda, 1958, pp. 72–4.

20. SL. Appendix 1, p. 142.

21. Xerez, *Verdadera Relación*, p. 152.

22. José Antonio del Busto Duthurburu, *La Pacificación del Perú*, Lima, Studium, pp. 279, 280.

23. Xerez, *Verdadera Relación*, p. 156.

24. Hemming, *The Conquest of the Incas*, p. 82.

25. Chroniclers. Porras, *Los Cronistas*. Philip Ainsworth Means, Biblioteca Andina, Yale University Press, 1973. Lockhart, *The Men of Cajamarca*.

26. Xerez, *Verdadera Relación*, p. 28; Jiménez Placer, *Vida de Francisco López de Xerez*, Madrid, 1911.

27. MSL, 51.

28. Lockhart, *The Men of Cajamarca*, p. 266.

4. *The City of the Sun God*

1. Waldemar Espinoza Soriano, *La Destrucción del Imperio de los Incas*, Lima, Retablo de Papel Ediciones, 1974, p. 132.

2. MSL, 5.

3. Ibid., 6.

4. Ibid., 6.

5. Ibid., 6.

6. Ibid., 7–11.

7. Trujillo, *Relación*, p. 205.

8. MSL, 7–11.

9. Ibid., 7–11.

10. Horacio Villanueva Urteaga, 'Documento Sobre Yucay en el Siglo XVI', in *Revista del Archivo Histórico del Cuzco*, XIII Cuzco, 1970, p. 165.

11. Ibid., p. 163.

12. MSL, 12.

13. Espinoza, *Los Orejones*, p. 95.

14. MSL, 12.

15. Hemming, *The Conquest of the Incas*, p. 546.

16. MSL, 12.

17. Francisco López de Gómora, in Garcilaso de la Vega, *Comentarios Reales de los Incas, Historia General del Perú*, ed. José de la Riva Agüero, Buenos Aires, Libro 2, 1944, Vol. VII, p. 127.

18. Santa Cruz Pachacuti, in *Antegüedades del Perú*, p. 206.

19. Gobernantes del Perú, Vol. 2, pp. 139–40.

20. Manuel de Mendiburu, *Diccionario Histórico-Biográfico del Perú*, Lima, 1874–90, Vol. V, pp. 426, 427.

21. MSL, 15.

22. Ibid., 15.

23. Pedro Pizarro, *Relación*, p. 60.

24. SL. The lands and Indians of Callanga in the Yucay had belonged to Doña Beatriz and were later to be awarded by Pizarro to Paullu Inca; Cook, *Tasa*, p. 202.

25. JSL.

26. Villanueva, *Documentos sobre Yucay*, p. 178.

27. Trujillo, *Relación*, p. 206.

28. Carlos Sempat Assadourian, *Transiciones Hacia el Sistema Colonial Andino*, México, Colegio de México, Fideicomiso Historia de las Americas, 1944, p. 144.

29. Cristóbal de Molina, *Conquista*, pp. 340, 341.

5. *The Fall of Tahuantinsuyo*

1. MSL, 13–14.

2. Ibid., 13–14.

3. Ibid., 16–19.

4. Ibid., 16–19.

5. Mendinburu, *Diccionario*, Vol. V, p. 434.

6. Rostworowski, *Doña Francisca Pizarro*, p. 22.

7. Soto's offer to Almagro. Lockhart, *The Men of Cajamarca*, p. 197.

8. Assadourian, *Transiciones*, pp. 55, 56.

9. Molina, *Conquista*, pp. 345, 346.

10. Lockhart, *Spanish Peru*, p. 15.

11. MSL, 20–1.

12. JSL, 3.

13. Beauty of Rahua Ocllo. *Las Crónicas de los Molinas*, Lima, 1943, p. 53.

14. Rape of Doña Juana. Gold given to Almagro. Molina, *Conquista*, pp. 342, 343.

15. Raúl Porras Barrenechea, *Cartas del Perú, Colección de Documentos Inéditos Para la Historia del Perú*, Lima, Sociedad Bibliófilos Peruanos, 1959, p. 337.

16. MSL, 20–1.

17. Cieza de León, *Descubrimiento y conquista*, pp. 309, 310.

18. Rafael Varón Gabai, *La Ilusión del Poder, Apogeo y Decadencia de los Pizarro en la Conquista del Perú*, Lima, Instituto de Estudios Peruanos, 1977, pp. 77, 78.

19. JSL.

20. Gobernantes del Perú, Vol. 2, pp. 142, 143.

21. JSL.

22. Martín de Murúa, *Historia General del Perú*, Wellington MS, ed. Manuel Ballesteros, Vol. 1, p. 99.

23. Pedro Sancho de la Hoz, 'Relación de la Conquista del Perú', in Porras, *Los Cronistas*, p. 114.

24. MSL, 22–3.

25. Ibid., 22–3.

26. Ibid., 22–3.

27. Víctor Angeles Vargas, *Historia del Cusco Incaico*, Cuzco, Industrialgráfica, Tomo 1, p. 133.

28. MSL, 24.

29. López de Gómora, Garcilaso, *Comentarios*, Libro 2, pp. 165, 166.

30. Porras, *Cartas del Perú*, pp. 337, 338.

31. Espíritu Pampa. Hemming, *The Conquest of the Incas*, Chapter 25.

6. *The Wars of the Viracochas*

1. Pedro de Cieza de León, *Las Guerras Civiles del Perú*, ed. Carmelo Sáenz de Santa María, Madrid, Consejo Superior de Investigaciones Científicas, Vol. 2, p. 17; Garcilaso, *Comentarios*, Libro 2, p. 217.

2. Varón Gabai, *La Ilusión del Poder*, p. 92.

3. Porras, *Cartas del Perú*, p. 311.

4. Lockhart, *The Men of Cajamarca*, p. 154.

5. Garcilaso, *Comentarios*, Libro 2, p. 231.

6. Revista del Archivo Nacional del Perú.

7. Gobernantes del Perú, Vol. 2, p. 145.

8. MSL, 25.

9. Rómulo Cúneo Vidal, Obras Completas, Lima, Vol. 1, pp. 325, 328.

10. SL.

11. FSL.

12. MSL, 26–7.

13. Gobernantes del Perú, Vol. 2, p. 146.

14. Lockhart, *Spanish Peru*, p. 12.

15. Catherine Julien, *Condesuyo: The Political Division of Territories under Inca and Spanish Rule*, Bonn, Bonner Amerikanistische, 1991, pp. 17, 18.

16. Puente, *Encomienda*, p. 141.

17. Lockhart, *Spanish Peru*, p. 57.

18. Poma de Ayala, *Nueva Corónica*, Vol. 1, p. 288.

19. Gobernantes del Perú, Vol. 2, p. 138.
20. Garcilaso, *Comentarios*, Libro 3, IX, p. 265.
21. MSL, 28–31.
22. Revista del Archivo Nacional, Lima. Testamentos y Mayorazgos. Cartulario de los conquistadors del Perú. El Capitán Alonso de Mesa. Transcription, B.T. Lee.
23. Prescott, *The Conquest of Peru*, Appendix, pp. 496–7.
24. Promise of Indian women as booty. Delamarre y Bertrand Sallard, *Las Mujeres*, p. 60.
25. *La Iglesia de España en el Perú*, Colección de Documentos, ed. Emilio Lissón Chavez, Seville, 1943–7, Vol. 3, p. 13.
26. Prescott, *The Conquest of Peru*, pp. 365–6.
27. *La Iglesia de España*, Vol. 2, p. 116.
28. Ibid., Vol. 3, p. 68.
29. Ibid., Vol. 3, pp. 79–80.
30. Ibid., Vol. 3, pp. 87–8.
31. *Colección de Documentos para la Historia de Chile*, ed. José Toribio Medina, Santiago, 1888–1902, Vol. 5, pp. 341–3.
32. Puente Brunke, *Encomiendas*, p. 379.
33. The mummy of the Emperor Huayna Cápac was later rediscovered in Cuzco by the chronicler Juan Polo de Ondegardo. Teodoro Hampe, 'Los Momias de los Incas en Lima', in *Revista del Museo Nacional*, Lima, 1982, Tomo XIVI, p. 407.
34. Porras, *Los Cronistas*, pp. 747–51.
35. Garcilaso, *Comentarios*, Vol. 2, pp. 641–2.
36. *Relación de los Quipucamayos*, ed. Juan José Vega, Lima, 1974, p. 75.
37. Edmundo Guillén Guillén, *La Guerra de Reconquista Inka*, Lima, 1994, p. 126.
38. JSL, 4.
39. Hectór López Martínez, *Diego Centeno y la Rebellión de los Encomenderos*, Lima, Villanueva, 1970, p. 40.
40. Ricardo Palma, *Tradiciones Peruanas*, Lima, Obras Completas, Aguilar, 1968, pp. 65–6.

7. *The Devil on Muleback*

1. José Antonio del Busto Duthurburu, *Diccionario Histórico-Biográfico de los Conquistadores del Perú*, Lima, Studium, 1987, Vol. 1, p. 323.
2. Garcilaso, *Comentarios*, Libro 5, p. 260.
3. Zárate, *Historia del Descubrimiento*, Libro Cuarto, Capítulo XIV.
4. MSL, 32.
5. Ibid., 32.
6. Garcilaso, *Comentarios*, Libro 4, p. 37.
7. López Martínez, *Diego Centeno*, p. 32.
8. Garcilaso, *Comentarios*, Libro 4, pp. 65, 66.
9. Antonio de Ahumada. Busto, *Diccionario*, Vol. 1, p. 40.
10. Garcilaso, *Comentarios*, Libro 5, p. 270.
11. Ibid., p. 270.
12. Ibid., p. 270.
13. Ibid., pp. 269, 270.

14. MSL, 32.

15. *Documentos Relativos a Don Pedro de la Gasca*, ed. Juan Perez de Tudela, Madrid, Real Academia de Historia, 1964, Vol. 2, p. 354.

16. Ibid., Vol. 2, p. 357.

17. Ibid., Vol. 2, pp. 174, 175.

18. Cieza de León, *Las Guerras Civiles*, Vol. 2, p. 546.

19. Rivera, *El Primer Testamento*, p. 27.

20. Archivo de Indias, Legajo 5536, Libro 1, p. 428.

21. *Documentos – Gasca*, Vol. 1, p. 309.

22. Ibid., Vol. 2, p. 71.

23. Garcilaso, *Comentarios*, Libro 4, p. 133.

24. Lynch, *Spain under the Habsburgs*, Vol. 1, p. 61.

25. Ibid., Vol. 1, p. 62.

26. *Colección de Documentos Inéditos para la Historia de España*, Madrid, 1842–1895, Vol. XLIX, pp. 277, 278.

27. Diego Esquivel y Navia, *Noticias Cronológicas de la Gran Ciudad del Cuzco*, Lima, Biblioteca Peruana de Cultura, 1980, p. 145.

28. López Martínez, *Diego Centeno*, p. 93.

29. MSL, 32.

30. Ibid., 32.

31. María Calderón's death at Mansio's mansion. Víctor Angeles Vargas, *Historia del Cusco Colonial*, Vol. 2, p. 733.

32. MSL, 44.

33. Prescott, *The Conquest of Peru*, pp. 498, 499.

34. Garcilaso, *Comentarios*, Libro 4, p. 264.

35. Pedro Pizarro, *Relación*, p. 238.

36. *Documentos – Gasca*, Vol. 2, p. 258.

37. *Documentos Inéditos de Indias*, Madrid, 1873, Vol. 20, p. 522.

38. *Documentos – Gasca*, Vol. 2, p. 8.

39. Sir William Stirling-Maxwell, *The Cloister Life of the Emperor Charles V*, London, John Parker, 1891, p. 31.

40. Porras, *Los Cronistas*, pp. 216–19, 225–6, 255–7, 281–3, 392–408.

41. Manuel Ballesteros, in Cieza de León, *La Crónica del Perú*, pp. 31–40.

8. *The Coya of Cuzco*

1. Garcilasco, *Comentarios*, Libro 5, 111, p. 14.

2. Varón Gabai, *Francisco Pizarro*, p. 255; Puente, *Encomienda*, p. 379.

3. JSL, 3.

4. Antonio de Ribera, AGI, Patronato 188.

5. Number of colonists: Lockhart, *Spanish Peru*, p. 153; encomiendas: Puente, *Encomiendas*, p. 141; depopulation: Hemming, The Conquest of the Incas, p. 582.

6. Diego Fernández, *Crónicas del Perú*, Madrid, Biblioteca de Autores Españoles, 1963, p. 76.

7. Busto, *La Pacificación*, p. 377.

8. Ibid., p. 385.

9. Héctor López Martínez, 'Un Motín de Mestizos en el Perú', in *Revista de Indias*, Madrid, 1964, No. 97–8, p. 369.

10. Juan Olaechea Labayen, 'Recurso al Rey de la Primera Generación Mestiza', in *Anuario de Estudios Americanos*, Seville, Tomo XXX, p. 165. Villanueva, Documentos sobre Yucay, Información de Doña María Manrique Coya, p. 179.

11. Información Hecha en Cuzco, MS, AGI.

12. JSL, 3.

13. Ibid., 3.

14. Puente, *Ecomiendas*, p. 376.

15. Rostworowski, *Historia de Tahuantinsuyo*, pp. 148–53.

16. Marina de Córdoba. Alfonsina Barrionuevo, *Cusco Mágico*, Lima, 1980, p. 94.

17. Archivo de Protocolos de Córdoba, Oficio 29, Protocolo 35, 62.

18. JSL.

19. Ibid., 6.

20. Ibid., 7–8.

21. JSL, 7–8.

22. 'Testamento Inédito del Inca Sairi Túpac', in *Historia y Cultura*, Lima, 1965, p. 16.

23. JSL.

24. Informaciones Acera del Senorío de los Incas, p. 256.

25. Hampe, *Los Momias*, p. 405.

26. Puente, *Encomiendas*, p. 359.

27. JSL.

28. Ibid.

29. Ibid.

30. Date of Juan's death unknown. He was alive in 1570 when he made a last presentation of his Probanza. JSL. Dead by 1572. Cook, *Tasa*, p. 185.

31. Petitions. Ibid.

32. Date of Doña Beatriz's death – taken from John Hemming, *The Conquest of the Incas*, Genealogies.

9. *The House of the Serpents*

1. Bernabé Cobo, *Inca Religion and Customs*, tr. and ed. Roland Hamilton, Austin, University of Texas, 1994, pp. 70, 71.

2. 'El Monasterio de Sta Clara de la Ciudad del Cuzco', in *Revista del Archivo Nacional del Perú*, 11, 1938, pp. 55–95.

3. SL.

4. Diego de Mendoza, *Crónica de la Provincia de San Antonio de las Charcas*, Editorial Casa Municipal de la Cultura, Franz Tamayo, La Paz, 1976, Capítulo VII, Libro 3, pp. 399–405. Doña María is referred to by the surname of Saravia, an adaptation of the name of Serra. Her mother is referred to as Doña Lucía de Zuñiga, which was possibly her maternal grandmother's name.

5. Ibid.

6. Mansio's wife was buried at Santo Domingo. Rivera Serna, *Primer Testamento*, p. 27.

7. 'Carta de los Licenciados Cepeda y Vera a Felipe II, La Plata, 14 Febrero, 1585', in *Monumenta*

Misionem, Monumenta Peruana, ed. Antonio Egaña, Lima, 1961.

8. SL.

9. Archivo General de Indias, Seville. Contración, 5239, N.I., R.10.

10. Archivo General de la Nación, Lima, Sección Real Audiencia y Notarial, No. 604, 328.

11. Garcilaso de la Vega, Vol. 1, p. 189.

12. Rivera Serna, *Primer Testamento*, p. 28.

13. MSL, 45–7.

14. Puente, *Encomienda*, p. 251.

15. Though a number of historians, among them Raúl Porras Barrenechea and Guillermo Lohmann Villena, have regarded such restitutions as being solely influenced by the clergy, there is little evidence to support that the elderly conquistadors were entirely coerced into making such gestures. Neither does the fact that Mansio's last will was written in two sections imply anything other than it was dictated by him to two separate scriveners. Nor should the natural fear he expresses of damnation – omitted from Appendix 1 because of its length – be regarded as insincere. Lohmann Villena, 'La Restitución por Conquistadors y Encomenderos', in *Annuario de Estudios Americanos*, XXIII, Seville, 1966; Porras, *Los Cronistas*, pp. 575–80. Dr Porras quotes the fact that Mansio later inserted a clause in his will obliging Indians of his encomienda to pay the seasonal tributes he had previously waivered – something which is not so remarkable, taking into account the natural resentment of his children. There is no evidence he altered his restitution of his share of the Cajamarca or Cuzco treasure, nor of the Punchao, which he states in his will he obtained at Cuzco. In fairness, I should add that Dr Porras also discredits him for claiming in his will, dated 1589, that he was the last of the conquistadors and cites Pedro Pizarro as still being alive at the time in Arequipa. Pedro Pizarro, as Dr Porras himself correctly records in an earlier chapter, died in February 1587. Ibid., pp. 137, 579.

16. Rivera Serna, *Primer Testamento*, p. 27.

17. Cook, *Tasa*, p. 124. The encomienda of Alca consisted of eighteen villages that Toledo ordered be relocated to the neighbouring settlement of Santa Cruz de Ontiveros.

18. Ibid., p. 199.

19. SL.

20. Aurelio Miró Quesada, *El Inca Garcilaso*, Lima, Pontificia Universidad Católica del Perú, 1994, p. 373.

21. Lockhart, *Spanish Peru*, p. 194.

22. Palma, *Tradiciones*, p. 1210.

23. Ibid., p. 1213.

24. Josep Barnadas, *Charcas, Orígines Históricos de una Sociedad Colonial*, La Paz, Centro de Investigación y Promoción del Campesinado, 1973.

25. Miguel de Cervantes, 'El Celoso Extremeño', in *Novelas Ejemplares*, Madrid, 1917.

26. Bartolomé Martínez y Vela, Archivo Boliviano, Colección de Documentos Relativos a la Historia de Bolivia, ed. Vicente de Ballivían y Roxas, Paris, 1872. Bartolomé Arzans de Orsúa y Vela, *Historia de la Villa Imperial de Potosí*, ed. Lewis Hanke and Gunnar Mendoza, Brown University, 1965. Alberto Crespo Rodas, *La Guerra Entre Vicuñas y Vascongados*, Lima, 1965. John Lynch, *The Hispanic World in Crisis and Change 1598–1700*, Oxford, 1992, pp. 328–39.

27. Rubén Vargas Ugarte, *Historia del Perú*, Lima, 1949, pp. 36, 37.

28. John Julius Norwich, *Byzantium, the Decline and Fall*, London, Penguin Books, 1995, p. 421.

29. Stirling-Maxwell, *The Cloister Life*, p. 246.
30. Arthur Zimmerman, *Francisco de Toledo*, New York, Greenwood, 1968, p. 101.
31. Ibid., p. 103.
32. Gobernantes del Perú, Vol. 2, pp. 44, 45.
33. Harold Wethey, *Colonial Architecture and Sculpture in Peru*, Harvard, 1949, p. 39.
34. Juan de Matienzo was the author of 'Gobierno del Perú'. He died at Sucre in 1579. Juan Polo de Ondegardo, also a lawyer, wrote at length on Inca traditions and customs. He too died at Sucre, in 1575. Polo de Ondegardo, *El Mundo de los Incas*. Cristóbal de Molina, a native of Jaén, was for some thirty years a priest at Cuzco, and wrote extensively on Inca traditions and religion. He died at Cuzco in 1585. Cristóbal de Molina, *Fábulas y mitos de los Incas*, ed. Henrique Urbano y Pierre Duviols, Historia 16, Madrid, 1989.
35. Informaciones Acera del Señorío de los Incas, pp. 257–9.
36. Gobernantes del Perú, Vol. VII, pp. 117–28.
37. Stephen Clissold, *Conquistador*, London, Derek Verschoyle, 1954, Chapter 14.
38. Espinoza, *Los Orejones*, p. 67. A number of Inca lords were later forced to work for the Cañaris, who were exempt from the mita. Ibid., p. 81. Only in 1602 would the mita for Incas be abolished. Plight of lords: SL.
39. FSL.
40. Baltasar de Ocampo, Vol. VII, pp. 306–44.
41. Vargas Ugarte, *Historia del Perú*, p. 258.
42. The Mercedarian friar confuses Mansio's son, who was by then dead, with his grandson Juan-Pablo de Leguizamón.
43. Ghost dance: Dee Brown, *Bury My Heart at Wounded Knee*, London, Vintage, 1991, p. 431. Huacas and Taki Onqoy: *El Retorno de las Huacas*, Lima, Instituto de Estudios Peruanos, 1990, p. 214.
44. Palma, *Tradiciones*, p. 216.
45. Archivo General de Indias, Seville, Patronato, 216.
46. Mansio died sometime at the begining of 1590: FSL.

Appendix 1

1. The opening section of his religious declaration is omitted.

Appendix 2

1. The manuscript consists of fifty questions put to each of the twenty-one witnesses, two of whom, the conquistadors Diego Maldonado, el rico, and Nicolás de Ribera, el mozo, were at the time unable to attend the hearing, and whose subsequent testimonies have been lost. Though the evidence of most of the witnesses was given on separate days, and only relates to the events in which they were present, in order to maintain a sequence of continuity their answers are listed after each of Mansio's itemized statements, and translated in the first person singular.

FURTHER READING

SPAIN

Fletcher, Richard. *The Quest for El Cid*, Oxford University Press, 1989

Kamen, Henry. *The Spanish Inquisition*, London, Weidenfeld & Nicolson, 1997

Lynch, John. *Spain Under the Hapsburgs*, Oxford University Press, Vol. 1, 1981

Parker, Geoffrey. *Philip II*, Illinois, Chicago & La Salle, 1996

PERU

Garcilaso de la Vega. *The Royal Commentaries of the Incas and General History of Peru*, trs. Harold Livermore, 2 vols, Austin, University of Texas Press, 1966

Hemming, John. *The Conquest of the Incas*, London, Papermac, 1993

Lockhart, James. *The Men of Cajamarca*, University of Texas Press, 1972

———. *Spanish Peru 1532–1560*, University of Wisconsin Press, 1994

Zimmerman, Arthur Franklin. *Francisco de Toledo*, New York, Greenwood Press, 1968

INDEX